Contesting Sovereignty

Sovereignty is a foundational idea upon which regional organisation of nations is built, yet its demise has often been predicted. Regionalism, which commits states to common frameworks such as rules and norms, tests sovereignty as states relinquish some sovereign power to achieve other goals such as security, growth, or liberalisation. This book examines the practice of normative contestation over sovereignty in two regional organisations of Africa and Asia – the AU and ASEAN. A structured comparison of three case studies from each organisation determines whether a norm challenging sovereignty was accepted, rejected, or qualified. Joel Ng has carried out interviews about, and detailed analysis of, these six cases that occurred at formative moments of norm-setting and that each had very different outcomes. This study contributes to the understanding of norms contestation in the field of international relations and offers new insights on how the AU and ASEAN are constituted.

JOEL NG is a research fellow of the S. Rajaratnam School of International Studies, Nanyang Technological University, Singapore. He first worked in international affairs during the northern Uganda conflict, developing interest in security, human rights, and governance. He is in the Singapore member committee of the Council for Security Cooperation in the Asia Pacific (CSCAP).

Contesting Sovereignty

Power and Practice in Africa and Southeast Asia

JOEL NG
Nanyang Technological University, Singapore

Shaftesbury Road, Cambridge CB2 8EA, United Kingdom

One Liberty Plaza, 20th Floor, New York, NY 10006, USA

477 Williamstown Road, Port Melbourne, VIC 3207, Australia

314–321, 3rd Floor, Plot 3, Splendor Forum, Jasola District Centre, New Delhi – 110025, India

103 Penang Road, #05–06/07, Visioncrest Commercial, Singapore 238467

Cambridge University Press is part of Cambridge University Press & Assessment, a department of the University of Cambridge.

We share the University's mission to contribute to society through the pursuit of education, learning and research at the highest international levels of excellence.

www.cambridge.org
Information on this title: www.cambridge.org/9781108796064

DOI: 10.1017/9781108854320

© Joel Ng 2021

This publication is in copyright. Subject to statutory exception and to the provisions of relevant collective licensing agreements, no reproduction of any part may take place without the written permission of Cambridge University Press & Assessment.

First published 2021
First paperback edition 2023

A catalogue record for this publication is available from the British Library

ISBN 978-1-108-49061-0 Hardback
ISBN 978-1-108-79606-4 Paperback

Cambridge University Press & Assessment has no responsibility for the persistence or accuracy of URLs for external or third-party internet websites referred to in this publication and does not guarantee that any content on such websites is, or will remain, accurate or appropriate.

In memory of my father,
Dr Andrew Ng,
who set me on this journey of two continents

Contents

List of Figures page ix
List of Tables x
Preface xi
Acknowledgements xii
List of Abbreviations xiv

Part I Normative Contestation in Regional Organisations

1 Introduction 9
2 Theoretical Framework 30

Part II The African Union

3 The 'United States of Africa' Proposal 79
4 The Conference on Security, Stability, Development, and Cooperation in Africa 103
5 The Pan-African Parliament 133

Part III The Association of Southeast Asian Nations

6 Human Rights 'Protection' in the ASEAN Charter 169
7 The ASEAN Human Rights Mechanism 194
8 Extending the 'ASEAN Minus X' Formula 224

Part IV Comparative Findings

9	Assessing the Model	255
10	Conclusion	265
Appendix: List of Officials Interviewed		275
Bibliography		278
Index		296

Figures

1.1	Model of contestation	*page* 14
2.1	RO norm contestation: simple process flow	51
5.1	Consultants' proposed organisation chart of the African Union	143
5.2	The position of the PAP in present AU organisational structure	153

Tables

2.1	Comparison of realist and constructivist theories of norms	page 36
2.2	Sources of uneven structural power in regional organisations	45
2.3	Case studies	66
II.1	Timeline of the transition from the OAU to the AU	75
3.1	Contestation over the 'United States of Africa'	98
4.1	The rejection and acceptance of the CSSDCA	130
5.1	The contestation over the Pan-African Parliament	158
III.1	Timeline of ASEAN charter processes	166
6.1	Members of the Eminent Persons Group on the ASEAN Charter	174
6.2	Members of the High Level Task Force for the Drafting of the ASEAN Charter	178
6.3	Human rights 'protection' in the ASEAN Charter	191
7.1	Members of the High Level Panel for the Terms of Reference of the ASEAN human rights body	200
7.2	Inaugural representatives of the ASEAN Intergovernmental Commission on Human Rights	204
7.3	Representatives of the ASEAN Human Rights Declaration drafting group	206
7.4	Contestation over the ASEAN human rights mechanism	218
8.1	Recommendations on ASEAN decision-making compared with the result	239
8.2	Rejection of 'ASEAN minus X' as a procedural norm in ASEAN	250

Preface

Two seminal periods in the history of two of the most significant regional organisations in the Global South occurred at the beginning of the twenty-first century. The African Union (AU) and the Association of Southeast Asian Nations (ASEAN), together representing more than a quarter of the world's population, established their norms through new charters (and physical reorganisation). The AU's and ASEAN's processes of norm-setting were by no means pre-ordained from the outset. The norms held by these organisations' members, and the roles they implied for each region, were sharply contested as the political diversity of their member states brought differences to the fore during negotiations. The result is a story of the most fundamental political-normative debate of the two regions: the status of sovereignty of its member states. How are sovereignty norms contested, and what determines the outcomes? To answer this, I examine the negotiation of normative standards in regional organisations of the Global South.

The case studies cover the formative charter-drafting periods of 1999–2003 in the AU and 2005–12 in ASEAN, following cases where the institutional norms were contested and established. For the AU this involved the Conference on Security, Stability, Development, and Cooperation in Africa (CSSDCA), the Pan-African Parliament, and the proposal for the 'United States of Africa'. In ASEAN, the cases follow the ASEAN charter-drafting process on two normative questions – the inclusion of human rights and the use of the 'ASEAN minus X' formula – and look separately at the later establishment of an ASEAN human rights mechanism (comprising its declaration and commission). In studying this contest at a regional level, the book hopes to offer insights into comparative regionalism, institutionalisation, and theories of normative contestation.

Acknowledgements

This book has its origins nearly a decade ago when I began working on a project on global governance and regional interventions. The importance of comparative study across global regions became apparent then, and set me on a path over the next decade to more extensively treat these questions of sovereignty and its limitations. As a result, however, I am indebted to numerous people, far too many, indeed, to be able to recall all of them.

First and foremost, this work was greatly enriched by the numerous people in Africa, Europe, and Asia who took the time to give interviews and provide introductions and information, and without whose input this book would simply have been impossible. The flaws that remain in the analysis are entirely my own.

In Africa, I owe a great deal of thanks to Emmanuel Akeh, Agnes Asele, Chedza Molefe, Kidist Shawul, Sirak Tesfayi, and Thomas Tieku, all of whom aided me in various ways.

In Europe, I was deeply indebted to comments, critiques, and challenges by Quentin Bruneau, Cho Inyoung, Julian Gruin, Yuna Han, Paul Hansbury, James Hollway, Sa'eedu Hussaini, Sharinee Jagtiani, Arthur Learoyd, Julia Costa Lopez, Gjovalin Macaj, Jordan Mansell, Kate Millar, Fuadi Pitsuwan, Patrick Quinton-Brown, Nicole de Silva, Nora Stappert, Anette Stimmer, Sara Usher, and many others in the course of numerous seminars and interactions. Dave Elder-Vass, Louise Fawcett, Todd Hall, Eddie Keene, Andy Hurrell, Karma Nabulsi, Iver Neumann, Kalypso Nicolaidis, Ricardo Soares de Oliveira, Fredrick Söderbaum, and Jennifer Welsh provided sage guidance at key points during the research.

In Singapore, I appreciated the encouragement, discussions, and advice of Ong Keng Yong, Mely Caballero-Anthony, Alan Chong, Alistair Cook, Barry Desker, Ralf Emmers, Kwa Chong Guan, Joseph Liow, T. V. Paul, Angela Poh, Evan Resnick, Bhubhindar Singh, Elaine Tan, Tan See Seng, and Pascal Vennesson. Anugya

Chitransh provided helpful research assistance. Bridging these worlds was my indefatigable mentor, Khong Yuen Foong, whose interventions and support pulled me through many challenges and across the finish line.

I am enormously grateful to the Swire Educational Trust and the Tan Kah Kee Foundation for supporting my research immensely. I would also like to thank three anonymous reviewers for their exceedingly helpful comments.

Special credit must go to Walter Lotze and Andreas Stensland, who gave me my first taste of comparative regionalism so many years ago and have my endless gratitude for sparking the ideas that took me to this point; Densua Mumford, the most helpful peer and collaborator I could ever have asked for, whose parallel path provoked many critical discussions; and Farish Noor, both mentor and friend, whose focus and determination are something to which I will always aspire.

Finally, to my family – my parents, Andrew and Belinda, for supporting me in ways that can never be repaid; to my daughters, Simone and Corinne, for being constant sources of happiness, warmth, and joy; and to my beloved Bernadette, without whose belief and support this journey simply would never have begun.

Abbreviations

ABA-ROLI	American Bar Association Rule of Law Initiative
Abuja Treaty	Abuja Treaty Establishing the AEC (1991)
AEC	African Economic Community (Chapters 3–5) *or* ASEAN Economic Community (Chapters 6–8)
AEM	ASEAN Economic Ministers (Meeting)
AFTA	ASEAN Free Trade Area
AHRB	ASEAN human rights body
AHRD	ASEAN Human Rights Declaration
AICHR	ASEAN Intergovernmental Commission on Human Rights
AIPO	ASEAN Interparliamentary Organisation
ALF	Africa Leadership Forum
AMM	ASEAN (Foreign) Ministers Meeting
ANC	African National Congress (South Africa)
APSC	ASEAN Political-Security Community
ASCC	ASEAN Socio-Cultural Community
ASEAN	Association of Southeast Asian Nations
AU	African Union
AUC	African Union Commission (Secretariat)

List of Abbreviations

Bali Concord I & II	Declaration of ASEAN Concord (I – 1976; II – 2003)
Bangkok Declaration	Final Declaration of the Regional Meeting for Asia of the World Conference on Human Rights (1993)
Banjul Charter	African Charter on Human and Peoples' Rights (1981)
CEDAW	Convention on the Elimination of All Forms of Discrimination against Women (1981)
CEPT	Common Effective Preferential Tariff scheme (ASEAN, 1992)
CFTA	Continental Free Trade Area
Cha-Am Hua Hin Declaration	Cha-Am Hua Hin Declaration on the Intergovernmental Commission on Human Rights
CIDO	Citizens and Diaspora Directorate
CLMV	Cambodia, Laos, Myanmar, Vietnam
CPR	Committee of Permanent Representatives
CPTPP	Comprehensive and Progressive Agreement for a TPP
CRC	Convention on the Rights of the Child (1989)
CSCE	Conference on Security and Cooperation in Europe
CSO	civil society organisation
CSSDCA	Conference on Security, Stability, Development, and Cooperation in Africa
DSM	dispute settlement mechanisms
E10	Elected non-permanent 10 members of the UNSC
EAC	East African Community
ECOMOG	ECOWAS Monitoring Group
ECOSOCC	Economic, Social, and Cultural Council (AU)

ECOWAS	Economic Community of West African States
EDSM	Enhanced Dispute Settlement Mechanism (ASEAN)
EPG	Eminent Persons Group on the ASEAN Charter
EU	European Union
FAN	Forces Armées du Nord (Northern Armed Forces, Chad)
FAO	Forces Armées d'Ouest (Western Armed Forces, Chad)
Frolinat	Front de Libération National du Tchad (National Liberation Front of Chad)
FTA	free trade agreement
GUNT	Gouvernement d'Union Nationale de Transition (Transitional National Union Government, Chad)
HLP	High Level Panel (ASEAN)
HLTF	High Level Task Force (ASEAN)
ICC	International Criminal Court
IMF	International Monetary Fund
ISEAS	Institute for Southeast Asian Studies (now ISEAS-Yusof Ishak Institute), Singapore
Komnas-HAM	Komisi Nasional Hak Asasi Manusia (National Commission for Human Rights) (Indonesia)
MAP	Millennium Africa Recovery Plan
Maputo Protocol	Protocol on Amendments to the Constitutive Act of the African Union (2003)
MCPMR	Mechanism on Conflict Prevention, Management, and Resolution (OAU)
MPs	Members of Parliament
NAFTA	North American Free Trade Area
NAI	New Africa Initiative
NATO	North Atlantic Treaty Organisation

List of Abbreviations

NEPAD	New Partnership for African Development
NGOs	non-governmental organisations
OAS	Organisation of American States
OAU	Organisation of African Unity
OSCE	Organisation for Security and Cooperation in Europe
P2	Permanent 2 members (China and Russia) of the UNSC
P3	Permanent 3 members (Britain, France, and USA) of the UNSC
P5	Permanent 5 members of the UNSC
PAP	Pan-African Parliament (AU)
PTA	preferential trade arrangement
R2P	responsibility to protect
RCEP	Regional Comprehensive Economic Partnership
REC	regional economic community
RO	regional organisation
SAARC	South Asian Association for Regional Cooperation
SADC	Southern African Development Community
SAPA TFAHR	Solidarity for Asian People's Advocacy – Task Force on ASEAN and Human Rights
SCO	Shanghai Cooperation Organisation
SEOM	Senior Economic Officials Meeting (ASEAN)
SOM	Senior Officials Meeting (ASEAN)
SUHAKAM	Suruhanjaya Hak Asasi Manusia Malaysia (Human Rights Commission of Malaysia)
TAC	Treaty of Amity and Cooperation (ASEAN, 1976)
TFTA	Tripartite Free Trade Agreement
ToR	terms of reference
TPP	Trans-Pacific Partnership

UDHR	Universal Declaration of Human Rights
UMNO	United Malays National Organisation (Malaysia)
UN	United Nations
UNECA	UN Economic Commission for Africa
UNOCI	UN Operation in Côte d'Ivoire
UNSC	UN Security Council
UNSG	UN Secretary-General
VAP	Vientiane Action Programme
WTO	World Trade Organisation
ZOPFAN	Zone of Peace, Freedom, and Neutrality (ASEAN, 1971)

PART I

Normative Contestation in Regional Organisations

After the Cold War, regional integration was believed to be an inexorable force driving the world into regional communities with ever closer unions as the 'retreat of the state' paved the way for globalisation.[1] Growing transboundary challenges and multinational supply chains required increasing transnational governance, it was argued, which nation-states were ill-equipped to tackle on their own. The collapse of traditional notions of sovereignty was to be one inevitable outcome of addressing these challenges.

That was until integration efforts hit the immovable object of populism in 2016. While exemplified by Brexit, this case was hardly alone – the Eurozone crisis had earlier resulted in an array of candidates that toyed with the idea of leaving the European Union (EU). Globally, the USA pulled out of the Trans-Pacific Partnership (TPP) as free trade deals, once anathema only to the left, began to be targeted by the right. Nationalist movements called for curbs to immigration, and new populist governments turned away from regional commitments. Almost overnight, not only integration but multilateralism itself appeared to be in peril as nationalism or unilateralism obstructed or even reversed integration efforts. Underlying this trend was a resurgence in cleaving to sovereignty in the traditional sense – a notion that many once hoped would become obsolete, associated as it was with authoritarianism, conflict, and failures of cooperation.

Against this backdrop, the integration stragglers of Southeast Asia and Africa became hold-outs of multilateralism, contrasting with the reversals on integration in other regions. Rowing against the current, Africa redoubled its 2013 integration commitments that had marked the fiftieth anniversary of the founding of the Organisation of African Unity (OAU): from a frequently stalled process to sign a Tripartite Free

---

[1] Strange, *The Retreat of the State: the Diffusion of Power in the World Economy* (Cambridge: Cambridge University Press, 1996).

Trade Agreement (TFTA) to link three sub-regional blocs, it abruptly halted the TFTA to push for an even more ambitious Continental Free Trade Area (CFTA) and pushed this out in 2018. Southeast Asia too was bucking the trend: while the USA had withdrawn from TPP, the Association of Southeast Asian Nations (ASEAN) and its regional partners continued to push ahead with these initiatives, whether through the renamed Comprehensive and Progressive Agreement for a TPP (CPTPP – the TPP without the USA) or another configuration with slightly different membership, the Regional Comprehensive Economic Partnership (RCEP – an FTA that China could join).

These two regions that had so rigidly adhered to a restrictive notion of sovereignty in the 1990s were now pushing ahead with integration efforts while the rest of the world was at a standstill or in retreat. Even with explicitly populist-nationalist governments in several key member states in both regions, they did not appear to have slowed their resolve for integration. Why is this the case?

The relative switch in positions is partly down to what went wrong in the West. For a start, proponents of liberal integration had underestimated political dynamics, and largely assumed that functional-technocratic considerations superseded other factors. Collective rationality and bureaucratisation were drivers for institutional isomorphism,[2] and other regional projects were at least copying the European model if not going as far as behavioural change,[3] and these models were constantly held up against the EU[4] as the benchmark for 'successful' integration. The end of the Cold War also sparked research on normative change, and the 'spiral' or 'cascade' model of norm dynamics[5] came to be a leading view, predicting extensive expansion and internalisation of human rights norms, another force weakening the sovereignty of states. The politics surrounding integration and human rights debates in Southeast Asia and Africa seemed anomalous

---

[2] DiMaggio and Powell, 'The Iron Cage Revisited: Institutional Isomorphism and Collective Rationality in Organizational Fields', *American Sociological Review* 48, no. 2 (1983).

[3] Jetschke and Murray, 'Diffusing Regional Integration: the EU and Southeast Asia', *West European Politics* 35, no. 1 (2012).

[4] Lenz, 'EU Normative Power and Regionalism: Ideational Diffusion and its Limits', *Cooperation and Conflict* 48, no. 2 (2013).

[5] Risse, Ropp, and Sikkink, eds., *The Power of Human Rights: International Norms and Domestic Change* (Cambridge: Cambridge University Press, 1999).

and their failures to copy the European model due to an unfortunate lack of capacity (that could yet be corrected with more development assistance).

The African Union (AU) and ASEAN would be criticised for their failures to deepen liberal norms, rendering integration ineffective and piecemeal. Yet something rather different was playing out in their contestation over these debates about the locus of sovereignty. The member states had not simply been unable to implement them nor retreated into bubbles of denial. They had held intense debates about the nature and legitimacy of their regional norms as they embarked on charter-writing processes, and these contests accepted some qualifications on sovereignty while rejecting others. The debates, while fractious and remembered with misgivings by some, nevertheless relegitimised each region's processes, while bringing their resultant norms closer to their members' preferences.

At the time, there were some public disappointments as key regional initiators felt they had not obtained what they had originally pushed for. However, when the trend towards populism and anti-globalist forces surged, what was noteworthy was that both regions had already calibrated their respective paces for integration against a balance of sovereignty considerations. While questions have been raised about liberal values, the backlash against globalisation and regionalism has been far more subdued than in the EU.

This book investigates this key period of contestation in Africa and Southeast Asia with the following questions: Why were some sovereignty-limiting norms accepted while others were rejected? How did the contests play out, and what were the decisive factors to explain the outcome? Finally, what does the process of contestation tell us about the legitimacy of these outcomes and future prospects?

In examining the key question of outcomes from normative contestation, the book introduces a conceptual device from sociology, the 'norm circle' – groups committed to endorsing or enforcing a norm – to study domain-specified norm contestation (the regional organisation, or 'RO'). The model suggests that under conditions of contestation involving at least two closely matched norm circles, actors compete according to the terms of their domain, the RO. The differences involve actors' competencies in controlling the initiative, their mastery of other shared norms, and their ability to seek other opportunities of influence, termed 'metis'. Their relative success in these areas determines whether the norms in question are accepted, rejected, or qualified. Moreover, the future legitimacy and path dependencies are built into the contestation process: they depend on which of the above factors were critical in shaping the eventual norm, at least until new rounds of contestation play out.

Empirically, this book examines six case studies, three each from the AU and ASEAN, in which significant new norms were proposed testing member state sovereignty, after which the norms were either accepted, rejected, or qualified. Each case reviews the historical origins of the norm and the proposal, followed by analysis of how each norm circle used the factors mentioned above to seek approval for their proposals. It then assesses the relative importance of the factors, alternative explanations, and future implications for the norms in each case. In the AU, the three cases are the proposals for the 'United States of Africa', the Conference on Security, Stability, Development, and Cooperation in Africa, and the Pan-African Parliament. In ASEAN, this book examines the question of human rights in the ASEAN Charter, the attempt to formalise the 'ASEAN minus X' principle, also during the charter drafting, and the contestation over the creation of a regional human rights mechanism, which eventually became the ASEAN Intergovernmental Commission on Human Rights.

The rise of populism has challenged many preconceptions about a world order built on integration and liberalisation. The global order born after World War II had sought to bring the world closer together, and in so doing, reduce the prospect for conflict between states. Sovereignty, it was believed – particularly by early functionalists such as David Mitrany[6] – led to unilateral pursuit of national interests at the price of international security. However, the independence struggles of former colonies and then the outbreak of Cold War conflicts in Africa and Asia led to quite different understandings of sovereignty, a value that leaders in these regions felt was necessary to pursue their national aspirations. Africa and Southeast Asia both had their own share of debate between integration and sovereignty, though it looked very different from the European version. Africa was guided by a strong intellectual tradition of Pan-Africanism, which had originally emerged in the USA and Caribbean. Pan-Africanism sought unity to undo the

---

[6] Mitrany, 'The Functional Approach to World Organization', *International Affairs* 24, no. 3 (1948).

damage and divisions wrought by colonialism. The shared experience of slavery and colonialism gave a strong impetus to overcome the colonial legacy and limit its continuing influence beyond formal independence.

In Southeast Asia, the unification debate was less ambitious, given more varied experiences with colonialism. However, there was still a significant push for uniting the peoples of the Malayan archipelago by a newly independent Indonesia. As in Africa, it had been partitioned by colonial imperial markers, and the nationalist sentiments of some independence leaders were built on an identity that exceeded the boundaries of their independent nation-states. Unfortunately, Indonesia's independence leader, Sukarno, did this movement no good when he attempted to accomplish it by force, leading to a period known as *Konfrontasi* ('Confrontation'), which set neighbours Singapore and Malaysia against him. When the Association of Southeast Asian Nations was born shortly after Sukarno's desposal, Southeast Asian regionalism had quite a different sort of agenda: preventing the new Indonesian leadership from attempting another such military excursion again.

In both regions, the Cold War had seen states aligned with Western or Eastern blocs afflicted by conflicts as the global superpowers waged direct or proxy wars to try to preserve their spheres of influence. While some security guarantees were needed from a superpower, there was always the tension with the superpower's ability to wield undue influence in the regimes or policies of the states under its umbrella. Abstract appeals to sovereignty and non-interference were perhaps some of the least political ways to spell out this distance.

The end of the Cold War brought sovereignty back into question. Communist states, which tended towards authoritarian rule, had collapsed and much of this was ascribed to the failures of central planning. With the ascent of neo-liberalism in the 1990s, pressure was once again asserted against sovereignty, with free markets and regional economic communities being thought to be the most effective way of enabling development and economic growth. Civil conflicts in Africa also pressed against the political notions of sovereignty such as non-interference, as insecurity in one state could destabilise or even collapse neighbouring states, as the Liberia–Sierra Leone conflicts demonstrated.

Thus, the background to these episodes of contestation over sovereignty was informed by global and regional trends, but intimately related to each region's priorities. The relationship between regional integration and sovereignty in the Global South has always been complex, not only on account of protectionist sentiments, but also at an ideological level on the nature of integration itself. More than merely sovereignty as a norm, the question lay in deciding where the balance of member states' agency lay in the regional environment. Ultimately, these cases show how the dynamics of the regional organisations themselves were decisive in finally positioning the locus between regional and member state agency to deal with their governance imperatives and challenges as they saw them.

This book investigates normative change in a domain that has sometimes been overlooked for its potential in observing contestation – the regional organisation (RO). Focusing on political norms, it asks: What explains the acceptance or rejection of norms challenging sovereignty in regional organisations? If the members of ROs are states, having a quality of 'sovereignty', then the coming together as a 'region' involving iterated cooperation[7] necessarily risks some of that sovereignty (when understood as freedom to act) because it constrains certain courses of action while committing to others. The establishment of binding rules for members of an RO, and a commitment to abiding by them, reduces the total range of possible actions a state may take. For example, a regional nuclear non-proliferation treaty commits a state to not developing nuclear weapons, even though this may be among its strategic options for defence. Thus, commitment to regional norms forms the basic tension within an RO for sovereign member states.

To answer the question about the acceptance or rejection of norms, I develop a contestation model at the intersection of functionalism and practice – two essential elements for the study of regional organisations and diplomacy. This model borrows a concept from sociology – the 'norm circle', defined as 'groups of people who share a commitment to endorse and enforce a particular norm'[8] – to differentiate actors and measure differences between the groups in opposition during

---

[7] Krapohl, ed., *Regional Integration in the Global South: External Influence on Economic Cooperation in ASEAN, Mercosur and SADC* (Cham, Switzerland: Palgrave Macmillan, 2017), 5.

[8] Elder-Vass, 'Towards a Realist Social Constructionism', *Sociologia, Problemas e Práticas*, no. 70 (2012): 11–12.

Normative Contestation in Regional Organisations

contestation. This allows it to bring in the insights from coalition literature[9] that are rarely employed in norms and constructivist literature. Finally, a conscious analysis of 'power in practice'[10] brings insights from diplomatic studies and negotiation theories to bear on normative outcomes. Greatly unequal norm circles follow power dynamics in that the lesser side is likely to concede, but 'contestation' arises when the sides are relatively equal, for example owing to institutional rules that negate power differentials (such as veto or consensus mechanisms).

My central argument is that three processual factors of diplomatic practice play out in regional norm contestation: (1) the control of the initiative, (2) the actors' use of other existing shared norms and practices, and (3) their 'metis' or agential power to change relations – which, in the conceptual framework of norm circles, is the ability to bring actors into their preferred norm circle. These competencies form a diplomatic 'power', distinct from material conceptions of power, which has significant effects on normative outcomes. Through this model and studying contestation at a regional level, the book hopes to offer insights into comparative regionalism, institutionalisation, and theories of normative contestation.

---

[9] For example, Krehbiel, *Pivotal Politics: A Theory of US Lawmaking* (Chicago: University of Chicago Press, 1998); Gehlbach, *Formal Models of Domestic Politics* (Cambridge: Cambridge University Press, 2013).

[10] Adler-Nissen and Pouliot, 'Power in Practice: Negotiating the International Intervention in Libya', *European Journal of International Relations* 20, no. 4 (2014).

1 Introduction

The beginning of the twenty-first century saw a rapid period of institution-building in regional organisations (ROs) of the Global South. The decade started with the Organisation of American States (OAS) adopting the Inter-American Democratic Charter in 2001. In 2002, the African Union (AU) was established, succeeding the ineffectual Organisation of African Unity (OAU), with its Constitutive Act giving members the right to intervene in grave circumstances of war crimes, genocide and crimes against humanity,[1] overturning a long-standing non-interference principle that was blamed for the ineffectiveness of the old OAU. In 2004, the League of Arab States established an Arab Charter on Human Rights. In 2007, the ASEAN Charter was established that gave the Association of Southeast Asian Nations (ASEAN) a legal identity for the first time and formalised a set of norms that guided the relations of its members both among themselves and in relation to external states. By 2012, it had adopted the ASEAN Declaration on Human Rights. During this flurry of regional norm-setting, the 2005 World Summit at the UN General Assembly unanimously agreed an array of human rights commitments, including the principle of the 'responsibility to protect' (R2P), as key norms that were universally accepted by its member states.

Yet the period that followed immediately after – involving the first real tests of the extent of these normative commitments in Africa and Southeast Asia – did not result in agreement on the needed courses of action, nor did it establish which norms took precedence in cases of contestation. Instead it exposed the thinness of the commitment to principles such as R2P and considerable disagreement on actions needed in crisis situations.

---

[1] African Union, 'The Constitutive Act of the African Union' (Lomé 2000), Art. 4(h).

While AU interventions on the grounds of R2P increased, particularly against non-state actors in Sudan, Somalia, Mali, and so on, this contrasted with the organisation's stonewalling against intervention in 2011 that would have confronted state actors in Côte d'Ivoire and Libya. While sub-regional organisations such as the Economic Community of West African States (ECOWAS) and the Arab League favoured intervention, and despite the AU's precedence-setting on the right to intervene as provided for in its Constitutive Act, it nevertheless favoured political mediation and blocked intervention plans in both cases. The (non-)decisions were then overtaken by circumstance as ECOWAS and French forces pushed ahead to intervene directly in Côte d'Ivoire under UN authorisation, while an Arab League-sponsored UN Security Council (UNSC) resolution resulted in NATO intervention in Libya. Meanwhile, despite the acknowledgement of principles of human rights and democratisation in its charter, ASEAN did not change its stance over the longstanding issue of human rights violations in Myanmar, preferring to continue its quiet diplomatic pressures internally, while rebuffing overt pressure externally. Liberal optimism about the inclusion of human rights in the ASEAN Charter dissipated when the ASEAN Intergovernmental Commission on Human Rights and Human Rights Declaration were eventually adopted with no protection, monitoring, or even communication mechanisms.

Taken together, these two sets of observations – rapid formalisation or commitment (possibly short of 'institutionalisation') followed by contestation – are difficult for existing theories to explain. Realist theories would have dismissed the charter revisions as 'theatre',[2] pointing out that in actual events, interests would prevail. But that begged the question: Why would member states create new, permanent rules with which they had no intention of complying, and the superficiality of which would be exposed as soon as an actual crisis occurred? How could Muammar Gaddafi, representing one of the 'big five' donors[3] to the OAU, fail so utterly to achieve his aims of influence in his region? A liberal constructivist account might have described the new Constitutive Act or ASEAN Charter as the tipping

---

[2] Wigstrom, 'Beyond Theatre Regionalism: When Does Formal Economic Integration Work in Africa?' (PhD dissertation, University of Oxford, 2013).

[3] The 'big five' donors to the OAU/AU were South Africa, Nigeria, Egypt, Algeria, and Libya, which, in the 2000s, together accounted for a larger share of contributions than the other fifty members.

point of a norm cascade that would lead to a deepening of respect for human rights and progressive norms, but how could this cascade stumble at virtually its first hurdle in two different regions? Institutional isomorphism would at best explain the creation, but leave the problems of implementation as anomalous or the organisations lacking political will in its theory – without an adequate theoretical treatment of 'political will'. These puzzles lead to deeper theoretical questions. What explains the acceptance and rejection of norms challenging sovereignty in regional organisations? If structural conditions of member equality hold in the formal rules of the organisations, how do actors exercise differences in power to achieve their normative aims? Further, what normative trajectories or path dependencies develop out of the nature of contestation that takes place, particularly norms that challenge sovereignty?

This book examines the practice of normative contestation over sovereignty in the AU and ASEAN. Norm contestation refers to the ways in which actors 'dispute the validity, the meaning or the application of norms'.[4] While increasing attention to normative contestation has taken place in recent years, our understanding still involves several gaps, including the dynamics of contestation in two major regional organisations of the Global South.

In international relations, theories about normativity are young, having emerged barely twenty years ago.[5] The first wave of norm theorists investigated normative development *within* a liberal post-Cold War order and, facing a realist orthodoxy, were more concerned with demonstrating that norms had a significant effect at all. With the overarching order ensconced by the collapse of communism and global US hegemony through the 1990s, norms studied in this period seemed to point to the norm 'cascade' theory driven by 'norm entrepreneurs',[6] as developed by Risse, Ropp, and Sikkink.[7] In these models,

---

[4] Wolff and Zimmermann, 'Between Banyans and Battle Scenes: Liberal Norms, Contestation, and the Limits of Critique', *Review of International Studies* 42, no. 3 (2015): 518.
[5] Finnemore, 'Norms, Culture, and World Politics: Insights from Sociology's Institutionalism', *International Organization* 50, no. 2 (1996): 344.
[6] Finnemore and Sikkink, 'International Norm Dynamics and Political Change', *International Organization* 52, no. 4 (1998).
[7] Risse, Ropp, and Sikkink, *The Power of Human Rights*; Risse, Ropp, and Sikkink, *The Persistent Power of Human Rights: From Commitment to Compliance*, Cambridge Studies in International Relations (Cambridge: Cambridge University Press, 2013).

contestation is a characteristic at the start of the process, but is overcome by the actions of norm entrepreneurs who eventually remove obstacles in a 'cascade'.

Whereas challenges to this theory emerged,[8] the alternative models continued to presume the existence of the liberal order, such as that of Amitav Acharya, who offered 'norm localisation', a theory on how transnational norms might take root, without investigating where or how the transnational norm originates (perhaps taking a norm cascade as given).[9] Other approaches to contestation searched for contestation within the meaning of broader norms,[10] but again such a framework assumed the norm to already be widely accepted, with only the specifics to be determined. Finally, Wiener identifies contestation as an output to fill a legitimacy gap that exists because of tensions between broadly accepted fundamental norms and actually existing rules and practices[11] – but permits few pathways to investigate challenges to fundamental norms and requires a specific circumstance (that a legitimacy gap is the fundamental problem facing contestants) and ontological assumption (that competing norms are reconcilable), incongruent with the cases that will be presented.

Non-constructivist approaches such as realist or rational choice theories were relatively uninterested in the qualitative content of norms. Realist approaches are premised on the notion that 'the logics of consequences dominate the logics of appropriateness',[12] i.e. that

---

[8] For a constructivist critique, see Hurrell, 'Power, Institutions, and the Production of Inequality', in *Power in Global Governance*, ed. Barnett and Duvall (Cambridge: Cambridge University Press, 2005). For a quantitative critique, see Hafner-Burton and Ron, 'Seeing Double', *World Politics* 61, no. 2 (2009).

[9] Acharya, *Whose Ideas Matter? Agency and Power in Asian Regionalism* (Singapore: Institute of Southeast Asian Studies, 2010). He has since addressed this through a new model of 'norm circulation' in 'The R2P and Norm Diffusion: Towards a Framework of Norm Circulation', *Global Responsibility to Protect* 5, no. 4 (2013). However, whereas the former was agent-centred, it is difficult to see the continuity of agency in his circulation model, in which the localising agents are expected to be equally influential at both global and regional levels, while the resistance to these agents is not theorised.

[10] Wiener, *The Invisible Constitution of Politics: Contested Norms and International Encounters* (Cambridge: Cambridge University Press, 2008).

[11] Wiener, *A Theory of Contestation* (Heidelberg: Springer, 2014).

[12] Krasner, *Sovereignty: Organized Hypocrisy* (Princeton: Princeton University Press, 1999), 6.

Introduction 13

self-interested, calculated behaviour in the pursuit of states' goals trumped norms as predictors of their behaviour. Rational choice theories that used mathematical models required cases where cost-benefit analysis was quantifiable, i.e. 'the conflicts of interest over the distribution of those adjustment costs',[13] treating preferences exogenously, and with relatively firm rules of enforcement. Norms that were ambiguous, hard to quantify, or weakly enforced were difficult to model under such conditions.

The contents of political norms were thus left relatively unexplained in realist or rationalist models. Whereas both approaches offered useful tools that might have been brought to bear on the question of norms, namely power (realism) and utility and preference ordering (rational choice), the disinterest left normativity theories in international relations to largely be dominated by discourse analysis[14] and constructivists,[15] and thus focused on persuasion or diffusion as mechanisms for transmission.[16] The efforts to demonstrate normative *change*, however, left resistance and contestation unexplained: at best they were failures of the scope conditions for change; at worst, they delivered teleological accounts with Whiggish interpretations of history.

There is now an increasing literature on norm contestation, particularly starting from the recognition that norms contain ambiguities that allow space for contestation.[17] What these studies hold in common is

---

[13] Buthe and Mattli, *The New Global Rulers: the Privatization of Regulation in the World Economy* (Princeton: Princeton University Press, 2011), 42.

[14] For example, Ramos, *Changing Norms through Actions: the Evolution of Sovereignty* (Oxford: Oxford University Press, 2013); Krook and True, 'Rethinking the Life Cycles of International Norms: the United Nations and the Global Promotion of Gender Equality', *European Journal of International Relations* 18, no. 1 (2012); Booth Walling, *All Necessary Measures: the United Nations and Humanitarian Intervention* (Philadelphia: University of Pennsylvania Press, 2013).

[15] Goodman and Jinks, *Socializing States: Promoting Human Rights through International Law* (Oxford: Oxford University Press, 2013); Risse, Ropp, and Sikkink, *The Persistent Power of Human Rights*.

[16] Checkel, 'International Institutions and Socialization in Europe: Introduction and Framework', *International Organization* 59, no. 4 (2005).

[17] Wiener, *The Invisible Constitution of Politics*. See also Panke and Petersohn, 'Why International Norms Disappear Sometimes', *European Journal of International Relations* 18, no. 4 (2011); Sandholtz, 'Dynamics of International Norm Change', *European Journal of International Relations* 14, no. 1 (2008); Moses, *Sovereignty and Responsibility: Power, Norms and Intervention in*

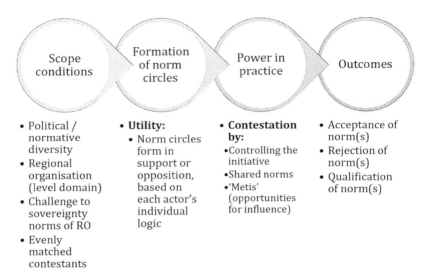

Figure 1.1 Model of contestation.

that effective normative opposition must draw on different sources for legitimacy to contest the norm in question. The practices and presumptions of both protagonists and their opponents must be impartially investigated to understand the outcomes that result. Presuming an overarching normative order tends to skew results, which is precisely why this book focuses on contestation – the 'critical practice with the purpose of participating in the process of negotiating normativity'.[18] The argument of this book is that in politically diverse ROs where material inequalities are relatively constrained (such as through funding rules, consensus decision-making processes, or individual member votes), when contestation arises, successful norms are determined by a relational notion of power driven by practice (see Figure 1.1). First, a proposal is made that invokes or implies certain norms. Norm circles form according to different actors' perceived

> *International Relations* (Basingstoke: Palgrave Macmillan, 2014); Gordon, 'Human Rights as a Security Threat: Lawfare and the Campaign against Human Rights NGOs', *Law and Society Review* 48, no. 2 (2014); Dietelhoff and Zimmerman, 'Things We Lost in the Fire: How Different Types of Contestation Affect the Validity of International Norms', *Peace Research Institute Frankfurt Working Paper* 18(2013); Wolff and Zimmermann, 'Between Banyans and Battle Scenes'.

[18] Wiener, *A Theory of Contestation*, 8.

utility of the norms (in relation to their national interests). Next, the competing norm circles contest: if the difference in size is overwhelming, it is unlikely that the smaller norm circle will put up much resistance. However, with more moderate differences in power (especially where domain rules like consensus decision-making provide minority states with significant degrees of power), then the contest is determined by the exercise of competence along three lines: (1) controlling the initiative, (2) the mastery of other shared norms of that domain, and (3) metis, the actors' skill in 'obtain[ing] the maximum number of effects from the minimum force',[19] that uses contingent opportunities to wield influence and change social relations – in particular, the weight of opinion or distribution of norm circles in favour or opposition to the norms.

In searching for a space that is both contested and normative, I have chosen regional organisations in the Global South, wherein normative barriers to entry are thin, and therefore the normative positions of states vary widely. By historical period, I also seek periods of greater normative openness at critical junctures, where norms were rapidly being developed – and two recent periods work particularly well: the transition from the Organisation of African Unity to the African Union from 1999 to 2003, and the period around the establishment of the ASEAN Charter until the ASEAN Human Rights Declaration from 2004 to 2012. The use of ROs from two distinct regions also hopefully avoids the over-specification common in area studies, which obstructs the ability to draw out generalisable characteristics or observations, and sharpens the nature of differentiation between them where variation exists.

Finally, despite studying rather narrow, limited cases of contestation over individual (if sometimes wide-ranging) proposals, each case study has significant implications tracing back to the broad study of regionalism. If the governance of regions is conducted through regimes,[20] part of which include the clusters of norms that grant

---

[19] De Certeau, *The Practice of Everyday Life* (Berkeley: University of California Press, 1984), 84, quoted in Neumann, 'Returning Practice to the Linguistic Turn: the Case of Diplomacy', *Millennium: Journal of International Studies* 31, no. 3 (2002): 633.
[20] Fawcett, 'Exploring Regional Domains: a Comparative History of Regionalism', *International Affairs* 80, no. 3 (2004): 433.

regimes both order and legitimacy,[21] then the study of how these norms came to be accepted or even identity-forming suggests significance beyond the simple explanation of their acceptance, rejection, or qualification. Furthermore, the nature of contestation also suggests important path dependencies in the life cycle of such norms, something that often goes amiss in independent–dependent variable analyses. Given the focus on sovereignty-challenging norm proposals, in studying both failed and successful proposals, this book offers possible explanations for the continued resilience of nation-state sovereignty in a world of regionalisms.

Outline

The current chapter begins with the research question that guides the entire study. This is followed by a review of norms literature, including problems with its application to regional organisations and the Global South more generally. I argue that earlier scholars of normative change have tended to undertheorise opposition to the norm, especially the opposition's means of resistance and therefore their power, as well as how the norms are selected. In this book, these are central components of the model, though specific to the domain. Chapter 2 then constructs the theoretical framework, stressing an anti-foundationalist account of how norms are selected. This avoids privileging some norms, or treating the preference as fixed and entirely exogenous. I then consider how groups of norm followers or proponents emerge, which I introduce through the 'norm circle' following sociologist Dave Elder-Vass. This permits the further specification of several variables, such as their size, power, and their competence in a given domain.

I argue that 'competence' is measured by the respective norm circles' performance in three key areas: (1) controlling the initiative, (2) their mastery of shared norms, and (3) their ability to identify and exert opportunistic possibilities for influence, including bringing material factors back into play, given that the domain of the RO ostensibly excludes this or maintains a putative equality of members. These therefore form the key set of independent variables that affect the outcome of the cases.

---

[21] Hurrell, *On Global Order: Power, Values and the Constitution of International Society* (Oxford: Oxford University Press, 2007), 83–7.

I then turn to investigating the two regional organisations – the AU and ASEAN – giving a brief background to their respective normative trajectories, given their historical experiences. From this I select six cases – three from each organisation, and with one of three outcomes: acceptance, rejection, or qualification – for norms that tested the sovereignty of the member states of the RO. The six empirical case studies then follow as individual chapters (3 to 8).

Chapter 9 brings in a comparative lens to look at the relevance of the different factors across the two regions, drawing from all six case studies. It also reviews the empirical evidence against the model's deductive inferences. The Conclusion (Chapter 10) considers the wider implications of this study against several themes in international relations. First, it shows that competing norms usually represent competing logics that are difficult to reconcile, and this has considerable and underrecognised implications for several linear theories of normative and institutional change. Second, it draws from this notion to the wider impact on comparative regionalism, with the observation that an era where political and economic logics are not aligned will be highly contested. Third, it discusses the impact that contestation has on legitimacy. Finally, it closes with some policy implications.

Norms Literature

Norms are the building blocks of institutions, but before we can investigate institutional change through norms, it is worth exploring theories of normative change. In the 1990s, liberal constructivists faced a realist orthodoxy that asserted that norms did not really matter because 'clubs can always be trump',[22] and this led, among other things, to two characteristics of the empirical cases they studied. First, they sought cases that played down the importance of power, and second, they sought cases where new norms had profound influences on behaviour in international relations. Contested norms tended not to have these characteristics: power was typically a significant factor in contestation, and contested new norms did not necessarily lead to behavioural change, least of all from the norm's opponents, who may have considered the contest unfinished. Unsuccessful attempts at spreading a norm also went unstudied.

[22] Krasner, *Sovereignty: Organized Hypocrisy*, 238.

In searching for significant normative *change*, liberal constructivists sought a 'winner' that drove new normative characteristics and behaviours. The most influential theory of norm dynamics suggested that human rights norm acceptance moves through five stages of a 'spiral' or 'cascade' model: (1) repression, (2) denial, (3) tactical concessions, (4) prescriptive status, and finally, (5) rules-consistent behaviour. Risse et al. argued that the spiral model of human rights adoption might be able to account for broader 'socio-political change processes, where such change involves norms other than human rights'.[23] They believed that the phases of their model were shortening, correlating with 'the growing robustness of international human rights norms and increasing strength of transnational advocacy networks'.[24]

Yet fourteen years later, their review of their case studies was more guarded. By their own admission, some human rights progress has failed, as in the case of Guatemala.[25] In other cases, such as Uganda, they would surely have withdrawn their claim that President Yoweri Museveni was a '"true believer" in human rights',[26] as documented by numerous violations in the northern Uganda conflict and the criminalisation of homosexuality. Both Uganda and Guatemala had been cited as examples of states in the latter stages of the spiral, predicting that it was 'very likely' that these countries would move from prescriptive status to rules-consistent behaviour regarding human rights.[27]

Instead, they had to deal with setbacks in these and many other cases, including the USA's use of torture,[28] while still using the model to argue that the USA eventually returned to a compliant international standard on torture. Conceding they were wrong to expect their model to be unidirectional,[29] this still left unexplained how normative change in the opposite direction occurred, including what the driving interests, legitimation claims, or assumptions might be for protagonists on the other side. They were also criticised for failing to demonstrate any deepening of human rights changes.[30]

---

[23] Risse, Ropp, and Sikkink, *The Power of Human Rights*, 273. [24] Ibid., 266.
[25] Risse, Ropp, and Sikkink, *The Persistent Power of Human Rights*, 75.
[26] Risse, Ropp, and Sikkink, *The Power of Human Rights*, 16. [27] Ibid., 248.
[28] Sikkink, 'The United States and Torture: Does the Spiral Model Work?' in *The Persistent Power of Human Rights*, ed. Risse, Ropp, and Sikkink.
[29] Risse, Ropp, and Sikkink, *The Persistent Power of Human Rights*, 285.
[30] Hafner-Burton and Ron, 'Seeing Double.'

Risse et al. tightened their scope conditions, withdrew their more ambitious claims, but still maintained the salience of their model. However, these beg some questions. Why, if their arguments on the *intrinsic* properties of the norm are correct,[31] would human rights progress stall or reverse?[32] If human rights acceptance is a legitimating factor that drives its acceptance and the global human rights regime is generally strengthening, how can illegitimate acts or pushbacks be carried out so frequently? Under what conditions are norms contested? Thus, models focused on explaining normative *change* were insufficient for explaining normative contestation, because of their prerequisite for a successful norm to be the subject of analysis. They thus did not adequately theorise resistance to it – a critical question for norm contestation.

A fresh wave of norm research did focus explicitly on norm contestation. Antje Wiener pioneered one aspect of norm contestation, highlighting that the meanings of norms themselves were not fixed and this provided space for disagreements.[33] Yet Wiener does not tackle the question of how norms succeed or fail, instead using 'the principle of contestedness as a meta-organising principle of governance'.[34] For her, the *access to* contestation drives its legitimacy, and she assumes norm contests can be resolved – an assumption that does not necessarily hold for all cases.[35] Dietelhoff and Zimmerman suggest another bifurcation between 'applicatory' and 'justificatory' contestation: applicatory contestation relates to questions about which or whether a norm applies for a given situation, while justificatory contestation looks at what norms the group wants to uphold. The validity of a norm is not questioned under applicatory contestation, but is questioned under justificatory contestation.[36]

Another corrective to the missing theorising of norm resistance comes from Bloomfield's idea of 'norm antipreneurs', 'actors who

---

[31] See especially Finnemore and Sikkink, 'International Norm Dynamics.'
[32] According to Freedom House, 'freedom in the world' had decreased for ten consecutive years since 2006. Freedom in the World Index 2016 (https://freedomhouse.org/report/freedom-world/freedom-world-2016).
[33] Wiener, 'Contested Meanings of Norms: a Research Framework', *Comparative European Politics* 5, no. 1 (2007).
[34] Wiener, *A Theory of Contestation*, 3.
[35] Bloomfield, 'Norm Antipreneurs and Theorising Resistance to Normative Change', *Review of International Studies* 42, no. 2 (2015): 315–16.
[36] Dietelhoff and Zimmerman, 'Things We Lost in the Fire', 5.

defend the entrenched normative status quo against challengers'.[37] What these cases have in common is a central emphasis on the role of discourse in shaping the norms,[38] and this leaves relatively interesting questions about power and practice out of the picture.[39] This emphasis on discourse is not unimportant, but to ignore power and practices would be to overlook what are argued to be central dynamics in, for example, international institutional[40] or diplomacy[41] literature, clearly important characteristics for the study of norms in ROs.

Norms and Power

Risse et al.'s spiral/cascade theory of norm dynamics was probably the most general theory of normative change in international relations, but it tried to explain change without the use of physical power, ascribing influence to the power of the idea, rather than agents. But within a given domain and given the existence of opposition to a norm, power may still be a factor and must be considered accordingly. This section discusses the basis of norm formation to argue that power is intrinsically a part of norms and must be included in a thoroughgoing analysis of normative contestation.

Barnett and Duval define power as 'the production, in and through social relations, of effects that shape the capacities of actors to determine their own circumstances and fate'.[42] They further identify four forms of power:

---

[37] Bloomfield, 'Norm Antipreneurs', 321.

[38] Other examples in the new contestation literature include Sandholtz, 'Dynamics of International Norm Change'; Bower, 'Arguing with Law: Strategic Legal Argumentation, Us Diplomacy, and Debates over the International Criminal Court', *Review of International Studies* 41, no. 2 (2014); Krook and True, 'Rethinking the Life Cycles of International Norms'; Acharya, 'Norm Subsidiarity and Regional Orders: Sovereignty, Regionalism, and Rule-Making in the Third World', *International Studies Quarterly* 55, no. 1 (2011); van Kersbergen and Verbeek, 'The Politics of International Norms: Subsidiarity and the Imperfect Competence Regime of the European Union', *European Journal of International Relations* 13, no. 2 (2007).

[39] Hurrell, 'Power, Institutions, and the Production of Inequality.'

[40] Woods and Mattli, eds., *The Politics of Global Regulation* (Princeton: Princeton University Press, 2009).

[41] Sending, Pouliot, and Neumann, *Diplomacy and the Making of World Politics* (Cambridge: Cambridge University Press, 2015).

[42] Barnett and Duvall, *Power in Global Governance* (Cambridge: Cambridge University Press, 2005), 3.

1 *compulsory* power: the 'relations of interaction that allow one actor to have direct control over another';
2 *institutional* power: 'when actors exercise indirect control over others, such as when states design international institutions in ways that work to their long-term advantage and to the disadvantage of others',
3 *structural* power: 'the constitution of social capacities and interests of actors in direct relation to one another'; and
4 *productive* power: 'the socially diffuse production of subjectivity in systems of meaning and signification'.[43]

These distinctions are important for the study of the establishment of norms, where both the factors for their establishment and their influence tend to be diffuse rather than direct.

As will be discussed later, establishing the domain around the regional organisation delineates institutional and structural power, but suggests the core factors entail forms of productive power. In some cases, institutionalisation of certain norms could be a means of promoting interests through indirect power, which might be understood as embedding an actor's particular logic of appropriateness over others as a more efficient means of enforcement than physical measures. This nuanced definition of power permits examining the kinds of processes that are overlooked in certain constructivist frameworks.

If norms constrain or enable actors, then changing norms affects the relative distribution of power. While the costs may not be easily quantifiable, this is consistent with the idea that when proposing new norms, there are 'conflicts of interest over the distribution of those adjustment costs',[44] for those furthest from the proposed norms. Norms, once embedded, constitute a diffuse form of power – they form a key component of institutions, defined as 'systems of established and prevalent social rules that structure social interactions'.[45] The establishment of norms, then, affects forms of institutional power as defined above.[46]

---

[43] Ibid. [44] Buthe and Mattli, *The New Global Rulers*, 42.
[45] Hodgson, 'What are Institutions?' *Journal of Economic Issues* 40, no. 1 (2006): 2.
[46] See also Mahoney and Thelen, eds., *Explaining Institutional Change: Ambiguity, Agency, and Power* (Cambridge: Cambridge University Press, 2010), 8–9.

Thus, if norms affect power relations and attributing power is to politicise it, how are norms generated? Norms, as a component of institutions, comprise elements of both rules and regularities. As Hurrell notes:

> [N]orms are identified by regularities of behaviour among actors. Norms reflect actual patterns of behaviour and give rise to expectations as to what will in fact be done in a particular situation ... [N]orms reflect patterned behaviour of a particular kind: a prescribed pattern of behaviour which gives rise to normative expectations as to what ought to be done.[47]

A rule may take the logical form, 'If X, do Y,'[48] while a regularity would take the form, 'If X, Y occurs.' Even a rule to which no one (alive) subscribes would still be a rule – for example, the Babylonian Code of Hammurabi or the grammatical rules of the extinct language Linear B – and requires no intersubjective agreement to *exist* (though it would need such agreement to be *effective*, however). As 'social' facts, however, norms require intersubjective agreement to have a 'normative' character or *causal* influence. A degree of regularity is thus a necessary component, and the greater its regularity of use, the stronger we would observe that the norm held. Norms can thus be understood to be particular instances of both rules and regularities, that is, equilibria of social expectations. I thus frame a norm as taking the form, 'If X, one is *expected* to do Y.'[49] This leaves open the question of the source of expectation (and its enforcement) which we will look at in the next section discussing norm circles. However, because of the social component not present in conventions or rules, norms occupy a special position in the process of social validation.[50]

---

[47] Hurrell, 'Norms and Ethics in International Relations', in *Handbook of International Relations*, ed. Carlsnaes, Risse, and Simmons (London: Sage, 2002), 142.

[48] Hodgson, 'What are Institutions?' 3.

[49] Expectation is built into other theories of norms. Habermas describes it as 'the problem of how social order is supposed to emerge from the processes of consensus formation that are threatened by an explosive tension between facticity and validity'. One of the solutions institutionally is through the 'stability of behavioural expectations' that secure a 'spellbinding authority'. Like Kratochwil, Habermas sees a functional role for norms as coordinating social action. Habermas, *Between Facts and Norms*, trans. Rehg (Cambridge: Polity Press, 1996), 21, 24.

[50] Ibid.

Foundational or Anti-Foundational Approaches?

The above formulation renders redundant an additional distinction inserted by constructivists who draw on Fearon (*Rule*: 'Do X to get Y'; *Norm*: 'Good people do X')[51] which sets rules up as instrumentalist (without bounded circumstances) as opposed to norms as 'moral' (distinguished from 'constitutive' and 'regulative' norms, as Searle classifies them[52]). Their source of 'oughtness' derives ultimately from morality claims (perhaps via social expectations, whereas this thesis suggests morality is only one of multiple sources of social expectations, and often weaker in pluralist societies), where they understand human rights to be within this subset of moral norms.

Their formulation has several fundamental problems. First, in appealing to morality, they rely on foundationalist principles of natural law in what is purportedly an anti-foundationalist account of norm cycles. That is, trying to explain norms' success involved a combination of arguments about both the intrinsic properties of the norm (i.e. that humans are destined to accept them as inherently superior), as well as external variables (such as changing preferences through persuasion, building coalitions, and forming a norm cascade). This precludes a theory of norm decline, because the 'intrinsic' properties can never dissipate if they are truly intrinsic, and also leads to several contradictions (some mentioned above) and the accusation that they are trying to smuggle in liberal normative values when explaining the global orientation of norms.[53] The main problem with a foundationalist account of historical norm development is that it privileges 'good' norms because morality must be a significant factor, and therefore tends towards the teleological.

Second, in discussing the emergence of norms, Kratochwil observed that 'all rules and norms are problem-solving devices for dealing with the recurrent issues of social life: conflict and cooperation',[54] and growing anthropological research suggests that norms pre-date us as *Homo sapiens*, being a functional development from the needs of social

---

[51] Finnemore and Sikkink, 'International Norm Dynamics', 891–2.
[52] Searle, *The Social Construction of Reality* (London: Allen Lane, 1995), 28–9.
[53] Moses, *Sovereignty and Responsibility*, 80–3.
[54] Kratochwil, *Rules, Norms, and Decisions: On the Conditions of Practical and Legal Reasoning in International Relations and Domestic Affairs* (Cambridge: Cambridge University Press, 1989), 69.

animals (such as monkeys and apes) to maintain cohesion.[55] Furthermore, where actors of distinct moral systems meet (for example, Muslims and liberals[56]), establishing common grounds on utilitarian or contractarianist[57] rather than deontological principles is more common. Put differently, the incommensurability between different moral systems may be mitigated by agreeing on common goals, rather than trying to reconcile the systems. However, this leaves the normative systems as non-overlapping *magisteria*. Utility becomes a crucial common language of normative discourse in pluralist settings. If norms exist at the intersection of regularities and rules, and if power drives rule-making, it is utility that drives recurrence, i.e. their regularity: one would not follow or appeal to a norm consistently unless its functions were *useful*. Anti-foundational approaches are the only consistent means of investigating their spread or contestation without privileging some values.

Even in cases where norm entrepreneurship is an important factor in driving change, utility still plays a role. For example, although the abolition of slavery is often credited to the hard work of abolitionist 'norm entrepreneurs',[58] Mazrui points out that by the late eighteenth century, capitalist economies had already discovered that wage labour was cheaper and more efficient than slave labour, and it is no coincidence that the leading abolitionist states were the most advanced capitalist powers.[59] News of the Haitian revolution and France's involuntary abolition of slavery in response would surely have reached British shores, along with the tremendous costs of trying to enforce a slavery regime that the slaves wished to destroy. Thus in empirically observing the establishment and prevalence of norms, their moral content is always only a partial factor in explaining their success (or failure), contingent on other factors that require explaining, even if we have a tendency to ascribe normative change as moral victories. For

---

[55] Brosnan and de Waal, 'Evolution of Responses to (Un)Fairness', *Science* 346, no. 6207 (2014); De Waal, 'The Antiquity of Empathy', *Science* 336, no. 874 (2012).
[56] Dalacoura, *Islam, Liberalism and Human Rights* (London: I. B. Tauris, 1998).
[57] Scanlon, *What we Owe to Each Other* (Cambridge, MA: Harvard University Press, 1998).
[58] Finnemore and Sikkink, 'International Norm Dynamics.'
[59] Mazrui, *The African Condition*, The Reith Lectures (London: Heinemann, 1980), 31–2.

diverse actors to coalesce around a common norm which they did not hold previously, multiple reasons for the change might be expected.

Recent studies on norm contestation illustrate this point. Sandholtz acknowledges the ambiguity in meaning of norms as a starting point for contestation, then goes further to observe that separate and conflicting bodies of rules can lead to contestation, itself resulting in norm change.[60] Bloomfield offers 'norm antipreneurs' that oppose the standard accounts of progressive activists ('norm entrepreneurs'), significant for granting opponents of norm entrepreneurs their independent agency.[61] Gordon introduces elements of law as alternative sources of power in the contest, when authoritarian states use indirect measures in domestic law to suppress human rights activism.[62] This is expanded in Stimmer and Wisken's account of norm contestation involving both 'discursive' and 'behavioural' contestation.[63] Moses posits two norms – sovereignty and the responsibility to protect – against one another, and reintroduces power, though in a very Foucauldian sense.[64] Finally, Panke and Petersohn give an account of norm death.[65] What these studies have in common is that effective opposition to a norm must draw on different sources for legitimacy[66] to counter the norm in question. The practices and beliefs of both proponents and their opponents must be investigated to understand the outcomes that result.

A measure of a norm's function is thus expected if norms are constitutive parts of the international order 'that sustains the elementary or primary goals of the society or states, or international society'.[67] The corollary is that norm diversity is reflective of *what* and *whose*

---

[60] Sandholtz, 'Dynamics of International Norm Change.'
[61] Bloomfield, 'Norm Antipreneurs.' Cf. Bob, *The Global Right Wing and the Clash of World Politics* (Cambridge: Cambridge University Press, 2012).
[62] Gordon, 'Human Rights as a Security Threat.'
[63] Stimmer and Wisken, 'The Dynamics of Dissent: When Actions are Louder than Words', *International Affairs* 95, no. 3 (2019).
[64] Moses, *Sovereignty and Responsibility*.
[65] Panke and Petersohn, 'Why International Norms Disappear Sometimes.'
[66] Clark, *Legitimacy in International Society* (Oxford: Oxford University Press, 2005).
[67] Bull, *The Anarchical Society: a Study of Order in World Politics*, 2nd ed. (London: Macmillan, 1977), 8.

problems they were originated to solve.[68] If we treat human rights in functionalist terms – as norms that check the relationship between a state and its citizens – the norm's source of expectation derives not from deontological principles but from different actors' sets of values and experiences, derived in different ways in pluralist settings. Likewise, while international actors may sometimes make normative decisions based on what they believe to be morally right, they could also make such decisions for instrumental reasons.[69]

It is thus unsurprising that Finnemore and Sikkink recognised domestic mobilisation, regime type, and other structures that shape the nature of power relations in states as key scope conditions.[70] The emergence of human rights occurs in tandem with changing power relations in a state, the norm and its function (constraining the state) developing together with the mobilisation of actors interested in limiting the state's power. Yet, in leaving the element of power beneath these conditions untheorised (or attributed largely to the ideational 'power' of human rights[71]), they cannot explain norm dynamics if domestic mobilisation around an external norm does not occur, such as with gay rights struggles in Africa. These tensions they try to resolve by appealing to foundationalist claims (bodily integrity and legal equality of opportunity[72]) of the norms they believe in,[73] while concurrently trying to explain their 'success' in anti-foundationalist terms[74] – either limiting what they can explain or creating inconsistencies in trying to reach generalisable principles.

---

[68] Conversely, conformity in international law might be demonstrative of hegemony. See Koskenniemi, 'International Law and Hegemony: a Reconfiguration', *Cambridge Review of International Affairs* 17, no. 2 (2004).
[69] Krasner, *Sovereignty: Organized Hypocrisy*; Towns, 'Norms and Social Hierarchies: Understanding International Policy Diffusion "from Below"', *International Organization* 66, no. 2 (2012).
[70] Risse, Ropp, and Sikkink, *The Persistent Power of Human Rights*, 287–93.
[71] Sikkink, 'Transnational Politics, International Relations Theory, and Human Rights', *PS: Political Science and Politics* 31, no. 3 (1998): 518.
[72] Finnemore and Sikkink, 'International Norm Dynamics', 907.
[73] Keck and Sikkink, eds., *Activists beyond Borders: Advocacy Networks in International Politics* (Ithaca: Cornell University Press, 1998).
[74] Moses, *Sovereignty and Responsibility*, 78–85.

Selection, Iteration, and Normativity

Non-foundationalist approaches such as evolutionary models posit that actions that are successful are likely to be repeated, and as they are repeated, they become a norm, avoiding outmoding through disuse. These approaches do not require foundational presuppositions of rationality or morality, since ineffective norms will be selected out of a system (or else the systems themselves collapse and more effective systems remain).[75] 'Selection' in the evolutionary sense could allow for multiple logics to apply, including moral suasion, utility, power, and so on. The reason behind each choice may vary, but it is the repeated iteration of the actions that embed a norm: the consistent preference for a norm (for whatever reason) strengthens it, while failing to select it or to punish non-compliance leads to disuse.[76] New norms must also fit into an existing 'norm complex' of social structures that pre-dates them in order to be selected as solutions.[77]

Rational choice explanations for the existence of norms may be classed in four ways: the coincidence of interests, coercion, cooperation, or coordination equilibria. Coincidence of interest involves private benefits for all parties involved (which may not necessarily be the same). Coercion involves a powerful state threatening or inducing weaker states to follow its lead. Cooperation results from a repeated prisoner's dilemma in which defection is costly on one side or both. And coordination involves states' interests converging according to the moves of other states.[78]

The treatment of norms as equilibria in a coordination game[79] sheds some light on contestation. In repeated instances of the game, the equilibria giving the greatest Pareto-optimal results should be selected,

---

[75] Axelrod, 'An Evolutionary Approach to Norms', *American Political Science Review* 80, no. 4 (1986): 1097.
[76] Panke and Petersohn, 'Why International Norms Disappear Sometimes.'
[77] Bernstein, 'Ideas, Social Structure and the Compromise of Liberal Environmentalism', *European Journal of International relations* 6(2000).
[78] Goldsmith and Posner, *The Limits of International Law* (Oxford: Oxford University Press, 2005), 26–34.
[79] For example, Myerson, 'Justice, Institutions and Multiple Equilibria', *Chicago Journal of International Law* 5, no. 1 (2004).

and demonstrated through practice.[80] Technically, utility is measured by the actors' rank-order preferences of the available choices, though because of uncertainty at the decision-making point, one can only have an expected or projected measure of utility.[81] This suggests that normative contestation could be understood as equilibrium selection problems where multiple equilibria exist. This becomes especially difficult if the actor's perceived 'costs' start to blend into areas such as ideological integrity or social identity, which defy quantification.

While neither evolutionary nor rational choice approaches require social expectation within their models, the norm that proffers the winning strategy or optimal outcome is the one that ought to be followed if the goal is efficiency or maximising utility. Thus, norms that are more beneficial or serve a greater utility than their counterparts (under their models' scope conditions) are likely to spread and embed themselves. These notions of regularity and selection through utility suggest how norms might spread organically rather than being imposed. Yet the difficulty with these kinds of approaches, especially those involving mathematical modelling, is that they require stable structures in which patterns of relations form. What happens when informality is intentionally built into the process, when there exist more ambiguous relationships between actors, or when the structure itself is endogenous to the contest, is usually not considered amenable to such types of study.

This chapter introduced our puzzle in understanding the advance and retreat of regional checks on sovereignty in the Global South at the outset of the twenty-first century. It then explored the problems in the existing literature with respect to these questions. I argued that power was a significant variable, and that more attention should be given to the iterative character of 'norms', requiring repeated selection even if for different reasons (broadly, their 'utility' function capable of validity in multiple logics or systems) – that is, an anti-foundational approach. Indeed, the selection of the same norm for very different reasons would

---

[80] Patrick, 'The Evolution of International Norms: Choice, Learning, Power, and Identity', in *Evolutionary Intepretations of World Politics*, ed. Thompson (New York: Routledge, 2001), 146–8.

[81] Bjola and Kornprobst, *Understanding International Diplomacy: Theory, Practice and Ethics* (Abingdon: Routledge, 2013), 98.

Selection, Iteration, and Normativity

arguably demonstrate a strong norm or at least one with great potential. I now turn to constructing the model that will be used to explore the case studies, paying special attention to power, considerations for how it can explain both norm stability and change, and resisting the privileging of certain kinds of norms in order to understand contestation from a more neutral vantage.

2 | Theoretical Framework

> Normative change, however, is increasingly common and any adequate general theory of normativity must be able to accommodate both stability and change.
>
> Dave Elder-Vass[1]

The previous chapter discussed some of the inherent difficulties with the norm cascade theory in addressing the trajectory of sovereignty norms, particularly aspects relating to power, utility, and selection. A final question also involves the question of expectation – the social aspect of norms. The question of collective expectation leads to identifying the primary actors driving this, which I will argue, constitute the 'norm circle'[2] of the decision-making actors in an RO. This provides a causal mechanism that leads to changes in the normative environment of an institution. This discussion then suggests a model that generates the hypotheses in this study.

Norm Functions and Utility

Norms have latent functions: they guide actors on what to do under certain circumstances or conditions. That function in turn has a utility value. Does it improve the situation of the actor following the norm, or not, relative to the cost of action? How might the distributional costs of change be allocated in the RO? For instance, a democracy would have few or no perceptible costs creating a democratic regional charter that commits to elections, representation, and other democratic norms, but the costs for an authoritarian regime would be high. Functional analysis precedes other factors because it implies the differences in benefits and costs that affect member states differently, even if only

---

[1] Elder-Vass, *The Causal Power of Social Structures: Emergence, Structure and Agency* (Cambridge: Cambridge University Press, 2010), 133.
[2] Ibid., 11–12.

perceived implications, particularly in the case of political norms that are difficult to quantify.

This measure is a *perceived* utility, based on causal beliefs rather than hard quantification. Thus, I use it primarily as a sorting mechanism for allocating actors into norm circles, rather than as a predictive variable. It has an intersubjective quality as it evaluates norms across different logics of behaviour (such as the logics of consequences, appropriateness, or practice) – a necessary condition or else the model would inherently prefer some modes of decision-making or preferences over others. The alternative has been to treat preferences as simply exogenous, but as I will argue later, contestation outcomes require some preferences to be dynamic, changeable, or not yet established at the onset of a debate. At the same time, this is not an attempt at a theory of preference formation, but a means of understanding the expectations of actors, and potentially the directions in which norms may drift or evolve under contestation.

Norm Circles

How might the power of a norm be measured, particularly its *generative* power to influence the normative environment? I suggest it is best done through the concept of 'norm circles' which constitute the capacities of the followers of a particular norm. While the reasons members of a norm circle follow a particular norm may be based on history, function, beliefs, or other logics, the manner in which a norm becomes *selected* as a more broadly applicable standard is hypothesised in this thesis to be a combination of its utility and power. Norm circles offer a conceptual tool to define and contrast the actors behind separate norms, and measure their power to affect this selection.

The sociologist Dave Elder-Vass explains how normative social institutions emerge as causal powers from the agents that form them. He argues that 'normative social institutions are emergent properties – causal powers – of normative circles',[3] and these norm circles are 'groups of people who share a commitment to endorse and enforce a particular norm'.[4] This formulation does not require ideational commitment alone, but allows that they may share goals, identities, or values, and those shared areas may be their reason for endorsing or

---

[3] Ibid., 122.   [4] Elder-Vass, 'Towards a Realist Social Constructionism', 11–12.

enforcing a norm. He describes three approaches to understanding the norm circle: the *proximal* norm circle is the set of actual actors that have influenced a particular normative disposition; the *imagined* norm circle is the actors' beliefs about the extent of the norm circle; and the *actual* norm circle is the network of actors who endorse and enforce the norm concerned.[5] For him, the social institution is the causal power that these circles have to produce corresponding practices among their members.[6] The proximal norm circle explains the origins of an actor's preferences, but forms of power are inherent in the norm circles: if an actor believes that their norm is shared only by other weak actors, they may not be as strident in making demands of others to come into line. Conversely, if they believe that their imagined norm circle is large and powerful, they may be more assertive about what ought to be done. The actual norm circle describes the enforcement mechanism, which may be weak or powerful as well.

For example, the norm of territorial integrity creates a social institution amongst states that inhibits states from invading one another. State actors believe in territorial integrity thanks to influence from their *proximal* norm circles (e.g. education and learning), *imagine* others also believe in territorial integrity, and these may be enforced by *actual* norm circles (such as the International Court of Justice, hegemonic powers, or alliance systems). In this example, the specific costs and benefits of invading another territory are just one part of a matrix of calculations that they must consider, and the norm circles illustrate how non-material factors could play an additional part in affecting an actor's behaviour.

Furthermore, this may avoid ambiguity, such as uneven application of which norm circle applies, especially if it does not map neatly on to other identities (most usually states). Coalitions are defined as teams of 'individuals or groups that unite for a common purpose'.[7] To the extent that a 'commitment to endorse and enforce a particular norm'[8] is a shared goal, norm circles are a subset of coalitions, dealing with

---

[5] Elder-Vass, *The Causal Power of Social Structures*, 127–9.   [6] Ibid.
[7] Strom and Nyblade, 'Coalition Theory and Government Formation', in *The Oxford Handbook of Comparative Politics*, ed. Boix and Stokes (Oxford: Oxford University Press, 2009), 783.
[8] From the definition of 'norm circle', above. Elder-Vass, 'Towards a Realist Social Constructionism', 11–12.

normative matters.[9] Put differently, the 'norm circle' is a more basic ontological unit, forcing one to theorise other factors such as intent, capacities, and so on. In this conception, the spread of a norm absent its agents (the norm circle) cannot be meaningfully studied.

Because coalition literature is so extensive in comparative politics, it is useful to have a separate term that is unencumbered with baggage to use in this theory,[10] as well as emphasise the underlying normative question at the heart of this study. With much of coalition literature based on US two-party dynamics, some caution is necessary on the extent to which such dynamics may apply to normative contests, but given domain constraints of the regional organisation (as will be described later), the overlap allows insights from coalition literature,[11] which has sometimes been overlooked in norms literature. Various conceptions of normative actors such as 'norm entrepreneurs'[12] or 'antipreneurs'[13] (though they may consist of a single individual) can be understood as members that transform norm circles into coalitions, having added an additional scope condition that they have purposive intent to spread their norm and coalesce the grouping around the norm.

---

[9] Another view is offered by the 'linked ecologies' framework of Andrew Abbott via John Karlsrud. However, Karlsrud's emphasis is on shared professional 'ecologies' that are the basis of association. His contribution in observing alliances in these ecologies as fundamental for norm change is similar to the norm circle idea espoused here, but with a different ontological starting point more heavily favouring practice. See Karlsrud, *Norm Change in International Relations: Linked Ecologies in UN Peacekeeping Operations* (London: Routledge, 2015); Abbott, 'Linked Ecologies: States and Universities as Environments for Professions', *Sociological Theory* 23, no. 3 (2005). A good exposition of this approach is also found in Seabrooke, 'Epistemic Arbitrage: Transnational Professional Knowledge in Action', *Journal of Professions and Organization* 1, no. 1 (2014).
[10] Particularly the strong association with government formation, cf. Strom and Nyblade, 'Coalition Theory and Government Formation.'
[11] A good example of work on coalition-building given institutional constraints is Krehbiel, *Pivotal Politics*. In these case studies, the regional organisation is the institutional constraint, and the actors are state and sub-state groupings and individuals. However, the lack of formality in structures in the cases at hand prevents an overly structuralist account of the process. Cf. Gehlbach, *Formal Models of Domestic Politics*.
[12] Keck and Sikkink, *Activists beyond Borders*.
[13] Bloomfield, 'Norm Antipreneurs.'

Existing Theories in Light of Utility and Power

The next question is how norm outcomes are affected by their functional utility and relative power. Returning to Krasner's analysis of human rights norms, he asserts:

> [Human rights conventions] never violate a basic tenet of international legal sovereignty, which is that juridically independent territorial entities should not be subject to coercion. Conventions can but do not necessarily compromise Westphalian sovereignty.[14]

He stresses that conventions endorsed by their members are 'voluntary, Pareto-improving agreements' – that is, they do serve a useful function, but are secondary to international legal sovereign principles and only challenge Westphalian sovereignty where enforcement procedures exist.

In contrast are the spiral model theorists. Like Krasner, they accept that initial adoption of a norm may be for instrumentalist reasons with Pareto-improving (functional) effects.[15] However, the process of engaging in the 'moral discourse' that follows results in shifting identities and interests:

> The logic of discursive behavior and of processes of argumentation and persuasion rather than instrumental bargaining and the exchange of fixed interests prevails when actors develop collective understandings that form part of their identities and lead them to determine their interests.[16]

While they do not explicitly discuss the effect of their norm's functions in the spread of its adoption (aside from brief mention of Pareto-improving effects), they appeal to the 'intrinsic characteristics' of a norm as a factor in its success,[17] though it remains implicit in the rest of their work. This is a gap because when they discuss stages such as a state in a phase of instrumental adoption or tactical concessions, they implicitly make functional claims about the norm. The internalisation

---

[14] Krasner, *Sovereignty: Organized Hypocrisy*, 106.
[15] Finnemore and Sikkink, 'International Norm Dynamics', 903.
[16] Risse, Ropp, and Sikkink, *The Power of Human Rights*, 14.
[17] Finnemore and Sikkink, 'International Norm Dynamics', 906–7.

of human rights then extends to supersede sovereignty principles, for example, in their discussion of R2P and the International Criminal Court (ICC).[18]

The net effect of these two views is that they select cases where, *functionally*, their norm has already been presumed the winner. Put differently, in their logical framework, the norm they favour is already superior to its opposing norm – an implicit result of their own causal beliefs.[19] For Krasner, sovereignty always precedes human rights considerations. For the spiral model theorists, human rights eventually overtake sovereignty norms. The balance of power between proponents then determines the nature of normative outcomes: if the human rights advocates are weak in Krasner's cases, the status quo results, while if they are powerful, an instrumental adoption may take place, but it necessarily remains secondary to sovereignty principles. For the spiral model theorists, when proponents of human rights are weak, they must use persuasion and states can repress or deny human rights abuses, but when they have mobilised, a norm cascade becomes inevitable. Neither looks at cases where other norms might have more utility than those they favour.

Thus, when one applies the two litmus tests – the assumption of a norm's utility, and the power of the circles behind the competing norms – a non-overlapping framework shows how both explain different parts of a broad spectrum of attitudes towards each norm and observed outcomes. Moreover, the implication is that it is not power that predicts normative decisions, but utility, contingent on an implicit value system or logic. A norm's utility to various actors' logical systems explains its prevalence as a preference, and power inflects the type of observed outcomes. The implicit utility assumptions illustrating a spectrum of stances towards human rights and sovereignty norms is illustrated in Table 2.1.

---

[18] Risse, Ropp, and Sikkink, *The Persistent Power of Human Rights*, 278–83.
[19] Goldstein and Keohane, eds., *Ideas and Foreign Policy: Beliefs, Institutions, and Political Change* (Ithaca: Cornell University Press, 1993).

Table 2.1 *Comparison of realist and constructivist theories of norms*

Theory	Functional assumption (relative utility)	Power of norm circles	Observed outcomes
Krasner: *Sovereignty: Organized Hypocrisy*	Sovereignty greater than (>) human rights	Sovereignty > human rights	Authoritarianism, voluntary social contracts possible
		Human rights > sovereignty	Spread of human rights according to powerful states' interests
Risse, Ropp, and Sikkink: *The Power of Human Rights/The Persistent Power of Human Rights*	Human rights greater than (>) sovereignty	Sovereignty > human rights	Instrumental adoption, tactical concessions towards human rights
		Human rights > sovereignty	Prescriptive status and rules-consistent behaviour on human rights

Empirical Investigation

I now turn to converting these concepts into a research design, focusing first on regionalism as an ideal site of studying contestation, then translating the concepts of power and utility as they apply to this domain. 'Regions' are defined as being 'located in between the "national" and the "global"'.[20] As Söderbaum explains, 'old' regionalism focused on characteristics that emerged during the Cold War and in conjunction with post-colonialism. 'New' regionalism developed after the Cold War and saw globalisation as the major challenge facing nation-states, to which 'regionalism' provided one avenue of response.

---

[20] Borzel and Risse, eds., *The Oxford Handbook of Comparative Regionalism* (Oxford: Oxford University Press, 2016).

And finally, 'comparative' regionalism considers the emerging multipolar order and regional institutions as an important part of multi-layered global governance.[21]

The broad changes brought about by the end of the Cold War resulted in new challenges facing both the OAU and ASEAN, of which they were acutely aware. The period of the 1990s spurred on regional projects such as the EU and the North American Free Trade Area (NAFTA), and both the OAU and ASEAN considered the possibilities of their marginalisation, to which a response was needed. The creation of the African Economic Community (1991) and the ASEAN Free Trade Area (1992) must be seen against this backdrop, but both were also deemed to be insufficient. It is not entirely coincidental that periods of norm-setting followed as both sought to strengthen their regional identities. However, ASEAN was delayed by the Asian financial crisis of 1997–8 and its main initial response was simply expansion (to embrace Cambodia, Laos, Myanmar, and Vietnam) by the end of the 1990s. In contrast, the Rwandan genocide and growing intra-state conflicts in Africa quite likely accelerated the OAU's impetus for reforms, and the 1999 Algiers Summit, which endorsed its stance against unconstitutional changes of power – primarily military coups – foreshadowed the rapid changes that would culminate in the establishment of the African Union just one year later.

The study of normative contestation therefore covers an overlapping period between the 'new' and 'comparative' approaches to regionalism in the discipline. Hettne and Söderbaum suggested that:

[T]he 'new regionalism' is simultaneously linked with domestic factors, sometimes challenging the nation-state while at other times strengthening it. Thus the renewed trend of regionalism is a complex process of change, simultaneously involving state as well as non-state actors, and occurring as a result of global, regional, national and local level forces. It is not possible to state which level is dominant, because actors and processes at the various levels interact and their relative importance differs in time and space.[22]

---

[21] Söderbaum, 'Old, New, and Comparative Regionalism: the History and Scholarly Development of the Field', in *The Oxford Handbook of Comparative Regionalism*, ed. Borzel and Risse (Oxford: Oxford University Press, 2016).

[22] Hettne and Söderbaum, 'Theorising the Rise of Regionness', *New Political Economy* 5, no. 3 (2000): 457.

However, comparative regionalism offers some ways out of this dilemma by structuring the comparison to create like units of study, using similar levels of analysis. The key factors are 'utility' and 'power', using ROs as the sites of study and using comparative analysis of norm circles composed of the negotiating actors to make sense of the levels in which actors become more or less influential. This breaks down aspects of the challenge that Hettne and Söderbaum believed insurmountable in 2000. Understanding that regions share common characteristics and challenges,[23] the next step is to understand ROs as arenas, capable of being studied by the same lenses through a focused, structured comparison.

Regional Organisations as Sites of Contestation

Regional organisations may be characterised as 'region-specific but not issue-specific cooperation projects',[24] and broadly committed to a loose definition of 'regional integration', defined as 'a process of iterated cooperation that leads to an ever-increasing web of substantive and procedural institutions at the regional level'.[25] At the same time, since 'regional solutions to regional problems'[26] became an organising principle in global governance, ROs have become key sites of normative interpretation, implementation, or contestation.[27] There is a marked tension between national interests (which might explain why a state joined an RO in the first place) and sovereignty (as commitment to cooperation narrows the universe of choices available to any state for dealing with particular challenges).

Moreover, ROs are useful for a structured comparison of norm contestation in international relations because they are both

---

[23] Fawcett and Gandois, 'Regionalism in Africa and the Middle East: Implications for EU Studies', *Journal of European Integration* 32, no. 6 (2010): 618.
[24] Krapohl, *Regional Integration in the Global South*, 5.
[25] Ibid. This definition deliberately avoids narrower definitions of regional integration as involving the transfer or pooling of sovereignty to supranational levels, as sovereignty is one of the norms in question. See Borzel, 'Comparative Regionalism: European Integration and Beyond', in *Handbook of International Relations*, ed. Carlsnaes and Simmons (London: Sage, 2013).
[26] Acharya, 'Norm Subsidiarity and Regional Orders', 102.
[27] Ibid., 100; Alden, '"A Pariah in our Midst": Regional Organisations and the Problematic of Western-Designated Pariah Regimes – the Cases of SADC/Zimbabwe and ASEAN/Myanmar', *Crisis States Working Paper Series* 2 (2010).

institutions and organisations – having normative effects as well as structuring the relationship of actors who form them. As Hurrell writes, 'institutions act as platforms for normative debate, for the mobilisation of concern, and for debating and revisiting ideas about how international society should be organized'.[28] Methodologically, organisations have the added advantage that the institutional rules that govern interactions between members (as well as secretariats) are well defined as 'organisationally dependent capabilities' and individual states' powers are constrained by the organisational environment they are in.[29] Norms are always in some flux in the RO.[30]

ROs that do not have normative political criteria for membership (such as levels of democratisation, commitments to human rights, etc.) may be characterised by political diversity[31] and therefore contain more divergent norm circles. In contrast, the entry requirements of entities such as the EU are significant, which means that norm contestation will frequently be within the bounds of broader normative agreement on fundamental principles of governance such as the Copenhagen criteria. 'Low' institutional environments, by contrast, have fewer formal institutional structures and therefore greater scope for change but also disagreement. Organisations with extensive enforced rules that limit the scope for change are less useful for observing contestation since many of the contests have already been 'settled' and the only significant way for a dissenting state to break from the institution is by withdrawing[32] (e.g. Brexit or African states applying to withdraw from the ICC).

At the same time, even these normatively diverse ROs have still agreed on some shared norms, including political ones. There may be varying levels of commitment to or enforcement of these norms, but their formation was often marked by contestation. Contestation is particularly amenable to investigation via practice theory because it illuminates how practices are created or performed, which in turn shows how different, especially conflicting, practices interact with

---

[28] Hurrell, 'Norms and Ethics in International Relations', 147.
[29] Keohane and Nye, *Power and Interdependence*, 3rd ed. (New York: Longman, 2001), 48.
[30] Bjola and Kornprobst, *Understanding International Diplomacy*, 105.
[31] See Hurrell, 'Power, Institutions, and the Production of Inequality', 35–6.
[32] Morse and Keohane, 'Contested Multilateralism', *Review of International Organizations* 9, no. 4 (2014): 391.

one another.[33] Adler and Pouliot's definition of practices is 'socially meaningful patterns of action which, in being performed more or less competently, simultaneously embody, act out, and possibly reify background knowledge and discourse in and on the material world'.[34] Put simply, it takes 'the perspective of everyday performances that embody shared knowledge'.[35] Such a practice cannot be removed from explanations of the outcomes that result as it is 'a generative force in and of itself',[36] and this has important implications for research on norm dynamics.

The book will look at two ROs of the Global South – the AU and ASEAN. The focus on the Global South matches the need for normatively diverse ROs, but also crucially addresses a neglected area in the study of international institutions, which has focused on either global or Eurocentric organisations and norms.[37] This therefore addresses gaps in both the comparative regionalist and normative change literatures.

Both the AU and ASEAN share some similarities, being inspired by the Bandung Conference in 1955, being formed in 1963 (as the OAU) and 1967 respectively, and crucially for the nature of cases sought, having witnessed a flurry of normative openness and norm-setting in the 2000s, much of which was contested. While dissimilar in size, they are the pre-eminent ROs of their respective regions, with only the UN system above them as far as international organisations are concerned. This is not true of African sub-regional organisations, such as ECOWAS or the Southern African Development Community (SADC), which are components of the AU and building blocks for continental integration. For various reasons, there has never been a pan-Asian RO, and other RO contenders such as the South Asian Association for Regional Cooperation (SAARC) or Shanghai Cooperation Organisation (SCO) have been far less successful in virtually every aspect of regional integration or normative development.

---

[33] Adler and Pouliot, eds., *International Practices* (Cambridge: Cambridge University Press, 2011), 20.
[34] Ibid., 6.   [35] Adler-Nissen and Pouliot, 'Power in Practice', 2.   [36] Ibid., 3.
[37] Acharya and Johnston, eds., *Crafting Cooperation: Regional International Institutions in Comparative Perspective* (Cambridge: Cambridge University Press, 2007), 13–14.

ASEAN, as the most successful in this regard, is a 'least likely' case from which to study contestation. That is, if it has been more successful at creating regional norms than the others, why would they *not* have applied these lessons from other norms they successfully agreed on, to drive consensus on the remaining contested norms?

However, there are also significant differences between the AU and ASEAN, most obviously their respective sizes and representation (continental vs sub-regional). While this difference is a weakness in a comparative sense, it may be an asset for explanatory power if the dynamics of norm circles operates in both large and small organisations. Second, they also have different historical trajectories, having faced different sorts of challenges to sovereignty. This affects the type of norms being debated – while ASEAN members have seen mass atrocities, these occurred before they became members – and so the frames of the debate may be much different. While the problems are clearly different, I hope to show that the use of shared norms, which may be specified for each RO, allows comparative study inasmuch as they are individually specific to the RO.

While the OAS and Arab League could also have qualified, I exclude them for different reasons. The OAS counts the USA as a member, and many of its normative agreements occurred during the Cold War.[38] Given the unique circumstances of bipolarity during the Cold War, but with the most significant actor of the opposing pole, the Soviet Union, excluded from the RO, it is more difficult to establish the effects of contestation within such a domain. The power imbalance is too great and risks banal observation. The Arab League, meanwhile, has largely been overshadowed by the Israel–Palestine conflict, and this makes comparison with the AU or ASEAN difficult. The Middle East has also lacked the broad inter-state stability of these two regions which would be a necessary condition for regional norm-setting.[39] Nevertheless, further investigation as to how the two ROs relate to the research questions could be a worthwhile and fruitful endeavour, but probably too complex to be incorporated into a book-length investigation.

---

[38] On OAS human rights, the Commission, Convention, and Court were adopted in 1959, 1969, and 1979 respectively.

[39] Fawcett and Gandois, 'Regionalism in Africa and the Middle East', 622–3.

Operationalising the Variables

For the RO, dynamic interaction involves the passing or rejection of resolutions, decisions, policies, budgets, and so forth. These, and their qualitative content, are what are debated by competing norm circles. As Florini has pointed out, the appropriate level of analysis must be at the level of selection: like genes, which provide individual instructions but nevertheless reproduce or die based on the organism they comprise,[40] individual norms sit within a larger text that may or may not be passed *in toto*. As such, in the cases that follow, the unit of analysis is a normative *proposal* within the RO. These are the vehicles on which their norms sit: If, for example, one proposes a policy for regional integration, it will pass or be rejected *in toto*, usually requiring rounds of debate and revision to pass. The qualitative content within the policy will imply the norms that are accepted, whether on trade, labour rights, mutual recognition, or other requisites for regional cooperation.

This puts us some distance from the norm directly, but it is not to duck the question. As Bjola and Kornprobst argue, 'Global diplomacy is, *inter alia*, constituted by the weakening of some norms and the strengthening of others.'[41] Proposals are the gambits by which these challenges come about – once adopted, they change the normative complexion of the RO, even when non-binding, because they define or reinforce a set of norms but also imply a certain support for them, and may form a precedent, even if only used discursively. The proposals must navigate their way through the existing cloud of norms within the RO, challenging some while claiming to be the legacy or continuation of others.

Norm Circles via Utility

The case studies all employ the measurable variables – norm circles, utility, and power – to study the normative contest. The first stage is to split the members of the RO into two opposing norm circles at an originary point in time (e.g. when a proposal is first formally introduced, or even informally floated), t,[42] based on their rank order

---

[40] Florini, 'The Evolution of International Norms', *International Studies Quarterly* 40, no. 3 (1996): 370.
[41] Bjola and Kornprobst, *Understanding International Diplomacy*, 105.
[42] I specify the time because during the contest (i.e. at time = $t + 1, t + 2, \ldots$), the productive power of the actors is in play (see Hypothesis, below, particularly 'Control'), and the membership of respective norm circles may subsequently change.

preference of the proposal against existing structures, aims, or policies. This is drawn from empirical observation rather than using an ex ante judgement such as ideational preferences – the usual source of accusations against states for taking 'hypocritical' positions, when it is simply that states have always considered a range of interests in deciding policy positions, aside from even their official ideational narratives. If the proposal has more utility than existing mechanisms or supports some other external national objectives, then they join the norm circle 'for' the proposal. If it has less utility or clashes with national interests, they join the norm circle 'against' the proposal. We will investigate the interaction of the norm circles and the use of power, including social construction power (that may affect the perceived 'utility' of the norm) in $t + 1$.[43]

There may be multiple reasons for taking any particular stance, whether it be realist calculus, shared interests, signalling, or ideological stances. Indeed, states may not even have set positions at the start of a debate, only 'brackets' of the bounds of acceptable outcomes,[44] and this dynamic is rarely captured in traditional international relations approaches, yet essential to understanding the unfolding contest.

Although the norm circles may not be able to quantify all their respective costs and benefits, the distribution of costs of political norms are judged to be unequal depending on the perceived distance of the actor from the norm and its ability to achieve their goals. That is, a state that was furthest from adhering to new norms would perceive itself as requiring the most change to see them implemented, and therefore estimate its expected costs to be the greatest. For the state

---

[43] The problem of circularity between power and utility is that some forms of power can affect preferences and therefore the assessed utility. This problem can be described as the problem of retroduction and retrodiction, introduced if we believe that multiple interacting causes affect any event. If retroduction is the identification of causal powers and mechanisms, and retrodiction is the interaction of those multiple causes, one has an infinite regress problem untangling the two. Here we start with the physical proposal as our starting point, and then move forward accepting that socially productive power will change utilities, and therefore the composition of norm circles. For a full discussion, see Elder-Vass, 'Developing Social Theory Using Critical Realism', *Journal of Critical Realism* 14, no. 1 (2015).

[44] Adler-Nissen, 'Conclusion: Relationalism or Why Diplomats Find International Relations Theory Strange', in *Diplomacy and the Making of World Politics*, ed. Sending, Pouliot, and Neumann (Cambridge: Cambridge University Press, 2015), 288.

to want to shift to this new norm, it must perceive the benefits of the norm to outweigh other costs, or that the costs are not as significant as assumed.

Riders may exist who are silent or seemingly invisible in the documentary evidence, but whose support bulks up the respective size of norm circles. These will be investigated on a case-by-case basis. The point is not to assume that 'liberal' states will take 'liberal' positions on any given proposal, nor that 'authoritarian' states will take 'authoritarian' positions, nor to overplay the RO's existing normative environment. Other models simply treat preferences as exogenous, but this is unsatisfactory if one wants to explain how reconfigurations of actors occur – which may be essential to the passage of a proposal.

In the case studies that follow, it is important to understand how or why the key actors take the positions they do, which also may have implications for switches and the strength of support or objection. There may also be attempts to amend the proposal considerably to satisfy different parties – this is important in coalition-building, but some amendments may start to shift the normative implications, and these will be watched for. This is an important part of the process trace, as the initial normative implications may change significantly and therefore what starts out as a relatively radical proposal may not end up as such.

Finally there may be neutrals and undecideds, and some members may also switch sides midstream (indeed they frequently do, which may be an important factor for success or failure). We assume neutrals or undecideds will not affect the outcome, and in some cases, may even serve as useful conduits for negotiations. Having parted the actors into two discrete groups, we can now assess their relative power and performance.

Power in an Organisation of Equals

The choice of RO as the domain of the contest has several advantages. First, the rules of the organisation specify what kind of decision-making powers members formally have in that domain. Both the AU and ASEAN have ostensible equality between members, with both preferring consensus decision-making,[45] which limits use of compulsory power within the domain of the regional organisations.

---

[45] The AU has a two-thirds majority vote if consensus cannot be reached. 'The Constitutive Act of the African Union', 2000, Art. 7. Unlike the AU, in ASEAN,

Table 2.2 *Sources of uneven structural power in regional organisations*

Type	Regional organisation	
	AU	ASEAN
Decision-making	Two-thirds majority (consensus preferred)	Consensus
Funding contribution	Unequal	Equal
Veto	None	Potential consensus obstruction
Membership size[a]	55	10
Chair (agenda setting)	Regional rotation	Alphabetic rotation

[a] A larger membership permits greater flexibility in coalition formation.

ASEAN furthermore stipulates that members support an equal share of funding to its Secretariat,[46] levelling another potential source of inequality of influence (this stipulation does not exist in the AU, however, and is an important source of unequal power within that organisation). Physical numbers may still have an effect even in consensus-based decision-making, since the appearance of unity lies at the bottom of a consensus decision, and would be impossible with equally opposed numbers. Finally, the chair of the RO rotates by region or country each year, giving the sitting chair in both some degree of influence in agenda setting. These differences are summarised in Table 2.2 and their use will be treated in depth in the empirical chapters.

The structures and rules of an RO are designed to negate inequalities in structural or compulsory (coercive) power.[47] If use of compulsory

there is no standard recourse to majoritarian voting, though an 'ASEAN minus X' formula allows member states to opt out of some economic agreements and the ASEAN Summit has powers to decide how to proceed if no agreement can be reached (so characterising consensus as every-member-has-a-veto is not exactly correct). ASEAN, 'Charter of the Association of Southeast Asian Nations' (Singapore 2007), Arts. 20 and 21.

[46] 'Charter of the Association of Southeast Asian Nations', 2007, Art. 30(2).
[47] Full discussion of these forms of power can be found in Barnett and Duvall, *Power in Global Governance*.

and structural power is constrained by the institutional rules of the RO, then differential power stems from institutional and/or productive power. This makes even solitary states, or small norm circles, relatively powerful in the RO, since they may withhold support and thus consensus and may not necessarily be overridden even with a straight vote. The counterweight to this is the use of social pressures for conformity or demonstrated unity to reach consensus on issues under debate. How this might take place in these ROs, however, is not well understood.

There are many theories of influence or mechanisms for norm diffusion, often revolving around persuasion and socialisation.[48] However, I find these too unspecified and not reflective of the dynamics in an RO, that is, diffusion theories provide insufficient causes and overlook power. Rebecca Adler-Nissen and Vincent Pouliot have extensively examined how capabilities relate to influence through their framework of 'power in practice'. Recognising the value of both the 'capability' and 'relational' approaches to power, they conceive of power in practice as an emergent property of both, that is, the effort to convert capabilities in specific interactions of actors, and thus not reducible to either: 'The way in which the game is played, not just its rules or the distribution of tokens among players, is crucial for explaining its outcome.' This brings them to focus on the idea of competence:

> Any social context produces a notion of what it means to be an able player at the game. Being so recognised typically allows one to wield a form of endogenously generated power often called influence, that is, power without apparent coercion. The exercise of power in practice, thus, rests on a never-ending struggle for recognition as competent in a given practice.[49]

This intersubjective understanding of power – the recognition of competence – helps to explain how actors achieve their objectives despite resistance in diplomatic settings and putative equality amongst members in an RO. Using this approach, one need not quantify the respective norm circles' power (which merely results in a capabilities assessment), only demonstrate the intersubjective agreement on

---

[48] Emblematic of this trend is Goodman and Jinks, *Socializing States*. While thorough, it never reaches a great deal of specification in its model, which compares 'coercion', 'persuasion', and 'acculturation' mechanisms for norm diffusion; indeed their third factor – acculturation – which they favour, is the most ambiguous.

[49] Adler-Nissen and Pouliot, 'Power in Practice', 6.

competence. In their study of how actors influenced decision-making in the 2011 Libyan crisis, Adler-Nissen and Pouliot identified numerous ways in which British and French diplomats succeeded in getting their objectives achieved at the UN Security Council (UNSC). I have distilled these into three broad categories that I can generalise to my model. Given structural equality in ROs as a constraining difference, I will thus use this 'power in practice' framework as the basis for identifying three competence (power) sub-variables.

1 Control of the Initiative and Narrative (Taking a Leading Position)
The first set of observations was of the way diplomats controlled the narrative. By taking initiative and managing the pace of development (such as controlling the release of information on Libya), and by controlling the text of UNSC Resolutions 1970 and 1973 (literally, as Britain was the 'penholder' country), these diplomats effectively defined the image of the crisis to imply the solutions they preferred. Carrie Booth Walling similarly finds that the types of causal stories are significant factors in determining whether a decision is made to intervene or not.[50] Broadly, these recall Barnett and Finnemore's reminder:

> The heart of bureaucratic power, as Weber argued, is control based on knowledge ... bureaucratic knowledge not only reflects the social reality as defined by the bureaucracy but also constructs that reality.[51]

Whereas they look at the international organisation as a unit, we expect the actors that constitute the IO to have the same capacity on a lesser scale, and the contestation within an IO is the contestation for that licence to wield precisely this influence beyond the IO. This control of the narrative and initiative is a form of 'social construction power'.[52] Similarly, the classic Romer–Rosenthal model in public choice theory suggests that agenda control is influential on political resource allocation.[53] It may also be described as a first-mover advantage observed in other international

---

[50] Booth Walling, *All Necessary Measures*.
[51] Barnett and Finnemore, *Rules for the World: International Organizations in Global Politics* (Ithaca: Cornell University Press, 2004), 29–30.
[52] Bjola and Kornprobst, *Understanding International Diplomacy*, 83.
[53] Romer and Rosenthal, 'Political Resource Allocation, Controlled Agendas, and the Status Quo', *Public Choice* 33, no. 4 (1978). Cf. Agenda setting in Gehlbach, *Formal Models of Domestic Politics*, 77–81.

organisational dynamics.[54] Finally, the idea of credible leadership must be considered here, and the ability to mobilise people around an initiative. In the cases that follow, I look at how the narrative is controlled, the leadership of the process, and how initiative is wrested back and forth.

2 Use of Shared Areas of Agreement (e.g. Use of Existing Norms, Procedures, Precedents, Practices)

While one norm is being contested, there are always other constellations of norms and practices that are agreed upon. Adler-Nissen and Pouliot observed that 'the "tremendous institutional memory" that P5 [Permanent 5] missions have is a huge source of influence at the [UN Security] Council — perhaps the greatest difference, in the struggle for diplomatic competence, between them and E10 [elected non-permanent] delegations, according to one insider'.[55] Additionally, the P5 are skilful masters of the procedures at the UNSC, allowing them to use the timings and schedules to prevent the formation of 'counter-blocks' against them (i.e. an opposing norm circle).[56] In the media, they were keen to portray the Libyan scenario as a 'responsibility to protect' case (which was ostensibly universally adopted in 2005), though in the actual debates this term was rarely used.[57]

The general point is that there are shared agreements that all the actors have prior agreement to accept. There will also be other shared norms that may be constitutive of the identities of the actors in that domain. Earlier decisions create precedents, and indeed may become shared norms, with which any new proposal may or may not be congruent. Framing one's argument as a continuation of certain norms, while downplaying contradictions with other precedents or practices, is important and grants legitimacy to the novel proposal. This concept is not new: it is analogous to Acharya's use of 'cognitive priors' that are crucial in establishing the potential for norm localisation.[58] Ann Florini also points to the need for 'coherence' where norms must fit with the existing milieu of other norms,[59] while

---

[54] Mattli and Buthe, 'Setting International Standards: Technological Rationality or Primacy of Power?' *World Politics* 56, no. 1 (2003): 4.
[55] Adler-Nissen and Pouliot, 'Power in Practice', 10.   [56] Ibid., 13–14.
[57] Morris, 'Libya and Syria: R2P and the Spectre of the Swinging Pendulum', *International Affairs* 89, no. 5 (2013).
[58] Acharya, *Whose Ideas Matter?*, 21–3.
[59] Florini, 'The Evolution of International Norms', 376.

Empirical investigation 49

Steven Bernstein has argued the fit with the existing social structure or 'norm complex' is a key factor.[60] Frank Schimmelfennig argues that a key to successful 'rhetorical action' is that 'actors who can justify their interests on the grounds of the community's standards of legitimacy are able to shame their opponents into norm-conforming behavior and to modify the collective outcome that would have resulted from constellations of interests and power alone'.[61] What the 'power in practice' model suggests here is that it is not only existing norms, but also existing practices, that new ideas must fit into to be accepted. We will thus investigate how the proposers use other norms, procedures, practices, and precedents to get their proposal passed.

3 'Metis': Identification and Conversion of Opportunities for Influence

Finally, in any situation, there are opportunistic elements that may appear – empirical facts pertinent to the situation under debate - and which may be turned into sources of influence. These are hard to define, and indeed may map back on to forms of 'power' in the preceding two factors. In Adler-Nissen and Pouliot's case, such examples are many: the P3's[62] use of a defection of a Libyan diplomat and their deployment of him to support them at the UNSC allowed them to claim legitimacy from the Libyan 'people'. They simultaneously put him up as an African voice behind a referral to the ICC (to pre-empt the continental complaint about the ICC that it was always targeting Africans), while making use of Lebanon's position on the UNSC to speak for the Arab world. Finally, they got the Bosnia-Hercegovina member of the UNSC to invoke Srebrenica and vouch for the effectiveness of airstrikes.[63]

Iver Neumann has introduced this as the concept of 'metis', originally used by sociologist Michel de Certeau.[64] He describes metis as the

---

[60] Bernstein, 'Ideas, Social Structure and the Compromise of Liberal Environmentalism.'
[61] Schimmelfennig, 'The Community Trap: Liberal Norms, Rhetorical Action, and the Eastern Enlargement of the European Union', *International Organization* 55, no. 1 (2001): 48.
[62] P3 is the common designation for Britain, France, and the USA, as opposed to the P2 (China and Russia), of the Permanent 5 members at the UNSC.
[63] Adler-Nissen and Pouliot, 'Power in Practice', 12–13.
[64] Neumann, 'Returning Practice to the Linguistic Turn.'

way to 'obtain the maximum number of effects from the minimum force'.[65] Put differently, 'Metis is the agential power to change relations.'[66] This corresponds well with Adler and Nissen's observations in which diplomats at the UNSC were able to identify opportunistic ways in which they could shape the outcome in their favour given limited means and ostensibly level playing fields, a key component, therefore, of competence. For them, they found a similar concept, *ars inveniendi*, 'the creativity that comes with the feel for the game', from Bourdieu.[67] However, whereas they term all of these competence notions as forms of *ars inveniendi* (i.e. including initiative control and mastery of shared norms), I limit it to just this third group of abilities, and specify it around the ability to marshal facts as resources in a discursive contest, especially to change the norm circle compositions.

Hypothesis

As Stinchcombe states, 'A power is legitimate to the degree that, by virtue of the doctrines and norms by which it is justified, the powerholder can call upon sufficient other centers of power, as reserves in case of need, to make his power more effective.'[68] For this volume, the above three factors, which I will render in shorthand as Control (C), Shared norms (S), and Metis (M), are the differences in productive power that determine the outcome of a contest in an RO.

These three factors can be thought of as procedural, ideational, and material. Controlling the initiative is a procedural factor that uses momentum within the dynamics of the organisation. The use of other shared norms aside from the contested norms is an ideational factor, yet contingently so: it recognises that it is largely the shared norms of the actors in the specific domain that matter. Finally, metis, while requiring actor interpretation and attributing meaning to facts or material circumstances, nevertheless shows how practices translate these into relevant factors for the contest. Indeed all three factors are mediated through practice, to explain how they have effects in ROs.

---

[65] De Certeau, *The Practice of Everyday Life*, 84, quoted in Neumann, 'Returning Practice to the Linguistic Turn', 633.
[66] Bjola and Kornprobst, *Understanding International Diplomacy*, 126.
[67] Quoted in Adler-Nissen and Pouliot, 'Power in Practice', 6.
[68] Stinchcombe, *Contructing Social Theories* (Chicago: Chicago University Press, 1987), 162.

Empirical investigation 51

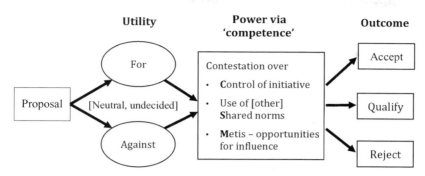

Figure 2.1 RO norm contestation: simple process flow

The process trace through each case study will thus work as follows. I identify the norm circles as far as possible (not all states' preferences may necessarily be known, if their position is a 'bracket' or range of possible acceptable outcomes, no votes are taken, and/or discussions happen behind closed doors – which are common practices in both the AU and ASEAN). I then assess the contest according to Control, use of Shared norms and practices, and Metis, and then observe the result that follows, classed as acceptance, rejection, or a qualification. This is illustrated in Figure 2.1.

Whereas these are qualitative factors, putting it in formal terms will help to clarify the immediate implications. As mentioned earlier, I use utility to split the members of an RO into for or against. If A is the proposing (for) norm circle, and B is the opposing (against) one, then my hypothesis is that the proposal's chance of success is given by the probabilities that (1) A's Control over the initiative is greater than B's; (2) A's use of Shared norms and practices exceeds B's; and (3) A's Metis or opportunity for influence is greater than B's. The relative factoring of these measures (greater or less than) as probabilities builds the relational nature of power[69] into the formula. This is annotated as:

$$P (\text{Proposal success}) = P (C_A > C_B) \cdot P (S_A > S_B) \cdot P (M_A > M_B)$$

I count a 'qualified' result as a weak success, and define being 'qualified' as when the proposal has been modified sufficiently that some of the implicit or inferred norms have changed, in the course of being

---

[69] Adler-Nissen, 'Conclusion: Relationalism or Why Diplomats Find International Relations Theory Strange.'

accepted. Qualification is expected if any of the factors are close, as the proposer strives to maximise their chances of success. If the proposal is rejected, then it is a failure in a specified time period, and new strategies or circumstances are required for the proposer to succeed at a second attempt.

Inferences and Observations from the Model
1 Utility is analytically prior to competence in this model. When the utility of a particular norm is overwhelmingly beneficial to the majority of actors it is likely to pass without significant resistance. Material power or ideational preferences may be sufficient explanations for many types of norm change. The 'competence' variables are mainly significant under situations of contestation (where norm circles are not extremely mismatched in relative strength or size, or if a special mechanism, e.g. a veto or consensus decision-making, is a factor).
2 Even without knowing the exact weights, outright successes (acceptance with no significant changes) are unlikely under situations of contestation. If the norm circles' competencies are closely matched on any one variable, the proposal's chance of success is reduced accordingly across the board. The only escape is if one of these variables in contest has a negligible weight (i.e. if our model contains a spurious factor). This brings the first observable implication: that in situations where even a single factor is evenly matched, the chance of outright success is immediately limited. We therefore expect a strong tendency to qualify the proposal to enlarge the norm circle backing it.
3 Veering far from the norm is hard to do. $P(S_A > S_B)$ explains the inherent conservatism of regional organisations' norms. We would expect 'realistic' proposals to be built around the actors' *imagined* norm circle of who shares the same beliefs. Building out of existing norms is important, as Acharya's localisation theory showed.[70] The second observable implication is that very successful radical changes will only be expected under extreme conditions (where the utility of the proposal is high for many members) or in periods of normative openness (where actors have agreed a 'reset', which implies S_B is

---

[70] Acharya, *Whose Ideas Matter?*

Empirical investigation 53

low). Otherwise, extreme proposals are likely to either fail or be continually watered down until they are more acceptable.

4 Coalitions are important and, since utility is the most important cut (see point 1), reconfiguring the norm circles to be more favourably inclined is more effective than attempting to win by brute force via the competence factors. Therefore, some strategic ambiguity in the proposal may be used to change the utility perception to prevent opposition from key actors. Ambiguity promotes agreement, but is costly ex post as implementation is weakened. Conversely, precision is costly ex ante, it promotes compliance ex post.[71]

5 Vetoes in this model[72] are the ability of opponents to cause:

$$C_A = 0 \Leftrightarrow P(C_A > C_B) = 0$$

Not causing the opposing faction to trigger a veto (formal or informal) is obviously crucial, and any actor with this capability is especially powerful.[73] The implication is that if there is a high likelihood of triggering a veto (assuming this is an independent probability), we would expect more conservative proposals or more adjustments to make the proposal universally accepted.[74] A low likelihood of veto may conversely encourage more radical proposals. A persistent 'spoiler' actor could result in either timid proposals, or indeed calls to change the rules to get around the spoiler, depending on the urgency of the situation.

6 The decision not to oppose or convert power into influence in opposing the proposal has the opposite effect ($C_B = 0$) of a veto, guaranteeing passage of the proposal. States that do not pay attention do so at their peril. 'Quiet' proposals (e.g. in 'lame duck' sessions[75]), or amendments slipped into long texts, rely on the strategy of avoiding the attention of other actors to succeed.

---

[71] Goodman and Jinks, *Socializing States*, 116.
[72] Cf. the definition of 'veto players' in formal analysis as 'actors whose agreement is both necessary and sufficient for a bill to become law.' Gehlbach, *Formal Models of Domestic Politics*, 81.
[73] Aside from formal vetoes, there is also the 'pivot veto', if an actor sits on the line between a majority and the stipulated minimum to pass. Krehbiel, *Pivotal Politics*.
[74] Weingast, 'A Rational Choice Perspective on Congressional Norms', *American Journal of Political Science* 23, no. 2 (1979).
[75] Wawro and Schickler, 'Where's the Pivot? Obstruction and Lawmaking in the Pre-Cloture Senate', *American Journal of Political Science* 48, no. 4 (2004).

7 This model sidesteps the structuralist's paradox,[76] usually posed against realists or those using power as an independent variable: why is it that the more powerful don't *always* win such contests? Or indeed why would the weaker side contest (spending significant resources in some cases) if the outcomes were predetermined by power? In this model, the domain constraints, multiple sources of power, and cumulative effects ensure power is never extremely unequal. This allows small states to punch 'above' their weight, and potentially block larger states from having their way (though of course it does not prevent forum shopping).

Metis has the greatest range of values. If norm circles are evenly matched but there is an exogenously-derived opportunity to influence the decision, it must be seized. Therefore, actors with this skill at identifying and converting such chances are extremely important. In the most extreme case, it may lead to reconfiguring of the norm circles (hypothetically, uncovering a mass atrocity might be used to change a government's national position on regional intervention measures, for example). However, this ambiguous variable limits the ability to further quantify the model.[77] The second shortcoming is that it is not known or may not be possible to quantify what the relative weights of each of the three factors are (except that the weights are non-zero). It is hoped that the cases that follow will shed light on this question.

Some of these implications are not entirely new, and may be described elsewhere in different contexts, particularly in coalition literature.[78] However, I list them to show where the model is consistent with past research, bringing the insights from coalition literature to norms literature. In some cases, it suggests which strategy might be

---

[76] Zartman and Rubin, eds., *Power and Negotiation* (Ann Arbor: University of Michigan Press, 2000), 3.

[77] This is compounded by the lack of formal structures in both ROs under discussion and the problem that in the period under study, the rules of the relationships between actors were themselves in contention. Moreover, quantifying the payoffs of the cases selected would lead, in my opinion, to oversimplification. As such, further formalization of the theory is not carried out here, though such practice may be useful in other case studies.

[78] For example. Krehbiel, *Pivotal Politics*; Wawro and Schickler, 'Where's the Pivot?'; Weingast, 'A Rational Choice Perspective on Congressional Norms', ; Strom and Nyblade, 'Coalition Theory and Government Formation.' For a theoretical summary, see Gehlbach, *Formal Models of Domestic Politics*, chapter 6.

more effective given certain circumstances (e.g. deadlock is best broken by reforming the norm circles, rather than by pushing through with brute force). In this way, one can systematically understand why these effects are observed, rather than claiming it is self-evidently so. In many cases, they also offer suggestions on how to proceed, if facing strong opposition.

Case Studies

Given the model above, the different variables relationship with outcomes can be examined through the 'congruence' method.[79] Did the contestation in these case studies play out according to these factors, and what does that imply about the importance of these factors in determining outcomes? Do alternative explanations adequately explain the characteristics of the outcomes? Given a limited number of historical cases, I choose one of each normative outcome (Accept, Qualify, Reject) for each RO. The norms of ROs are also specific to this study, which selects for norms that test sovereignty.

If the members of ROs are states, having a quality of 'sovereignty', then coming together as a 'region' through iterated cooperation (per Krapohl's definition of integration, above[80]) necessarily risks some of that sovereignty (when understood as freedom to act) because it constrains certain courses of action. If the expected pay-off for sovereignty concession is some form of legitimacy or problem-solving capacity,[81] then the relative utility as characterised by differing norm circles should play out in the analysis. While it would be impossible to find variation across outcomes for a single norm in both regional organisations under study, all the cases will examine a contest involving sovereignty, as the tension between sovereign members cooperating regionally plays out in the dynamics of an RO. Before moving to the case studies, I first briefly examine the normative trajectories of both ROs to give context to the selection of cases.

---

[79] George and Bennett, *Case Studies and Theory Development in the Social Sciences* (Cambridge, MA: MIT Press, 2005), 181.
[80] Krapohl, *Regional Integration in the Global South*, 5.
[81] Borzel, 'Theorizing Regionalism: Cooperation, Integration, and Governance', in *The Oxford Handbook of Comparative Regionalism*, ed. Borzel and Risse (Oxford: Oxford University Press, 2016), 47.

The Organisation of African Unity and African Union

The formation of the OAU was marked by a normative contest over the status of sovereignty and self-determination among newly independent states. However, in this case, the competing norm was Pan-Africanism, and its corollary, federalism.[82] Many post-independence African leaders had been active participants of the Pan-Africanist Congress of 1945, and it played a significant unifying role at independence. The idea went as far as Kwame Nkrumah's proposals for a 'United States of Africa' and this created competition for two very different regional architectures backed by two norm circles: the 'Casablanca' group led by Nkrumah sought a continental political union, while a 'Brazzaville' group (which eventually became the 'Monrovia' group), led by Tanzanian leader Julius Nyerere, emphasised sovereignty and independence. As Naldi describes:

> The Monrovia Group rejected political integration but stressed the sovereignty of States and non-interference in the internal affairs of States ... The Casablanca Group, led by President Nkrumah, sought a political union and the creation of a United States of Africa along federal lines under a High Command.[83]

Despite these initial tensions, the differences subsided as key issues dividing the groups were resolved.[84] Neutral states such as Ethiopia renewed efforts to forge consensus through a more limited Pan-African vision, and called for a summit in Addis Ababa in May 1963 that led to the creation of the Organisation of African Unity. Nkrumah's deposal via a coup in 1966 effectively ended his drive for Pan-Africanism on the continent, as other leaders turned towards opposition to apartheid in South Africa.[85]

---

[82] Tieku, 'Theoretical Approaches to Africa's International Relations', in *Handbook of Africa's International Relations*, ed. Murithi (Abingdon: Routledge, 2014).
[83] Naldi, *The Organization of African Unity: an Analysis of its Role*, 2nd ed. (New York: Mansell, 1999), 2.
[84] Matthews, 'The Organization of African Unity', in *African Regional Organizations*, ed. Mazzeo (Cambridge: Cambridge University Press, 1984), 52–4.
[85] Ayittey, 'The United States of Africa: a Revisit', *ANNALS of the American Academy of Political and Social Science* 632, no. 1 (2010): 90.

The OAU's purposes were thus to promote its ideals of African unity and solidarity as well as eradicate colonialism and promote cooperation and ties between African states. The emphasis on sovereignty in four of the seven principles in Art. 3 of the OAU Charter shows the extent to which the Monrovia group prevailed in these deliberations.[86] Moreover, for individual states, the 'functions and forms of state sovereignty' were soon to become vital for being adapted to 'the pressing task of building [internal] political authority in divided postcolonial African societies', putting paid to the Pan-Africanist ideals of the Casablanca circle.[87] Nevertheless, some of the norms stated in the OAU Charter began to be quietly dropped from mention, particularly self-determination – which had only been intended to refer to independence movements against colonialism – when it began to be used by new insurgencies with a view towards secession, such as in Biafra or Eritrea.[88]

While conflicts, coups, and political oppression in the 1970s appeared to have little effect on the OAU, it did finally respond to the excesses of the brutal regimes of Idi Amin in Uganda and Jean-Bedel Bokassa in the Central African Republic.[89] The OAU thus instituted the African Charter on Human and Peoples' Rights (hereafter the Banjul Charter) in 1981, as well as providing for the establishment of a commission to interpret and protect and promote rights guaranteed under the charter.[90] However, progress was relatively slow, with ratification of the Banjul Charter coming only in 1986, the commission set up in 1987, and agreement to establish an African Court on Human and Peoples' Rights in 1988 (the actual protocol coming in 1998).

Whatever the advances in legislation, the OAU precluded not only intervention but also discussion of grave situations of concern.[91] However, this began to change in 1990 when the heads of state

---

[86] Matthews, 'The Organization of African Unity', 58.
[87] Reno, *Warlord Politics and African States* (Boulder: Lynne Rienner, 1999), 21.
[88] Francis, *Uniting Africa: Building Regional Peace and Security Systems* (Aldershot: Ashgate, 2006), 24.
[89] Van Walraven, 'Heritage and Transformation: From the Organization of African Unity to the African Union', in *Africa's New Peace and Security Architecture*, ed. Engel and Porto (Farnham: Ashgate, 2010), 48.
[90] Stensland, Lotze, and Ng, *Regional Security and Human Rights Interventions: a Global Governance Perspective on the AU and ASEAN* Nupi Security in Practice 8 (Oslo: Norwegian Institute of International Affairs, 2012), 22.
[91] Van Walraven, 'Heritage and Transformation', 45.

assembly redefined non-interference to mean only tangible actions, rather than mention, debate, or adoption of resolutions. By 1992, the OAU Secretary-General, Dr Salim Salim, was arguing for a right to intervene in extreme breakdowns of order, though at this point he could not secure enough support for policies that would change the norm.[92] The collapse of the apartheid system in South Africa ended one of the OAU's main galvanising platforms, and South Africa also briefly experimented with an explicitly liberal foreign policy, before backing down as it was brought into contention with its OAU neighbours.[93]

Externally, the 1990s also saw a move to 'human security' and 'human development' discourses that increasingly called for regional approaches to tackle serious problems,[94] to which Africa was no stranger. The Rwandan genocide in 1994 and numerous civil wars throughout the continent brought the inaction of regional actors into sharp relief, and while the OAU had started to form nascent institutions for such problems, such as the Mechanism on Conflict Management, Prevention, and Resolution (MCMPR), its inability to tackle severe crises lay rooted in the non-interference clause of the OAU Charter.

However, events took a decisive turn when Muammar Gaddafi called an extraordinary summit in Sirte in 1999 and proposed the establishment of a new Pan-African entity (literally resurrecting Nkrumah's 'United States of Africa'). While Gaddafi's ambitious notions were roundly rejected, a remarkable convergence of Nigerian and South African foreign policy agendas did allow for not just the restructuring but the complete replacement of the OAU, while Thabo Mbeki's liberal agenda had a strong influence on the wording of the Constitutive Act that would follow.[95] At the Lomé Summit in 2000 where the new charter would be endorsed, the Eminent Panel's

---

[92] Ibid., 49–50.
[93] Johnston, 'Democracy and Human Rights in the Principles and Practice of South African Foreign Policy', in *South Africa's Foreign Policy: Dilemmas of a New Democracy*, ed. Broderick, Burford, and Freer (Basingstoke: Palgrave Macmillan, 2001).
[94] Söderbaum and Hettne, 'Regional Security in a Global Perspective', in *Africa's New Peace and Security Architecture*, ed. Engel and Porto (Farnham: Ashgate, 2010), 16–17.
[95] Tieku, 'Explaining the Clash and Accommodation of Interests of Major Actors in the Creation of the African Union', *African Affairs* 103, no. 411 (2004): 262.

report on the 1994 Rwandan genocide was also presented. In it, the OAU's failure to act was decried as a 'shocking moral failure',[96] in which Rwanda's Hutu regime attended the Tunis 1994 Heads of State Summit as a full and equal member while the genocide was in full swing. Against this shadow, Salim's call for a right to intervention appeared to have been finally heeded, enshrined in Art. 4(h) of the new Constitutive Act (CA) of the AU. However, the Maputo Summit of 2003 amended the Act to water down provisions on intervention and added the Peace and Security Council as a layer between the AU members and the decision to intervene.[97]

Finally, the Libyan and Ivorian crises in 2011 suggested limits to which certain actors within the AU interpreted the 'right to intervene'. Crucially, these cases departed from AU norms that had sanctioned numerous peace operations in other crisis situations such as Somalia, Darfur, South Sudan, etc. In Côte d'Ivoire, Laurent Gbagbo's rejection of the 2010 election results which declared challenger Alassane Ouattara the winner led to open hostilities. While the UN and ECOWAS made calls to intervene to avoid escalation, the AU viewed the incident as primarily political, and convened a high-level panel of African leaders to negotiate a settlement. ECOWAS then bypassed the AU, in effect forum shopping, to call on the UNSC to intervene. The UNSC unanimously adopted UNSC Resolution 1975, permitting the UN Operation in Côte d'Ivoire (UNOCI) and French forces (Force Licorne) to attack Gbagbo's troops.[98] A similar story unfolded in Libya, where despite international condemnation of Gaddafi's repression, the AU insisted events in the country were a domestic matter and rejected any notion of military intervention. It created its own High Level Committee and persisted in following its own roadmap, criticising the parallel UN roadmap.[99] Like in Côte d'Ivoire, external actions, this time by the Arab League and NATO forces, swiftly turned the tide of battle and rendered the AU's actions redundant. Gaddafi was killed outside Sirte in 2011, ending his rule.

[96] Masire et al., *Rwanda: the Preventable Genocide* (Addis Ababa: OAU, 2000), para. 15.87.
[97] Baimu and Sturman, 'Amendment to the African Union's Right to Intervene', *African Security Review* 12, no. 2 (2003).
[98] Stensland, Lotze, and Ng, *Regional Security and Human Rights Interventions*, 8.
[99] Omorogbe, 'The African Union, Responsibility to Protect and the Libyan Crisis', *Netherlands International Law Review* 59, no. 02 (2012): 160-61.

The nature of the AU's apparently progressive norms built out of the ineffectual OAU, compounded with its refusal to support those same norms in relation to Côte d'Ivoire and Libya, leave a puzzle for realist or constructivist theories. The AU's constitution should have represented a form of cascade for norm theorists, yet in practice there were and continue to be far more continuities with OAU practices at nearly every level, except for joint UN peace support operations which tend to support standing regimes.[100] I argue that these are explicable with close examination of the inner workings of the AU, particularly at the moment of creation. As such, the period from 1999 to 2003 is of special interest, and I choose three cases where proposals were either accepted, rejected, or qualified.

I begin with a 'rejected' case, but it involves the catalyst for the entire transition of the OAU to the AU which opened the normative space for the other proposals: Muammar Gaddafi's audacious attempt to reconstruct the OAU as the 'United States of Africa'. Recalling Nkrumah's suggestion in the 1960s, he argued that a united Africa could face down the major powers (as they had apparently done over the Lockerbie affair) and continental unity was now Africa's greatest imperative. As it happened, no part of his proposal made it through in terms of its actual institutional designs, though at a discursive level, great credit was given to him for his initiative and the principle of the idea.

Concurrently Nigerian President Olusegun Obasanjo successfully proposed the Conference on Security, Stability, Development, and Cooperation in Africa (CSSDCA). Obasanjo had tried to introduce the CSSDCA at Kampala and Abuja in 1991 while out of government. He failed then as authoritarian opponents argued these bore no resemblance to African norms and conflicted with the OAU's stance on non-interference. Repeated attempts to put the CSSDCA on the OAU agenda failed thereafter – until 1999. With the normative space opened by Gaddafi's 'US of Africa' proposal on the table, Obasanjo got it passed with no objections, only updates, to the proposal in 2000, and it would have a deep if under-recognised role in virtually all the norms of the new AU.

---

[100] De Oliveira and Verhoeven, 'Taming Intervention: Sovereignty, Statehood and Political Order in Africa', *Survival* 60, no. 2 (2018).

Case Studies

The final case is that of the Pan-African Parliament (PAP), which would promote democratic norms of participation in regional affairs. If Gaddafi's 'US of Africa' was rejected because the African Union had to be an organisation for the African people, it was curious that the PAP obtained no substantive functions despite its declared goal of becoming the full legislative organ of the AU. It faced further defeats on expansion of its powers during the review of its protocol. The qualification of the norms guiding its functions can be understood only in the context of the contest between Gaddafi and his opponents on the future of continental African federalism.

The Association of Southeast Asian Nations

After being formed in 1967 with the thinnest of declarations, ASEAN's first two binding multilateral agreements – the Declaration on the Zone of Peace, Freedom, and Neutrality (ZOPFAN, 1971) and the Treaty of Amity and Cooperation (TAC, 1976) – were established against a backdrop of disputes between Indonesia and Malaysia over Sabah and Sarawak on the island of Borneo (*Konfrontasi*), between the Philippines and Malaysia over the status of Sabah, and the Vietnam War. ASEAN had considered a charter as early as 1974,[101] but decided against it then, though the TAC and Declaration of ASEAN Concord (Bali Concord I, 1976), a statement of collective norms, were the results.

Vietnam's invasion of Cambodia in 1978–9 was universally condemned by ASEAN member states,[102] regardless of any abuses committed by the Khmer Rouge, and ASEAN continued to oppose any recognition of the Vietnam-backed Heng Samrin regime until the early 1990s, while supporting the Khmer Rouge's retention of its seat at the UN. ASEAN was thus founded on security concerns and driven by a desire to avoid conflict by emphasising cooperation in the economic domain.[103] Non-interference was a key norm – at least rhetorically[104] –

---

[101] Woon, *The ASEAN Charter: a Commentary* (Singapore: NUS Press, 2016), 14–19.
[102] ASEAN, *Joint Statement on Political Issues*, Kuala Lumpur, Malaysia (1980).
[103] Narine, 'Forty Years of ASEAN: a Historical Review', *Pacific Review* 21, no. 4 (2008).
[104] Cf. Jones, 'Asean's Unchanged Melody? The Theory and Practice of "Non-Interference" in Southeast Asia', *Pacific Review* 23, no. 4 (2010).

underpinning regional security. Regardless of power or normative differences between ASEAN member states, consensus on the need for regional security paved the way for the raft of security agreements through the 1970s and united opposition to the invasion of Cambodia.

In the 1990s, ASEAN members – still mostly comprising authoritarian or semi-authoritarian regimes – became involved in the 'Asian values' debate that emphasised public order and security alongside or as a priority over human rights.[105] While the debate was never completely resolved (most of its proponents becoming distracted by the Asian financial crisis of 1997–8), the 1993 Bangkok Declaration[106] inserted key clauses from Asian states qualifying their agreement to the Vienna Declaration, and many ASEAN leaders continued to view human rights as irrelevant Western notions, particularly rebuffing Western pressure over Myanmar. ASEAN's expansion in the late 1990s and early 2000s, incorporating four authoritarian regimes – Cambodia, Laos, Myanmar, and Vietnam – also shifted the balance of non-democratic states to outnumber the democratic ones. Indeed, the West's overt pressure solely on Myanmar but not the other three (when all had poor human rights records) lent credence to the interpretation of human rights as a tool for advancing Western interests.

The rapid ascent of China in the 2000s precipitated rethinking about ASEAN's centrality in the region. Compounded with the slow pace of ASEAN integration efforts (and inability to enforce or implement agreements), ASEAN resolved to establish a charter for the organisation that would give it legal identity.[107] However, it also surprised observers by inserting significant commitments to human rights into its new charter in 2007, when it was under little pressure to do so.[108] It further provided for the establishment of a regional human rights body[109] (eventually named the ASEAN Intergovernmental Commission on Human Rights, AICHR) and subsequently proposed

---

[105] Kausikan, 'Asia's Different Standard', *Foreign Policy*, no. 92 (1993).
[106] UN, 'Report of the Regional Meeting for Asia of the World Conference on Human Rights' (A/Conf.157/ASRM/8) (Bangkok 1993),
[107] ASEAN, *Report of the Eminent Persons Group on the ASEAN Charter* (Jakarta: ASEAN, 2006).
[108] Some of these changes in stance towards human rights first appear in the Vientiane Action Programme in 2004. Tan, *The ASEAN Intergovernmental Commission on Human Rights* (Cambridge: Cambridge University Press, 2011), 249–50.
[109] 'Charter of the Association of Southeast Asian Nations', 2007, Art. 14.

to establish a declaration on human rights. If this marked the height of optimism for the establishment of human rights instruments in ASEAN, the subsequent debate on the ASEAN Human Rights Declaration (AHRD) was more sobering,[110] with civil society groups condemning the watering down of human rights provisions to levels lower than international standards as well as AICHR's track record and institutional weakness.[111] In spite of these changes, the question over what role ASEAN should play with regards to Myanmar's human rights remained unresolved until the dramatic détente between Aung San Suu Kyi and Thein Sein resulted in a sudden opening of the country.[112]

ASEAN's normative trajectory can thus be seen in the following stages. During the Cold War and the immediate post-independence period (1967–90), non-interference became a central guiding norm because of its function in ensuring security for its newly independent states with histories of territorial disputes. After the Cold War, the normative debate shifted to human rights, and these were initially resisted by an appeal to cultural particularity (i.e. 'Asian values'). However, the shadow of Myanmar's human rights record hanging over ASEAN led it to embrace a limited understanding of human rights. The extent of this interpretation was illustrated by the debate over the ASEAN Human Rights Declaration. As with the AU, optimism that democratisation in ASEAN would lead to a more liberal stance or that some normative cascade would ensue has largely been unfounded.[113] At the same time, its norms are difficult to explain in realist terms, having resisted US, Soviet, or Chinese influences during and after the Cold War. Non-liberal constructivist accounts have been

---

[110] Ng, 'The ASEAN Human Rights Declaration: Establishing a Common Framework', *RSIS Commentaries*, no. 114/2012 (2012).
[111] SAPA TFAHR, *Hiding behind its Limits: a Performance Report on the First Year of the ASEAN Intergovernmental Commission on Human Rights (AICHR) 2009–2010* (Bangkok: Forum Asia, 2010).
[112] Stensland, Lotze, and Ng, *Regional Security and Human Rights Interventions*, 55–56.
[113] Jones, 'Democratization and Foreign Policy in Southeast Asia: the Case of the ASEAN Inter-Parliamentary Myanmar Caucus', *Cambridge Review of International Affairs* 22, no. 3 (2009).

most successful at characterising ASEAN norms, but they largely explain 'successful' cases, rather than continued contestation.[114]

My first case will involve the adoption of the ASEAN Charter, which introduced 'human rights' as a shared value into ASEAN, including its promotion and protection. This move surprised observers at the time, and was initially hailed as part of a global shift towards broad acceptance of human rights. Without the benefit of hindsight, this can be interpreted as an 'acceptance' of a proposal.

My second case involves the qualification of norms through the formation of the AICHR and its primary human rights text, the ASEAN Human Rights Declaration (AHRD), which collectively amount to ASEAN's human rights mechanism – an agreement and an institution for its promotion. The Working Group for a Human Rights Mechanism, a coalition of human rights NGOs based in Jakarta, had been advocating for a human rights body since the 1990s. With the mention of 'protection' of human rights in the ASEAN Charter, it was hoped that this body would become the regional mechanism for such. Ultimately, it received no protection powers and disappointed most activists for its 'toothless' nature, even though its work involved the promotion of human rights norms.

Finally, I contrast these human rights related cases with the idea behind a quite different norm of ASEAN, namely the use of the 'ASEAN minus X' formula, which economic officials hoped would be instituted as ASEAN developed a rules-based community. The concern was that economic integration had to be accelerated and could not always be held back by lagging member states. The 'ASEAN minus X' formula would allow integration efforts to bypass some member states and streamline decision-making processes. This reached its greatest elaboration in the ASEAN Eminent Persons Group (EPG) report on the ASEAN Charter. Ultimately, however, all their recommendations for more efficient decision-making processes were rejected, and 'ASEAN minus X' was permitted only in the economic domain, and only where consensus permitted it to be used. For the cases in ASEAN, the expansiveness of norms embedded in its charter allowed selection of two cases from the same proposal, though their momentum and trajectories do not quite overlap: debates about the economically

---

[114] Acharya, *Constructing a Security Community in Southeast Asia: ASEAN and the Problem of Regional Order*, 3rd ed. (Abingdon: Routledge, 2014).

driven 'ASEAN minus X' formula pre-date the charter drafting process, and also, by some years, the debate about the ASEAN human rights body.

Case Selection Criteria

Each of the cases selected represented a proposal for a significant change to the normative complexion of the RO in question and challenged the sovereignty rights of its members in some form. There was a novel characteristic to the norms and structures required of those norms that had previously not been practised or adhered to by the RO. The mere possibility of such far-reaching proposals was likely permitted by the foundational reflections that were ongoing in each RO as they thought through their charter-making processes. This critical juncture allowed more ambitious proposals than have typically been made in either. The cases are shown in Table 2.3. Each case involved a formal proposal, an inferred norm that was debated extensively (contested) within the RO, and an outcome for the norm (in relation to the proposal). The discursive debate may or may not have coincided with the timespan of the proposal: in many cases, the discursive debate extends beyond the proposal in question, but is nevertheless relevant to the success of the proposal.

Each outcome represents a variation on the outcome of our model, which is acceptance, rejection, or qualification of the norm, and each followed a period of contestation. The final criterion of the presence of observable contestation rules out certain possibilities, such as the adoption in the AU Constitutive Act's Art. 4(h) on the right to intervention, which passed without much contestation. While the idea was contested in the 1990s, during the actual process of charter writing it was accepted with little debate. The choice of contestation, which would present the obstacles to a proposal's acceptance, and three possible outcomes of acceptance, rejection, or qualification, is necessary to test the model's ability to describe both stability and change that was absent from many studies that emphasise only change, focused as they are on the significance of the norms in their study.

While the norm in question is embedded in a proposal, it is still possible to trace the impact of contestation on the norm as it is debated and amendments are made by looking at the discourses and actions taken by actors. It is of course exceedingly rare for any kind of motion

Table 2.3 *Case studies*

Case	Challenge to 'sovereignty' norm	Outcome
African Union (AU)/Organisation of African Unity (OAU)		
The 'United States of Africa'	Federalism	Rejected (2002)
The Conference on Security, Stability, Development, and Cooperation in Africa (CSSDCA)	Collective security responsibility	Rejected (1991); accepted (2000)
The Pan-African Parliament	Democratic legislation	Qualified (2002)
Association of Southeast Asian Nations (ASEAN)		
Human rights in the ASEAN Charter	Human rights 'protection'	Accepted (2007)
The ASEAN human rights mechanism (ASEAN Intergovernmental Commission on Human Rights (AICHR) and ASEAN Human Rights Declaration)	Human rights 'protection' mechanism	Qualified (2010 and 2012)
The 'ASEAN minus X' formula in the ASEAN Charter	Bypassing consensus (sovereign interests)	Rejected (2007)

to make it through an organisational process unrevised. Thus, an 'acceptance' does not mean *no* changes, but rather passage with *insufficient* changes to alter the normative content or implications of the proposal. A qualified acceptance should be ubiquitous, but here I mean acceptance that occurs after there are some changes that do not completely remove the normative intent of the original proposal – even if it entails some contradictions, ambiguities, or unresolved contentions – but that involves at least a weakening of the original proposers' intentions (particularly as interpreted by them). Each case study will examine the extent to which the norm survived passage through the contest to see the impact it had on its meaning, whether it was accepted or rejected, or qualified in the form of dilution or clarification. Finally, a rejection does not require that the proposal fails in toto, but only that the normative implications preferred by the sponsoring norm circle fail to pass.

First, the 'US of Africa', entailing a continental union government, may have been the catalyst for the African Union, but the AU bears so little resemblance to Gaddafi's vision that it can only entail a rejection of his intentions. The norms and institutional structures he sought are wholly absent from the AU. In contrast, the CSSDCA passed without changes to its normative intent, but its passage was surprising given the long debate and death by committee in 1991. The inclusion of human rights 'promotion and protection' in the ASEAN Charter also passed likewise, though narrowly. The Pan-African Parliament, a regional 'parliament' with no legislative but only advisory functions, constitutes a 'qualification' in which democratic participation was significantly watered down from its original proposal, even though the norm of participation or the creation of the AU 'for the African people' was allegedly the normative basis through which Gaddafi's opponents had deflected his 'US of Africa'.

The 'qualified' cases involve the watering down of the norms that were initially sought by their proponents. The AICHR's formation, while retaining the 'promote and protect' language of the ASEAN Charter, nevertheless involved no protection mechanism for the AICHR to carry out that aspect of its mandate, and its normative code, the ASEAN Human Rights Declaration, was largely condemned by human rights groups as being a dilution of commitments to human rights, requiring political statements alongside them to explain that there would be no such dilution in spite of the text produced. Unlike the charter, therefore, I consider it a qualified result. Finally, the 'ASEAN minus X' formula had gained considerable momentum up to 2006 as efforts to accelerate the ASEAN economic community gathered pace, but it was ultimately rejected as a general decision-making principle in the ASEAN Charter, being confined only to the economic sphere and only when there is consensus to proceed with it. These cases will be investigated for the influence of the norm circles and contestation between them.

The proliferation of approaches for studying norm contestation, from the very discursive normative approach of Wiener[115] to the very

---

[115] Wiener, *A Theory of Contestation*.

conflict-oriented styles of Bloomfield[116] and Bob,[117] suggests there is room for re-grounding the theory in a comparative approach. By creating a controlled comparison, differences can be identified to sharpen the model. Most interestingly, the relative importance of each of the factors may differ for each organisation, and respective variations in practices might be examined for having comparatively different effects. The key differences between the organisations, such as size and the majority vote in the AU, will be discussed in terms of how these affect the strategies actors use, what constitutes a 'critical mass' of proponents of a norm circle beyond which contestation dissipates, and how the members get around common problems, especially if different strategies are employed.

Methodology

The theoretical framework above allows for the study of norms with a special focus on ROs. The RO domain allows the use of approaches from negotiation and diplomacy studies, coalition theories, and the sociology of norms in a systematic way. The theoretical discussion earlier has framed the hypothesis and process flow around the key parameters, enabling the performance of a congruence check.[118] While the congruence method does not require process tracing,[119] I have done this to the extent possible because practices are necessary parts of the variables and these can only be measured through the way in which they were performed, and the effects they created. This also increases the confidence in ascertaining a causal relationship.

The primary data consists of archival material from the headquarters of both ROs. Speeches were useful especially when they were partisan, but these were checked against OAU Secretariat reports that tracked implementation and summary records of meetings (though there tended to be much less stated in these). In ASEAN, the most important documents – summary reports of meetings – are considered classified with no declassification system. Nevertheless, of the records that were obtained, many have not been used in academic literature

---

[116] Bloomfield, 'Norm Antipreneurs.'
[117] Bob, *The Global Right Wing and the Clash of World Politics.*
[118] George and Bennett, *Case Studies and Theory Development in the Social Sciences*, 181.
[119] Ibid., 182.

before, or their significance has been unrecognised. Even then, archives may be insufficient, as some states do not arrive at summits with written position statements.[120] In part this supports the need for a flexible 'bracketing'[121] conception of utility, when states' preferences become fixed only through the negotiation process itself, but care is taken not to simply allow such ambiguity to blur the norm circle distinctions.

The second point of data collection consisted of interviews with key informants, especially those who had participated in or witnessed the key debates. Senior officials in both ROs were interviewed, though because of the passage of time leading to retirement and return to their home countries, fewer AU officials were still accessible. Because of the paucity of ASEAN archival material, interviews here were much more important for understanding the contests. Fortunately, more ASEAN officials were available, though there is an acknowledged paucity of ASEAN informants from the more closed countries.

Because of the sensitivity of some of the information offered, all interviews were anonymised and the information given was stored securely at all times. Anonymous interviews allowed for more frank exchange and probing questions that I believe would not have been possible with the use of more intrusive recording. Indeed, several ministry officials communicated with me by emails classified under a 'Restricted' or 'Classified' level of secrecy. In this book, all RO officials, including those representing only specific foreign ministries, are abbreviated as either 'AU officials' or 'ASEAN officials' to preserve their anonymity. This comes at the expense of being able to invoke the significance of the actor who stated any particular comment, as well as the biases of the actor involved. Nevertheless, efforts were made to triangulate all statements, and material that could not be confirmed by at least one other source from a different member state (or the secretariats) was not used. A full list of all informants is found in the Appendix.

---

[120] Tieku, *Governing Africa: 3D Analysis of the African Union's Performance* (London: Rowman and Littlefield, 2016), 101.
[121] Adler-Nissen, 'Conclusion: Relationalism or Why Diplomats Find International Relations Theory Strange.'

PART II

The African Union

The partitioning of Africa in 1885 at the Berlin Conference is inscribed in the minds of Africa's political elite. On the one hand, it divided the continent artificially, and on the other hand, it represented the gravest violation of African polities' sovereignty until the wave of decolonisation in the 1950s and 1960s. Two counter-responses therefore developed: to reunite the continent from the colonial divisions, or to re-assert state sovereignties upon independence. The OAU eventually settled on the latter reaction and left colonial boundaries intact, while developing strict understandings of sovereignty and non-interference. However, the former response – to reunite Africa – has had the greater aspirational quality, and Pan-Africanism serves as an underlying norm for its continental international relations.[1]

The transition from the OAU to the African Union was, at the time, an unexpected sequence of events but a turning point for African regionalism. Commitment was made to establish the 'African Union' in 1999. Its charter, the 'Constitutive Act of the African Union', was adopted at the Lomé Summit in 2000. It then began a transitional period involving legal handover processes, and this was finally completed in 2003, shutting down the OAU permanently.

In July 1999, the Algiers Summit raised numerous discussions about the state of African regionalism, against a backdrop of the failures to make progress on the 1991 Abuja Treaty and recognition that continental security mechanisms were not working with the proliferation of conflicts around Africa. The summit ended leaving many issues unresolved. Muammar Gaddafi thus called for an extraordinary summit at Sirte in September, having just one item on its agenda: strengthening African capacity to deal with new challenges.[2] However, he surprised

---

[1] Tieku, 'Theoretical Approaches to Africa's International Relations.'
[2] Touray, *The African Union: the First Ten Years* (London: Rowman and Littlefield, 2016), 40.

delegates at a preparatory ministerial conference days before the summit with a proposal for a 'United States of Africa' as well as a draft Sirte Declaration that would enact it.

This proposal resurrected Nkrumah's Pan-Africanist vision, which itself recalled the 1924 poem, 'Hail United States of Africa', by the African-American writer, Marcus Garvey. From this extraordinarily ambitious proposal, the new 'African Union' would be born less than three years later, although it bore little if any resemblance to Gaddafi's vision. However, there were significant normative changes in the new organisation, as key elements that had straitjacketed the old OAU were introduced with the new Constitutive Act of the AU, such as a right to intervention, and these promised a new, more effective beginning to the region's continental institutions. However, the continental 'union government' that Gaddafi envisioned never materialised.

The Extraordinary Summit at Sirte was notable in many respects. Forty-three of fifty-three heads of state attended, and the remainder were represented by foreign ministers, the most senior representation in years.[3] The Sirte Declaration pronounced the creation of the African Union, and the Secretariat then began the drafting process for a new constitution and the protocol for a Pan-African Parliament (PAP), the only organ singled out for special mention in the Declaration.

After several disputes in the drafting process (see Chapter 5 on the Pan-African Parliament), the heads of state met again at Lomé in 2000. The Constitutive Act of the AU was adopted, although the PAP Protocol could not yet be agreed. The next Extraordinary Summit at Sirte was held in March 2001 when the Constitutive Act entered into force with the deposition of ratifications. The 'transition' period then began, to develop new rules of procedure and transfer the institutional arrangements from the OAU to the AU.

The 2001 Lusaka Summit adopted the rules of procedure for the AU, and was more of a logistics-focused summit on the day-to-day workings of the new institution. The former Ivorian foreign minister, Amara Essy, was elected as the transitional Secretary-General, replacing the outgoing Salim Salim. While Essy was trusted as a neutral actor,[4] it took eight rounds for him to acquire the necessary votes to defeat the last candidate, Theo Ben-Gurirab of Namibia.[5] He would then go on

[3] Ibid.   [4] Interview with AU official, 9 February 2016.
[5] Touray, *The African Union*, 44.

to become the Interim Chairperson of the AU Commission after the Durban Summit in 2002, which formally launched the African Union. This period, 2002–3, was named the 'interim period' as the OAU dissolved its remaining structures, handing them over to the AU. The Durban Summit uniquely contained both the last ever OAU summit and the first AU Assembly of the Heads of State and Government (the new name for heads of state summits). Durban was a ceremonial affair as the successful transition was celebrated and leaders reflected on the achievements of the OAU, especially relating to decolonisation and the fight against apartheid.

The 'interim period' of the establishment of the AU was declared over at the Maputo Summit in July 2003,[6] regardless of any other unresolved issues. This also provided for the election of the first chairperson of the AU Commission (AUC), and former Mali President Alpha Oumar Konaré was elected, the first time a former head of state had led the AUC.

What was eventually tabled and discussed as an 'African Union' had more in continuity with the OAU – albeit with some significant breaks, reflecting South Africa's and Nigeria's objectives – than with Gaddafi's US of Africa. African states continued to lavish praise on and give credit to Gaddafi for the idea,[7] even while nothing substantially remained of an actual union government.

The end of the 'interim period' in July 2003 at the Maputo heads of state summit closed the normative space, opponents of the 'US of Africa' having achieved their major goals, and pre-empted Gaddafi's further tampering with existing institutions. There was still unfinished business, such as establishing an African Court of Justice (to emerge from the mandated African Court of Human and People's Rights, establishment of which was still ongoing), the African Central Bank (still at a consultative stage), and so on.

Yet, interestingly, Gaddafi appears to have remained convinced for quite some time that his plan would succeed,[8] still tabling similar proposals for his standing army, the capital at Sirte, and others.

---

[6] Khamis, *Promoting the African Union* (Washington, DC: Liliane Barber, 2008), 157.

[7] Hindawi, 'In the Levant: Libya's Love Affair with Africa', *UPI*, 28 July 2001.

[8] For example, he still asserted that the term 'member states' had no meaning, and voting decisions should instead refer only to the 'Assembly' in the adopted Constitutive Act of the AU, one year later at Lusaka. Gaddafi, 'Speech by the

Nevertheless, Gaddafi's eagerness to be credited with whatever resulted also may have played a role in downplaying any objections.[9] His opponents allowed him the symbolic victories: Sirte is indelibly connected to the formation of the AU because of the 1999 Extraordinary Summit and Declaration, the 2001 Extraordinary Sirte Summit that declared the creation of the AU,[10] and the 2004 Extraordinary Summit that adopted the Common African Defence and Security Policy (in spite of the rejection of Gaddafi's common defence pact at Durban in 2002). This has sometimes been mistakenly understood to credit Gaddafi for the transformation of the OAU into the AU, but the structures and institutional features that resulted do not support this case. Gaddafi himself was clearly dissatisfied with the outcome, as he would continue to press for the 'United States of Africa' at 'The Grand Debate on the Union Government' in Accra in 2007,[11] and this continued at least until 2009, when Libya would last hold the rotating chairpersonship of the AU under Gaddafi. Interestingly, the 2007 Accra Declaration acknowledges his influence in stating:

We agree to accelerate the economic and political integration of the African continent, including the formation of a Union Government for Africa with the ultimate objective of creating the United States of Africa.[12]

Final attempts – such as the 2008 decision to try to transform the Secretariat, the African Union Commission (AUC), into an 'African Union Authority' – were scuttled in 2013 when an open-ended commitment was made to consider these issues 'at the appropriate time', while committing only to strengthen the AUC.[13] The departures of Alpha Oumar Konaré as chair and Abdoulaye Wade as president of Senegal, and Gaddafi's death, constituted the loss of the major

Leader of the Revolution at the Evening Session of the African Summit (Closed Session) on 10 July 2001' (Lusaka: Libyan Arab Jamahiriya, 2001), 7.
[9] Baimu and Sturman, 'Amendment to the African Union's Right to Intervene', 38.
[10] This was non-trivial as the Constitutive Act of the AU had not yet received enough ratifications to enter into force, and it was debated whether the AU should be declared created. The Constitutive Act eventually entered into force in May 2001, two months after the Sirte Summit.
[11] Akokpari, Ndinga-Muvumba, and Murithi, eds., *The African Union and its Institutions* (Auckland Park, South Africa: Fanele, 2008), 1–3.
[12] African Union, 'Accra Declaration' (Accra: African Union, 2007).
[13] African Union, 'Decision on the Transformation of the African Union Commission into the African Union Authority' (Assembly/AU/Dec. 454 (XX)) (Addis Ababa 2013),

protagonists for a more solid union government or supranational entity, which 'considerably weakened, if not killed, the spirit of the maximalists'.[14]

Part II will explore three normative challenges to sovereignty that took place during this transition, starting, of course, with the 'US of Africa' proposal itself, which proposed to federalise the continent. The second case is the longstanding issue of collective responsibility for regional security, following it through the ups and downs of the proposal for a 'Conference on Security, Stability, Development, and Cooperation in Africa' (CSSDCA) since 1991. Finally, an important check on the decision-making powers of the heads of state was potentially on offer with the Pan-African Parliament, another proposal that has its origins in 1991 but the form and structure of which would only be decided in this contest. The result of the three contests arguably placed a significant degree of nuance on the meaning of sovereignty in the AU and the locus between the agency of the RO and its member states as they emerged from the ashes of the OAU. The major events of the case study periods are listed in Table II.1.

Table II.1 *Timeline of the transition from the OAU to the AU*

Date	Event	Notable developments
May 1991	Kampala Forum	Conference on Sustainability, Stability, Development, and Cooperation in Africa presented to civil society
June 1991	27th Assembly of the Heads of State and Government, Abuja, Nigeria	CSSDCA sent back to committee for review Abuja Treaty Establishing the Africa Economic Community (AEC) signed
June 1998	34th Assembly of the Heads of State and Government, Ouagadougou, Burkina Faso	OAU decision to defy Western sanctions against Libya over Lockerbie bombing

[14] Touray, *The African Union*, 50.

Table II.1 (*cont.*)

Date	Event	Notable developments
February 1999	Nigerian elections after military rule	Olusegun Obasanjo elected president
July 1999	35th Assembly of the Heads of State and Government, Algiers, Algeria	Extraordinary summit at Sirte proposed
September 1999	Extraordinary Summit in Sirte, Libya	Forty-three of fifty-three OAU heads of state present 'United States of Africa' proposed Agreement to form 'African Union' in Sirte Declaration
June 2000	36th Assembly of the Heads of State and Government, Lomé, Togo	Constitutive Act of the African Union adopted
March 2001	2nd Extraordinary Summit in Sirte, Libya	Constitutive Act of the AU enters into force (May) Protocol to the Treaty Establishing the AEC Relating to the Pan-African Parliament adopted
July 2001	37th Assembly of the Heads of State and Government, Lusaka, Zambia	Amara Essy, former foreign minister of Côte d'Ivoire, elected transitional OAU Secretary-General/AU Interim Chairperson New African Initiative (NAI, later NEPAD) agreed
July 2002	38th Assembly of the Heads of State and Government (OAU) and 1st Assembly of the African Union, Durban, South Africa	Final OAU Assembly of the Heads of State and Government and first AU Assembly of the Heads of State held Interim period of transition from OAU to AU begins AU Peace and Security Council established

Table II.1 (*cont.*)

Date	Event	Notable developments
July 2003	2nd Assembly of the AU, Maputo, Mozambique	Interim period declared closed Former Mali President Alpha Oumar Konaré elected first chairperson of the AU Commission
December 2003		Protocol to the Treaty Establishing the AEC Relating to the PAP enters into force
March 2004	1st Ordinary Session of the Pan-African Parliament, Addis Ababa, Ethiopia	PAP inaugurated and adopts rules of procedure
July 2007	9th Assembly of the AU, Accra, Ghana	'Grand Debate on the Union Government' held, with agreement to work towards a union government
June 2014	23rd Assembly of the AU, Malabo, Equatorial Guinea	Protocol to the Constitutive Act of the AU Relating to the PAP adopted (not yet entered into force as of January 2021)

3 | *The 'United States of Africa' Proposal*

African states were born in an act that challenged the old norm of legitimate colonialism and established a new norm of self-determination.

Francis Deng and I. William Zartman[1]

Introduction

Treated in isolation, it is easy to reach the conclusion that Gaddafi was simply delusional and ego-driven, but this obscures the dynamics of this key period, and indeed would appear to offer few lessons to international relations as an exceptional event. As a result, the transition from the OAU to the AU has been historically described and its novel structures and innovations outlined,[2] but rarely adequately theorised,[3] a seeming one-off in the history of international organisations. Yet the unlikeliness of the event and the confluence of factors that led to the upheaval should create greater interest in this case. Even if Gaddafi's proposal were unacceptable to others, he could not be dismissed out of hand (and risk alienating future support for the OAU), but had to be carefully kept on board with the actual changes desired by other influential members, particularly South Africa and Nigeria.

---

[1] Deng and Zartman, *A Strategic Vision for Africa: the Kampala Movement* (Washington, DC: Brookings Institution Press, 2001), 141.

[2] See, for example, Akokpari, Ndinga-Muvumba, and Murithi, *The African Union and its Institutions*; Jeng, *Peacebuilding in the African Union* (Cambridge: Cambridge University Press, 2012); van Walraven, 'Heritage and Transformation'; Makinda and Okumu, *The African Union: Challenges of Globalization, Security, and Governance* (Abingdon: Routledge, 2008); Magliveras and Naldi, *The African Union (AU)* (Alphen aan den Rijn, Netherlands: Kluwer International Law, 2013).

[3] A notable exception being Tieku, 'Explaining the Clash and Accommodation of Interests.' However, Tieku's account focuses on the interplay between Gaddafi's, Mbeki's, and Obasanjo's motivations and how these affected the final shape of some AU norms, rather than following individual proposals from start to finish.

Moreover, as this case study will show, Gaddafi, despite being absent for nearly two decades at the OAU, behaved in a normatively compliant way with respect to OAU norms – including accepting decisions against his interests, but also appealing to OAU members' shared values and interests – in order to push his agenda, which he framed as an extension of existing values or aims. The contestation that erupted during the transition is also instrumental in explaining the norms that emerged out of such unlikely beginnings. I argue that it provides a salient example for the analysis of the effects of power and utility in explaining the norms of regional organisations, understood through categorisation by norm circles.

To explain the functional argument, it is necessary to step further back than Gaddafi's 'surprise' at Sirte in 1999, and review the long-standing debates in the OAU up to that time. By the 1990s, the difficulties the OAU had in addressing regional issues were apparent. While it had enjoyed success in hastening decolonisation, it was floundering in other areas that were increasingly coming to be viewed as the prerogative of regional organisations, such as conflict management and economic integration.

Regional Motivations

The 1980 Lagos Plan of Action, which had been devised to establish an African Economic Community (AEC), did not result in a treaty until Abuja in 1991, and even then it was missing several important parts, with a further twenty-nine additional protocols still formally required.[4] Many covered specialised technical areas, such as harmonisation standards, transit facilities, non-tariff barriers, and so on. However, missing even from the main Abuja Treaty were formal rules on the relations between the regional economic communities (RECs) such as the ECOWAS, SADC, and EAC, and the AEC proper. The AEC was also technically separate from the OAU as a legal entity. The draft protocol on relations between the AEC and RECs was only endorsed in November 1996, five years after Abuja, and only then could the ratification process commence.

In the 1980s and 1990s, Africa was also afflicted by civil wars and human rights abuses under authoritarian rule, with the 1994 genocide

[4] Khamis, *Promoting the African Union*, 39–41.

in Rwanda crowning a blight of protracted conflicts on the continent. In 1999, ongoing crises being discussed at OAU level involved Angola, Burundi, the Central African Republic, Comoros, Congo (Brazzaville), Congo (Kinshasa), Eritrea, Ethiopia, Guinea Bissau, Libya, Sierra Leone, Somalia, and Western Sahara.[5] This list omits several other ongoing conflicts at the time, including those in Uganda, Sudan, and Liberia. The OAU's role in these conflicts was limited to mediation at best or simply ignoring them at worst, having been chastened by the disastrous attempt at intervention in the Chadian Civil War in the 1980s,[6] and constrained by its charter commitment to non-interference.

Yet the OAU also had some successes. The collapse of apartheid rule in South Africa was one of its notable achievements, having long been the centre of a coalition of states in the Global South that applied pressure to isolate the apartheid regime internationally. Its defiance of Western sanctions against Libya in 1998, fatefully, would come to be viewed by Gaddafi as another such 'success'. The two underlying factors – poor economic performance and inability to deal with conflict – caused many in the OAU to desire strong reforms, but they had to overcome serious objections and open the normative space to do so. By the late 1990s, some within the OAU Secretariat had already openly discussed replacing the OAU's Charter and AEC's Abuja Treaty with a single act governing both.[7] However, until 1999, there had been no opportunity to do so.

Gaddafi's Motivations

Marginalised in the West since the 1986 Lockerbie bombing, Gaddafi had also been isolated in Sub-Saharan Africa over his war with Chad in the 1980s and support for numerous insurgencies against African states.[8] His actions towards the OAU were plainly transactional: for example, it was only during his bid to become president of the OAU in 1981 that he withdrew his troops from Chad (a precondition for the

---

[5] Introductory note to the Report of the Secretary-General, Algiers 1999, Part I.
[6] This is discussed in Chapter 4. For a full account, see Mays, *Africa's First Peacekeeping Operation: the OAU in Chad, 1981–1982* (London: Praeger, 2002).
[7] Tieku, *Governing Africa*, 86.
[8] Mays, *Africa's First Peacekeeping Operation*, 61–72.

OAU's first-ever deployment of peacekeeping troops[9]), though he still failed to secure the presidency. Failing in that bid, he stopped paying Libya's mandated contribution to the OAU, and after 1987, he would not attend another OAU summit until 1999, effectively boycotting it over the next decade.

However, in 1994, when the International Court of Justice ruled in favour of Chad over the disputed Aouzou strip, Libya surprisingly accepted the decision,[10] and this 'seemed to mark a significant change in Qadhafi's foreign policy towards Sub-Saharan Africa'.[11] This dovetailed his frustrations with the Arab world, which he felt had rebuffed him by accepting Western sanctions against Libya in response to the Lockerbie bombing.[12] In contrast, several African states had begun to plead on his behalf, and several leaders violated official sanctions to meet with him, including Nelson Mandela, following the decision at the 1998 Ouagadougou OAU summit. Gaddafi then refashioned himself from Pan-Arabist to Pan-Africanist, as he pronounced that 'the "Arab world is finished"', and declared Africans and not Arabs as Libya's real supporters.[13]

The willingness of African states to support his stance, and the act of no less a figure than Mandela to defy the sanctions, led him to believe that a united Africa could really face down the global 'imperialist' powers which had become preponderant after the Cold War.[14] The utility of this proposition was something he would later refer to continuously in speeches urging others to support his proposal.

As the Algiers Summit concluded in 1999 without resolution on several areas including economic integration and conflict management, Gaddafi invited the leaders to an extraordinary summit in Sirte, with the proposal 'to discuss ways and means of making the OAU effective so as to keep pace with political and economic developments taking place in the world and the preparation required of Africa within the context of globalisation so as to preserve its social, economic and

---

[9] The intervention was judged an 'abject failure' and caused a reluctance for any further missions by the OAU for several years thereafter. Naldi, *The Organization of African Unity*, 30–2.

[10] For context, see the background on the Chad civil war in Chapter 4.

[11] Huliaras, 'Qadhafi's Comeback: Libya and Sub-Saharan Africa in the 1990s', *African Affairs* 100(2001): 10.

[12] Africa Confidential, 'My Arabism Tired Me Out', *Africa Confidential* 39, no. 21 (1998).

[13] Huliaras, 'Qadhafi's Comeback', 11.   [14] Ibid.

political potentials'.[15] From his perspective, he believed he had a solution to the problems afflicting the OAU that would realise the long-lost dream of African unity. As Asteris Huliaras argues, Gaddafi wanted to seal his comeback to Sub-Saharan Africa with his grand vision of a US of Africa.[16]

Gaddafi's Gambit

Gaddafi held all the cards at the beginning. As Oche describes:

At [Sirte], the host, Colonel Muammar Ghaddafi, presented the respective African leaders that were present with a draft Charter in which he proposed the formation of The United States of Africa. His proposal described an African political configuration with one government, one leader, a single army, one currency, one central bank and one parliament that would legislate for a continent which would be essentially without borders as we know them today. The time period that was given for the realisation of this proposal was the year 2000.[17]

Gaddafi started off very well in terms of (1) controlling the initiative, (2) mastery of shared norms, and (3) identifying assets for influence, and clearly attempted to validate his proposal by making efforts on all three fronts. He had the clear initiative, having called the extraordinary summit, but may have misunderstood other considerations, having caught the delegates unawares, which may have alienated the response. Most of them would not have an immediate response, and some might have had to call their capitals (if they were not the heads of states themselves). Gaddafi pushed hard at Sirte to have the proposal accepted by consensus immediately,[18] when any of those opposed to the idea would not have a ready response. The Sirte Declaration, which he was instrumental in drafting, would become the guiding document (alongside the Abuja Treaty) for the formation of the AU, at least until

---

[15] OAU, 'Decision on the Convening of an Extraordinary Session of the OAU Assembly of Heads of State and Government in Accordance with Article 33 (5) of its Rules of Procedure' (AHG/Decl.140 (XXXV)) (Algiers 1999).

[16] Huliaras, 'Qadhafi's Comeback.'

[17] Oche, 'Nigeria, the AU, and the Challenge of Regional Integration', in *Nigeria and the Development of the African Union*, ed. Akinterinwa (Ibadan: Vantage, 2005), 142.

[18] Akinterinwa, ed., *Nigeria and the Development of the African Union* (Ibadan: Vantage, 2005), 20.

the Constitutive Act could be adopted, and this may have been a factor in the haste with which the Constitutive Act was adopted nine months later at Lomé. As far as the summit at Sirte was concerned, however, Gaddafi declared victory, confident that all his objectives would now be met following the adoption of the Sirte Declaration.[19]

The literal resurrection of a 'United States of Africa' was not accidental: it invoked Nkrumah's original Pan-African vision at the founding of the OAU, and indeed Gaddafi's supporters did compare him to Nkrumah.[20] Nkrumah's version had called for many of the same institutional features Gaddafi proposed to create: a combined continental government, leader, standing army, currency, central bank, and parliamentary institutions that would effectively merge Africa into a single country.[21] He framed his idea around the slogan, 'No future without unity',[22] a maxim impossible to disagree with at a meeting of the Organisation of African *Unity*. His proposal would merely be fulfilling the dreams of a liberation hero who was by now universally acclaimed among African leaders. He hoped to attract the support of avowed Pan-Africanists such as Abdoulaye Wade and Thabo Mbeki with such an appeal.

Arguably, few aspects of Gaddafi's proposal were original. The idea of transferring national sovereignties to the continental organisation had been suggested by Sekou Toure and Nkrumah in the 1950s and even enshrined in the constitutions of Guinea in 1958 and Ghana in 1960. He had even consulted ageing Nkrumahists who had been involved in the original proposal, with their version superseding the original more Marxist version he had originally developed.[23] The central bank and continental legislature were key elements to be formalised in unfinished protocols to the AEC. The standing army had been a longstanding (but always deferred) proposal since Nkrumah proposed the Defence Commission of the OAU. Gaddafi's influence was taken very seriously, and it is reflected in the language of the Sirte Declaration:

---

[19] Tieku, 'Explaining the Clash and Accommodation of Interests', 262.
[20] Makinda and Okumu, *The African Union*, 32.
[21] OAU, 'Draft of the Establishment of a State of the United States of Africa' (Sirte, Libya: Organisation of African Unity Archives, 1999).
[22] Africa Research Bulletin, 'Gaddafy Seeks United Africa', *Africa Research Bulletin* 36, no. 9 (1999): 13678.
[23] Interview with AU official, 22 February 2016

In our deliberations, we have been inspired by the important proposals submitted by Colonel Muammar Ghaddafi, Leader of the Great Al Fatah Libyan Revolution and particularly, by his vision for a strong and united Africa, capable of meeting global challenges and shouldering its responsibility to harness the human and natural resources of the continent in order to improve the living conditions of its peoples.[24]

Contemporary accounts of the Sirte Summit even described Nigeria and South Africa as supporting Gaddafi's initiative.[25] Even today, the idea of a federal or confederal 'United Africa' continues to appear in the AU's 'Agenda 2063', launched in 2015 after Gaddafi's death. While sparse on details, the Pan-African ideal retains serious traction in the AU,[26] even if individual members differ on the details or how this could be achieved.

With Libya's oil wealth, Gaddafi was also committed to financing his ambitious plans: he offered Sirte, his home town, to host the continental military base and be the new headquarters of the US of Africa, while also covering the arrears worth $4.5 million[27] of several states who owed contributions to the OAU at the time. Ouagadougou Hall in Sirte, constructed in honour of the Ouagadougou decision that defied Western sanctions against Libya, was offered as the new administrative and conference centre. He was strategic in offering choice roles to potential opponents too, hinting that Nkosazana Dlamini-Zuma, then South African foreign minister, should be the AU's first foreign minister, although Gaddafi believed he himself would be the leader.[28] Finally, since the Ouagadougou Summit in 1998, Libya had even been paying off the debts from unpaid dues of several OAU member states,[29] legally a precondition for having a vote (although votes are hardly ever taken).

---

[24] OAU, 'Sirte Declaration' (EAHG/Decl. (IV) Rev. 1) (Sirte 1999), para. 7.
[25] Africa Research Bulletin, 'Gaddafy Seeks United Africa', 13678.
[26] Tieku, 'Theoretical Approaches to Africa's International Relations.'
[27] Africa Research Bulletin, 'Gaddafy Seeks United Africa', 13678.
[28] Gumede, *Thabo Mbeki and the Battle for the Soul of the ANC* (London: Zed Books, 2007), 268.
[29] Oche, 'Nigeria, the AU, and the Challenge of Regional Integration', 153.

How the Opposing Norm Circle Fought Back

In 1999, Gaddafi had not countenanced strong opposition from other member states, and his lack of familiarity with the dynamics of the OAU would prove his undoing. His *imagined* norm circle for a Pan-African state far exceeded the *actual* norm circle. The dynamics of norm circles require allies, but this did not materialise the way he hoped. Although the 'Casablanca' norm circle at the formation of the OAU in 1963 had indeed supported a united Africa, subsequent governments of these states had now come to share the views of the Monrovia circle, that is, support for slow integration, or simply regional cooperation. The Monrovia and Casablanca divisions no longer existed by the time of Gaddafi's proposal,[30] and indeed the possibility of transfer of sovereignty to the OAU had disappeared from Ghana's and Guinea's later constitutions.

Gaddafi also alienated the norm circle of his erstwhile Lockerbie allies, in proposing an idea that was overambitious when so many OAU members were struggling to simply manage their own affairs. While authoritarian leaders such as Moi and Mugabe could normally be counted on for support in opposing liberal proposals, they would not accept the US of Africa plan without serious reservations or amendments. Gaddafi's reaction to some nascent opposition may have been even more alienating, as he derided those who stuck to 'their little kingdoms' to protect 'old-fashioned sovereignty of anthems and flags that should now be consigned to the museums'.[31]

Controlling the Initiative

Gaddafi was cognisant of his need to maintain control of the initiative, and anxious to have his proposal accepted immediately at Sirte, attempting to bypass the delegates' desires to receive instructions from their capitals.[32] However, attending delegates stalled him and, rather than make a wholesale commitment at Sirte, the eventual agreement was to establish an unspecified 'African Union', only committing to accelerating other, existing regional integration processes, in particular

---

[30] Interview with AU official, Addis Ababa, 3 February 2016.
[31] Quoted in Africa Research Bulletin, 'Continental Alignments: Conferences: the African Union', *Africa Research Bulletin* 37, no. 6 (2000): 13999.
[32] Akinterinwa, *Nigeria and the Development of the African Union*, 20.

strengthening the Abuja Treaty establishing the African Economic Community, and establishing the institutions it entailed, namely, the African Central Bank, the African Monetary Union, the African Court of Justice, and the Pan-African Parliament.[33] As one AU official describes:

> The conclusion was 'Yes' in principle, [we] agreed to the African Union government. Therefore, we accepted to change the name from OAU to establish the AU. However, on the union government, we said there should be greater consultation with the African people before we can form this union government. The opinion that led – became the dominant position – was that we should not create a union of governments or leaders, but of citizens.[34]

Gaddafi's framing of the matter as one of realising the dreams of the founding fathers of the OAU, and the utility that unity would have in staring down the major powers, was difficult to object to overtly. Thus the first objection raised against Gaddafi was to appeal to 'the African people' to create an additional procedural step, as it would involve returning to the national assemblies, and this precluded any firm decision at Sirte.

The following series of summits would begin to look in earnest in establishing the AU, but from then on, Gaddafi's advantage in holding the initiative would evaporate. Comparison with the European Union (EU) was a quirk of how events unfolded in Sirte, but the actual structure of the AU would be determined by the confluence of resolving the interests of the major actors of the other norm circle – the liberal wing led by Mbeki and Obasanjo[35] – and the existing OAU structures already created, such as the Mechanism on Conflict Resolution and the institutions of the AEC. Gaddafi invited the heads of state of Sudan, Mali, Ghana, Liberia, Senegal, Malawi, and Chad to the ministerial meeting in Tripoli ahead of the Lomé Summit to shore up support for his proposal,[36] turning it into a 'mini summit',[37] but as events transpired, this 'norm circle' could not persuade delegates to go further in his desired direction. At best, it was proposed

---

[33] 'Sirte Declaration' (EAHG/Decl. (IV) Rev. 1) 1999, para. 8(ii)(b).
[34] Interview with AU official, 9 February 2016.
[35] Tieku, 'Explaining the Clash and Accommodation of Interests.'
[36] Khamis, *Promoting the African Union*, 91.
[37] Touray, *The African Union*, 41.

that a confederal union could be formed over a fifty-year period, far too slowly for Gaddafi's liking.[38]

In subsequent summits, decisions on Gaddafi's proposals would be deferred (i.e. his proposal would be circulated amongst member states, or to be reviewed by ad hoc committees), which had the advantage of not provoking opposition from Gaddafi towards other initiatives. This effectively killed momentum wherever Gaddafi could muster it. Even in his home town of Sirte, at the Extraordinary Summit in 2001, he wanted the Constitutive Act to enter into force immediately, but this was met by opposition from Nigeria, Uganda, Tanzania, Namibia, Ghana, Lesotho, Zambia, Mali, South Africa, and Gabon. Amr Moussa, the Egyptian foreign minister, resolved that deadlock by allowing the Sirte meeting to announce the declaration of the AU, while delaying the entry into force of the Constitutive Act[39] (even though it was this document that was needed to create the 'African Union').

At Durban, for example, Gaddafi attempted to introduce numerous amendments into the Constitutive Act to recover his ideas for a continental army and a chairperson with presidential status.[40] However, rather than consider these amendments and put them up for debate:

> In his position as chairman, President Mbeki made the procedural argument that according to Rule 8 of the Rules of Procedure of the Assembly, items proposed by a Member State must be submitted 60 days and supporting documents and draft decisions communicated to the Chairperson of the Commission 30 days before the session.[41]

This passage encapsulates the performance of 'metis': here Mbeki had devised new shared rules that had been agreed only a year earlier at Lusaka, covering the putatively neutral area of procedure, and then opportunely deployed them to halt Gaddafi's attempts to reformulate the proposals in his favour. Finally, most of his proposals were quietly dropped by the review committee in January 2003.[42]

---

[38] Tieku, *Governing Africa*, 113.   [39] Touray, *The African Union*, 43.
[40] Libyan Arab Jamahiriya, 'Explanatory Notes on the Libyan Proposal for Amendment of the Constitutive Act of the African Union' (Addis Ababa: OAU, 2003), paras. 13–15.
[41] Baimu and Sturman, 'Amendment to the African Union's Right to Intervene', 38.
[42] Tieku, 'Explaining the Clash and Accommodation of Interests', 265.

When Gaddafi tried to return to the issue in 2005, he formed a commission of leaders from Uganda, Senegal, Libya, Mali, and Botswana. They recommended forming 'regional political federations' to accelerate Gaddafi's original plan. When their report was presented in July 2005, the AU decided immediately to form a second committee, this time chaired by Nigeria, and comprising mostly different countries: Algeria, Kenya, Lesotho, Senegal, and Uganda. The Gaddafi-backed committee's recommendations were quietly dropped.[43] Each time Gaddafi would raise his idea, the pattern would repeat itself, wherein Gaddafi would not be overtly opposed, but his project could always quietly be dropped in committee, usually formed of members of different norm circles than the ones who supported him.

Shared Norms: the African Economic Community

While Gaddafi's initiative gave the integration advocates a vital shot in the arm, as the African Union would turn out, he achieved very little of his vision in the final outcome.[44] Mastery of shared norms is a powerful factor in determining outcomes. Both South Africa and Nigeria expressed opposition to Gaddafi, and then began to attract a core of opposition around them, including Egypt and eventually Mali.[45] However, without a prepared response, it was difficult to present an alternative that could placate Gaddafi, draw others to an idea that had not been thoroughly thought through, and also fulfil the core interests of their own objectives (in this case, the 'African Renaissance', Mbeki's idea of a grand narrative where Africa would take united positions on a global stage). Obasanjo appears to have stepped in at Sirte, according to Akinterinwa's account:

President Obasanjo, at the 1999 Sirte (Libya) AU [sic] Summit, persuaded his colleagues to accept the concept of AU when there was a misunderstanding between several official delegates, on the one hand, and the host president, Muammar Ghaddafi, on the other ... It was thanks to Chief Olusegun Obasanjo, after consultations with like-minded leaders, that the lull was resolved. In this regard, he called on all his counterparts to begin implementing the [Abuja] Treaty Establishing the African Economic Community as a

---

[43] Khamis, *Promoting the African Union*, 192–3.
[44] Tieku, 'Explaining the Clash and Accommodation of Interests', 262.
[45] Van Walraven, 'Heritage and Transformation', 53.

prelude to the African Union. In fact [Nigerian Ambassador to the OAU, J. Kayode] Shinkaiye has it that the first draft of the Heads of State decision in Sirte II was hand-written by Obasanjo himself, and was given to Nigeria's representatives at the drafting committee meeting.[46]

While this account is flattering in respect of Obasanjo and probably overstates his role in resolving the deadlock, other sources agree that discomfort with Gaddafi's proposal was immediate, though not clearly expressed initially. Nigeria's attitude could be characterised as 'gradualist' and not in principle opposed to African unity.[47] As Akinsaya describes, according to Obasanjo,

> the nature of African Union should be understood to mean the pursuit of socio-economic integration of the continent as a first and necessary step towards the achievement of a political union … [W]hile a political union was desirable and *should be the ultimate objective of the Union*, the socio-economic conditions for its immediate implementation were not and are still not in place. It was noted, however, that closer socio-economic integration would, of necessity, require some degree of political cooperation.[48]

Recalling the Abuja Treaty proved to be the master stroke in refocusing attention on the difficulties African states had had up to this point at relatively less ambitious integration efforts, as well as drawing attention to one of Nigeria's neglected efforts at regional integration. Thus an 'African Union' was proposed, alluding to the European Union,[49] and this could have advantages in drawing in interest from EU donors, particularly at the forthcoming Africa–Europe summit in Cairo in 2000. While *Africa Confidential* would lambast the Sirte Declaration as 'a blank cheque' leaving entirely open the structure of what an 'African Union' would entail,[50] this was the result of the process of contestation underway, in which an alternative had not yet been fleshed out. The name would be as far as the similarity to

---

[46] Akinterinwa, *Nigeria and the Development of the African Union*, 20.
[47] Interview with AU official, Addis Ababa, 8 February 2016.
[48] Akinsaya, 'Nigeria at the African Union', in *Nigeria and the Development of the African Union*, ed. Akinterinwa (Ibadan: Vantage, 2005), 106–7, emphasis added.
[49] Salim, 'Statement by Dr Salim Ahmed Salim, Secretary General of the OAU at the Experts Meeting on the Establishment of the African Union and the Pan-African Parliament' (Addis Ababa: OAU, 2000).
[50] Africa Confidential, 'Organisation of African Unity: the Last Summit', *Africa Confidential* 42, no. 14 (2001): 1.

Shared Norms: the African Economic Community 91

the EU would go, as technical committees were formed in which to plan the new organs of the AU, modelled on *existing* but informal functional OAU structures.[51] Thus the EU was a temporary analogy, but not an actual model, for the future of African regionalism. Indeed, the final Sirte Declaration[52] was pared down to just eight paragraphs, against the rambling twenty-three-paragraph first edition drafted by Gaddafi.[53]

At the following Heads of State Summit at Lomé in July 2000, Yoweri Museveni (Uganda) and Abdoulaye Wade (Senegal) gave speeches in support of a 'United States of Africa', though they differed in the details and by now both referred to it as the 'African Union', albeit with strong supranational characteristics. Wade, having only been inaugurated as Senegal's president in April and probably not well briefed on events at Algiers and Sirte, proposed a constitution with structures taking after the United States of *America*, complete with upper and lower houses.[54] Having no precedent in existing OAU structures or organs and thus no immediately evident utility in addressing the continent's challenges, it was difficult to back and virtually ignored.

Museveni, then seen as a Gaddafi supporter, spared the details, only arguing that 'political unification is the only safe roof under which economic integration can take place', and that they should 'agree the modalities for the progressive establishment of the African Political Union and ... seek political mass support for these decisions'.[55] The implicit meaning was clear: that 'political mass support' for the US of Africa did not yet exist. Museveni argued that the African Union should start with regional political units, so that 'we would have 7 or less states (because some of them could be merged), each with a

---

[51] By 2001, the key AU structures were fleshed out in OAU, *Report of the Secretary General on the Implementation of the Lusaka Summit on the Texts Relating to the Key Organs of the African Union* (Addis Ababa: OAU, 2001), 29–31. All the organs previously existed in some form in the OAU or AEC.
[52] 'Sirte Declaration' (EAHG/Decl. (IV) Rev. 1) 1999,
[53] 'Draft Sirte Declaration' (Sirte, Libya: OAU Archives, 1999).
[54] Wade, 'Contribution de Sénégal à l'Union Africaine, Sommet de Lomé du 10 au 12 Juillet 2000' (Lomé: Republic of Senegal, 2000).
[55] Museveni, 'Statement by His Excellency Yoweri Museveni, President of the Republic of Uganda, at the 36th Summit of Heads of State and Government, Lomé, Togo, 10th–12th July, 2000' (Lomé, Togo: Republic of Uganda, 2000), 8, 13.

capacity comparable to the [United States of America] but fairly cohesive culturally'.[56]

Reaching for a compromise, Mali's President Alpha Oumar Konaré, who had been close to Gaddafi and one of the few constant invitees to his numerous preparatory meetings, gave his Lomé speech outlining existing integration efforts between the AEC and RECs (particularly ECOWAS, of which Mali was a member), and especially the difficulties:

> Certaines des Communautés existante connaissent des difficultés: absence de coordination et d'échanges entre Communautés, liens avec l'OUA mal définis et inappropriés; difficultés de fonctionnement, difficultés internes de politiques, et dans certains cas, manque de volonté politique.[57]
>
> (Some existing [Economic] Communities face difficulties: an absence of coordination and exchange between Communities, inappropriate and poorly defined links with the OAU, operational difficulties, internal political difficulties, and in certain cases, lack of political will.)

This laid down a challenge as to how integration would proceed, when existing efforts were already so weak. Ultimately, he argued:

> Il faut un dépassement de l'OUA à partir de l'OUA. C'est ce qui signifie pour nous l''Union Africaine', l'OUA avec une dimension économique. Les regroupements économiques avec une dimension politique plus affirmée.[58]
>
> (We must transcend the OAU from within the OAU. This is what the 'African Union' signifies for us. The OAU with an economic dimension. The economic groupings with a stronger political dimension.)

Despite having appeared to accept Gaddafi's arguments about the need and urgency for greater continental integration (exhorting his audience to do likewise, including the transfer of sovereignty), in his final proposal, Konaré put forward a simple merger of the AEC and OAU, but with the caveat that the AU would create the AEC, not the reverse (*'C'est l'Union Africaine qui créera la Communauté Economique Africaine et non l'inverse.'*[59]).

[56] Ibid., 13.
[57] Konaré, 'Allocution de son Excellence Monsieur Alpha Oumar Konaré, Président de la République du Mali, Trente-Sixième Session de la Conférence des Chefs d'État et de Gouvernement de l'Organisation de l'Unité Africaine (OUA) (Lomé, République Togolaise, 10–12 Juillet 2000)' (Lomé: Republic of Mali, 2000), 5.
[58] Ibid., 9.   [59] Ibid., 10.

Shared Norms: the African Economic Community   93

While rhetorically appearing to favour Gaddafi's arguments, the compromise Konaré tabled appeared to drive concessions from the US of Africa norm circle:

Cette Union pourrait être mise en place conformément au calendrier adopté à Syrte, si nous convenons d'un certain nombre de principes:

- la non-supranationalité, aujourd'hui, ce qui entrainera au départ un parlement non-souverain
- convenir du principe de démarche différenciée dans des domaines a définir pour ceux qui ne sont pas prêts
- concevoir que certains pays, ou groupes de pays, puissent jouer le rôle d'avant-garde et de locomotive sans domination particulière et sans exclusive, ni exclusion.[60]

(This Union could be set up according to the timetable adopted at Sirte if we agree on certain principles:

- Non-supranationality, today, which will result in a non-sovereign parliament
- Agree on a principle of a differentiated approach[61] in areas to be defined, for those who are not ready
- Appreciate that certain countries, or group of countries, may play a leading and driving role without individual domination and without exclusivity or exclusion.)

The concession that supranationality would be off the table at Lomé, with repercussions for the eventual structure of the Pan-African Parliament (see Chapter 5), was the key to this consensus. On top of this, Konaré suggested variable geometry (*démarche différenciée*) for those countries that were not ready, which put no onus on them to cede sovereignty then, and the Constitutive Act could therefore be agreed.

This merger of the OAU with the AEC, it turned out, was essentially the same as the proposal Konaré had made at Algiers in 1999[62] – before Gaddafi had opened the whole can of worms – but now, Konaré was poised to achieve his proposal, though it amounted to far less than what Gaddafi wanted. In this way, Gaddafi's support was dissipated:

---

[60] Ibid.
[61] In English, the term from the WTO used in relation to different speeds of economic integration is 'variable geometry'. See Gathii, *African Regional Trade Agreements as Legal Regimes* (Cambridge: Cambridge University Press, 2011), chapter 2.
[62] Khamis, *Promoting the African Union*, 92.

even those who ostensibly spoke in his favour, such as Wade, proposed items so far removed from Gaddafi's plan or any existing OAU institutions that they were of little use, and Senegal's and Mali's support dissipated during technical discussions as they were more willing to seek compromises.[63]

Efforts to centre the debate around the AEC succeeded. The pre-existing shared goal of economic integration was elevated to a place of central importance during this time, as a counter to Gaddafi's proposals. This was surprising given the excruciatingly slow pace that economic integration efforts had previously suffered until then. But, as a foil to Gaddafi, it became a top priority. Equally significant, the moribund OAU Charter Review Committee, which was established in 1980 to improve the functioning of the OAU but had got nowhere in eighteen years,[64] was superseded by the direct attention of the heads of states themselves. The Constitutive Act of the new AU was therefore agreed hastily at Lomé – initially as a transitional framework[65] – but had the effect of precluding the more ambitious US of Africa. Mbeki invoked millenarian urgency to dissuade Gaddafi, who still sought numerous amendments, from drawing out the process further,[66] reminding him that Gaddafi himself had set the 2000 deadline to accomplish his proposal. Gaddafi acquiesced on the understanding that changes could still be made later.[67]

Konaré's vision entailed a simple path: putting strong political will behind the floundering economic institutions. This appeal to strengthening and streamlining existing but neglected structures won out, and he would go on to become the first chairperson of the AU Commission, having considerable influence on the shape of the new institution.[68]

---

[63] Tieku, *Governing Africa*, 113.
[64] For example, the recommendation of the very first Charter Review Committee of 1980, and reiterated by the third (1982), fourth, and fifth (both 1989) sessions, to include mention of human rights in Article III of the OAU Charter, had not managed to make it into the charter by 1999. OAU, 'Background Information on the Work of the OAU Charter Review Committee' (paper presented at the 4th Extraordinary Session of the Assembly of Heads of State and Government, Sirte, 1999).
[65] Khamis, *Promoting the African Union*, 235.
[66] Gaddafi, 'Closed Session Speech, Lusaka 2001', 2.
[67] Khamis, *Promoting the African Union*, 236.
[68] Interview with AU official, 22 February 2016.

Metis: NEPAD vs Gaddafi Largesse

What then of Gaddafi's overt material incentives to various African states in exchange for support? Rather than assume that heads of states would cling to sovereignty as their fundamental political unit, Mbeki and Obasanjo were not prepared to leave it to chance. While they were not given to paying off members for support, they demonstrated their competence by identifying a key source of influence that did not require their own financial commitment.

Parallel to the AU debate were proposals that would eventually form the New Partnership for African Development (NEPAD). Africa's longstanding debt problems with the West had been a challenge for virtually every state on the continent. Foreign funding, while necessary for development financing, tended to come with external conditionalities which chafed against notions of sovereignty even among liberal African leaders, and strengthening African negotiating positions were a central focus of OAU discussions. Thabo Mbeki, while still South African foreign minister, had come up with an idea of 'African Renaissance' for the continent, key to it being negotiations for debt relief and establishing a common African position at global fora. Having been tasked with presenting a common African position to the G7 group alongside Obasanjo and Bouteflika, Thabo Mbeki began work on the 'Millennium Africa Recovery Plan' (MAP) to spur endogenous African growth. He had already presented an early draft at the World Economic Forum in Davos in 2001, before again presenting it at the second Extraordinary Summit at Sirte in March 2001.

However, at this summit, Senegal's Abdoulaye Wade, who had only been elected in April 2000, had come up with an alternative proposal, the 'Omega Plan for Africa', which focused on infrastructural investments. Wade had originally been critical of Mbeki's MAP and the African Renaissance concept generally.[69] However, existing overlaps enabled a consensus decision to be made that the plans be merged (infrastructure investment was a key strategic area within MAP), and this became the New Africa Initiative (NAI).[70] The fact that Wade was also a key supporter of Gaddafi's United States proposal[71] meant that

---

[69] Interview with AU official, 3 February 2016.
[70] OAU, 'Declaration on the New Common Initiative (Map and Omega)' (AHG/Decl.1 (XXXVII)) (Lusaka 2001),
[71] Wade, 'Contribution de Sénégal à Lomé.'

he could be peeled away from Gaddafi's norm circle through putting strong emphasis on the NAI/NEPAD and incorporating Senegal as a founding member.

Obasanjo and Mbeki, despite their normative similarities, would not align automatically. Obasanjo was suspicious that NEPAD would supplant his CSSDCA,[72] having thematic overlap (security and stability were also cornerstones of MAP) without a clearly delineated role for both. However, once Obasanjo saw that CSSDCA was not threatened, he began to back NEPAD strongly. Adding in the diplomatic nous of Algeria, the Pan-African trifecta of Mbeki, Obasanjo, and Bouteflika would go to the G7 and World Economic Forum summits to argue a common African position on development, to secure debt relief, and to establish NEPAD as the implementing agency.

Gaddafi initially railed against NEPAD, claiming, 'It's a creation of colonial capitalists and racists,'[73] but he appeared unable to marshal opposition to it, with South Africa, Nigeria, and Algeria supporting it, to whom would be added Egypt and Senegal as founding members of the steering committee. This committee noticeably comprised the OAU's 'big five' donor states *sans* Libya, but with Senegal added. However, some accounts suggest Gaddafi quietly removed his opposition when Libya was accepted into NEPAD as well.[74] At the same time, NEPAD was originally incorporated outside the AU system because of lingering opposition to the project[75] – so, clearly, not everyone was influenced.

In this way, NEPAD emerged out of NAI as a joint initiative backed by major voices from all parts of the continent, even if it was construed as a South African initiative, headquartered in Johannesburg and not even formally part of the AU at the time of creation. This externalisation made it difficult to oppose, as it did not need OAU/AU consensus to go ahead. The argument for debt relief and (putatively fairer) development financing from the West proved a more realistic and tangible alternative than anything Gaddafi could offer to distribute throughout the continent. NEPAD also addressed one of the major arguments Gaddafi had put forward on the necessity of the 'United States of Africa': that a united Africa was needed to face down Western

[72] Makinda and Okumu, *The African Union*, 31.
[73] Quoted in Gumede, *Thabo Mbeki and the Battle for the Soul of the ANC*, 267.
[74] Baimu and Sturman, 'Amendment to the African Union's Right to Intervene', 38.
[75] Interview with AU official, 22 February 2016.

powers – and indeed, inasmuch as a common negotiating position emerged out of the various proposals, African states could be united in such negotiations without ceding sovereignty.

Conclusion

This case study has shown how the interplay between interests and practices such as leading the initiative, using shared norms, and using external sources of influence was a key factor in explaining the normative complexion of the eventual AU. Gaddafi's attempt to recreate the OAU as a single continental state failed. Yet the dynamics involved offer rich and often overlooked lessons for understanding how key proposals either succeeded or failed in this period of remarkable normative openness. While Gaddafi attempted to harness old norms, lavished his own material resources, and drove the narrative of fulfilling the dreams of Africa's 'Founding Fathers', his attempts were thwarted at every turn by a combination of clever political manoeuvring by other OAU leaders who were not willing to concede sovereignty. Table 3.1 documents the key factors in the contest.

In this case study, the norm circles were contingent, and developed in reaction to Gaddafi's proposal. Because of the 'surprise' element employed by Gaddafi, quick reaction without necessarily having all the facts was required initially, but as the drama played out, the various groups came to see the competing ideas according to their broader national interests, and this spelled the end for Gaddafi's idea. However, with Libya's oil wealth and willingness to use it to support the OAU, they had to keep him on board, and this is the story of how they skilfully balanced the rejection of his proposal without alienating him completely.

The distribution of actors in the norm circles changed over time, with many wavering in their support for Gaddafi as time went on. This was down to the strategic direction of Nigeria and South Africa, prominent supporters of the opposing norm circle, who flexed their productive power emphatically to pre-empt Gaddafi's more physical rewards. It also made it more difficult for Gaddafi to marshal other forms of support and legitimacy as time wore on, even as his proposals kept being sent back to committees for further study.

The central question, 'Why did Gaddafi's "United States of Africa" fail?', is accounted for by the two levels this model has suggested –

Table 3.1 *Contestation over the 'United States of Africa'*

Factors	Proposing norm circle	Opposing norm circle
Members	Libya, Senegal, Mali, Burkina Faso, Uganda, Ghana, Liberia, Chad, Malawi, Sudan	Nigeria, South Africa, Algeria, Tanzania, Namibia, Lesotho, Gabon, Guinea, Madagascar
Control of initiative	• Hosting Extraordinary Sirte Summit • Monitoring of preparatory meetings	• Deferral of Libyan proposals to committees • Invoking urgency at Lomé to pass Constitutive Act • Use of procedural rules to block new proposals for amendments
Norms invoked	• Nkrumah's 'United States of Africa' • Pan-Africanism	• Abuja Treaty establishing AEC • Proposed merger of AEC and OAU
Metis	• Paying membership dues for OAU members (Libya) • Promising financial backing and offer of Sirte as capital • Offer of leadership positions in US of Africa to leading individual diplomats (failed)	• Merger of Omega and MAP into NEPAD (development financing and debt relief) • Defections or loss of support for proposal by Uganda, Mali, Senegal • Closure of interim period without amendments introduced
Outcome	Rejected	

norm circles and power based on competence. First, Gaddafi failed to organise sufficiently large norm circles to back his plan, and some of his early allies, like Wade, were successfully drafted into the opposing norm circle against the plan through external sources of influence. Unlike his opponents, he failed to bring new actors into his norm circle, insulting those who opposed him. Second, he failed to exercise sufficient skill in the three areas outlined in this book: controlling the initiative, the use of shared norms, and identifying opportunities for influence. His lack of familiarity with OAU procedures meant he was

Conclusion 99

often obstructed at crucial moments. He did not appear cognisant of how far Nkrumah's ideals had fallen out of favour since the 1960s. And his material offerings were insufficient incentives, especially for larger states.

The opposing norm circle performed much better. They successfully took the African unity narrative out of Gaddafi's hands to reformulate it around the AEC. They offered a bigger incentive to join up to their vision of NEPAD, against the physical largesse of Gaddafi's direct contributions. With NEPAD, they successfully merged aspects of several potentially competing proposals – CSSDCA, Omega, and MAP – to come up with a consensual framework that also functioned to reduce support for the union government plan. And finally, they used their much more skilful handling of AU rules of procedure and knowledge of technical problems around existing integration plans to thwart specific attempts to reintroduce Gaddafi's plans at all stages of the transition to the AU. In particular, Alpha Oumar Konaré, initially seen as close to Gaddafi,[76] achieved the proposal he made at Algiers in 1999, and would go on to lead the AU as its first chairperson.

The norm that all sides agreed on was significant and influential in the outcomes observed: the norm of African unity precluded overt objection to Gaddafi's proposal. The AEC proved the most tangible alternative and, despite languishing in the 1990s, it received a vital boost at that time as its importance suddenly became central to rejecting an immediate union government. Meanwhile, the appeal to African people and the existence of the Pan-African Parliament (PAP) in the AEC Treaty did create uncomfortable path dependencies that the norm circle opposed to Gaddafi could not entirely avoid.

This case study does have some weaknesses. The implications of Gaddafi's federalisation proposal are clearly much more extensive – a continental government, written on just fifteen pages – than the other cases this book examines. A claim could be made that it was doomed to failure from the outset. Yet even if that were so, it is most interesting that the contest played out exactly as the theoretical model structure suggests: Gaddafi tried to wield the initiative, appealed to shared norms, and attempted many other forms of influence beyond that. The model also suggests that overwhelming success requires imbalanced norm circles: Gaddafi was not nearly as marginalised on the

[76] Khamis, *Promoting the African Union*, 91.

continental stage as presented – he had at least ten states behind him, largely drawn from West Africa, where he had significant influence. And yet the success of the opposing norm circle in rejecting the US of Africa was not simply down to exercising their effective veto by withholding consensus or challenging its technical merits. Instead, they wrested control of the initiative from Gaddafi, appealed to different shared norms, and found creative ways to peel away his supporters. They could clearly have vetoed Gaddafi early on if they had overwhelming opposition to the proposal.

Furthermore, it must be remembered that Gaddafi's original proposal was initially *accepted* in principle,[77] and he originally saw the Sirte Declaration as a triumph,[78] before the resultant contestation would unwind his union proposal into the much more loosely integrated organisation we see today. Only this careful account of the shared (and unshared) practices and norms that drove decision-making from Sirte to Maputo can account for the resultant complexion of the AU, and the near-complete failure of Gaddafi to get *any* of the institutional structures in the form he desired, including the PAP.

Materialist or realist accounts would struggle with this total lack of success, given the resources Gaddafi had at his disposal, leaving only an explanation that Gaddafi was crazy. Yet this explanation is unsatisfactory given that he behaved in a norm-compliant manner within the OAU when he rejoined, and was well respected in the organisation long after the debate ended and even after his death and the collapse of his regime, when there would be little incentive to pay him further lip service.

Ideational or liberal accounts would struggle with the possibility of compromise or substantive agreement from such diverse member states. Furthermore, they would be challenged to account for the most liberal members (Nigeria and South Africa) being the most opposed to regional representation in the form of a Pan-African Parliament with real powers to promote integration, as is ostensibly its purpose and which aligned well with their shared interests or foreign policies.

One could argue that Gaddafi's 'United States of Africa', with such an extensive proposal involved, is the most 'unlike' of all the case studies involved in this book – i.e. that its rejection should have been

---

[77] Interview with AU official, 9 February 2016.
[78] Tieku, 'Explaining the Clash and Accommodation of Interests', 262.

obvious. Yet I would argue that if its rejection was such a foregone conclusion, then why was there even a contest? Why would all the actors involved, both for and against, act in such normatively compliant ways? Why wasn't the rejection simply made at the outset of the debate? The consensus mode of decision-making preferred in the AU could certainly have made it possible, with any one state having an effective veto to collapse the consensus. Instead, we see a contest that conforms to the structure of the theoretical model, and it played out over several years, meaning it was hardly coincidental, and this is a surprise.

Most interestingly, the 'accidental' success of these countries in thwarting Gaddafi cannot be taken lightly: this was not a foregone conclusion that it may appear to be today. The key institutions within the AU were all agreed as compromises for an 'interim period' before reaching full 'unity' – at a discursive level, Gaddafi plainly won the day and this continues to be reflected in the Agenda 2063 plans now being implemented.

While the transition from OAU to AU provided a unique moment of normative openness to various proposals, the fragility with which Gaddafi's opponents achieved their goals was apparent even to themselves, and they worked hard to close out the Constitutive Act to further changes at Lomé, despite numerous attempts at further intervention by Gaddafi. This proved a final act of metis, as it paid off in closing down the debate in future years. As one AU official recounts:

> Members were reluctant [to reopen the debate] in two aspects: One, some who were supporting Gaddafi said, 'We have something here – if we renegotiate, we can lose even this. As a compromise, we leave it as it is.' [Two,] Since the fundamental document was not finalised,[79] there have been so many misunderstandings. Some talk about the Abuja Treaty as if it still exists. But Article 33 [of the Constitutive Act] has replaced the OAU charter, to which Abuja was attached. But [some say] Abuja was never finished – so they have a point. We are [stuck] in these kinds of misunderstandings.[80]

---

[79] Here, the official argued that the Constitutive Act was drafted under the understanding that it was to be the constitution for the AU's *interim* period, and not intended to be its permanent constitution, and hence a 'fundamental document' that would have served as such (possibly referring to a version more aligned with Gaddafi's vision) was never drafted.

[80] Interview with AU official, 22 February 2016.

As an influential contributor to the OAU, Gaddafi could not be simply dismissed out of hand, but had to be outmanoeuvred in a way that did not jeopardise his sizeable financial support of the OAU, as had happened in the 1980s. The practice-oriented analysis sheds important light on how various aspects of opposition can be analytically broken down along the three competence variables. As noted above, even some Gaddafi supporters accepted this for fear of losing out more. The political will to allow any reopening of the debate is so weak that the 'Protocol on Amendments to the Constitutive Act of the AU' has yet to enter into force, as of December 2019.

4 | *The Conference on Security, Stability, Development, and Cooperation in Africa*

The security, stability and development of every African country is inseparably linked with those of other African countries. Consequently, instability in one African country reduces the stability of all other African countries.

The Kampala Document[1]

Introduction

The Conference on Security, Stability, Development, and Cooperation in Africa (CSSDCA) has had a remarkable, if little recognised, effect on regionalism in Africa. Conceived in 1991 by Nigerian leader Olusegun Obasanjo, then out of power, it was initially rejected by the OAU before its sudden adoption in 2000, and would go on to shape several of the regional norms and approaches to conflict resolution on the continent and beyond. Most prominently, the CSSDCA's approach of collective responsibility for regional security issues would, after much pressing, eventually overturn the strict stance on non-interference in the OAU, though it did so in the shadow of Gaddafi's 'United States of Africa' proposal.

However, the way the norms promoted by CSSDCA crept into the OAU structures is also notable. Whether inspired by or in competition with the CSSDCA, the OAU would devise the Mechanism on Conflict Resolution in 1993, the precursor to today's Peace and Security Council.[2] The CSSDCA's main economic thrust involved the acceleration of the regional economic communities to promote sub-regional integration. This would play a major role in the alternative to the 'US of Africa', which would become known as the 'African Union'. CSSDCA's social and economic components would be incorporated

---

[1] Africa Leadership Forum, *The Kampala Document* (Kampala: Africa Leadership Forum, 1991), General Principles, II.
[2] Deng and Zartman, *The Kampala Movement*, 113.

in the new initiative, NEPAD, to avoid duplication. And finally, a role for non-state actors to increase participation in the AU would eventually be formalised through the Economic, Social, and Cultural Council (ECOSOCC) in 2004.[3] Such was the success of CSSDCA that it was eventually dissolved (remnants contained in the Citizens and Diaspora Directorate, CIDO) with its major objectives considered accomplished by 2004.

This case study offers two observation points with separate episodes of contestation: the CSSDCA's initial rejection in 1991 by the OAU heads of state, and then its full acceptance in 1999–2000 during the transition from the OAU to the AU. Many of the factors can be observed to be held constant: the organisation, most of its influential member states (particularly CSSDCA's strongest opponents), the decision-making structure and procedural norms, and broader African norms overall. Other factors had changed in the intervening nine years: several states had democratised and their preferences radically shifted, Obasanjo had returned to power in Nigeria, the Rwandan genocide had occurred, and South Africa had emerged from apartheid rule.

This chapter first gives a historical account of the process, starting from its origins in 1990 through to its incorporation and eventual distribution of functions throughout the AU. It will then assess the 1991 rejection and 2000 adoption of the CSSDCA Solemn Declaration according to the parameters of competing norm circles' control of the initiative, use of shared norms, and use of opportunities for influence (metis). Finally, it concludes with some reflections on the impact of CSSDCA, a discussion of some competing explanations, and the importance of understanding practice for explaining the nature of outcomes in diplomacy.

Origins of the CSSDCA

The development of the CSSDCA is indelibly associated with Nigerian leader Olusegun Obasanjo. He first encountered the problems of African conflicts as Nigerian head of state during his first term in power from 1976 to 1979, particularly during the Chad civil war that lasted from 1966 to 1982 and witnessed Nigeria's first

---

[3] Interview with AU official, 22 February 2016.

unilateral peacekeeping mission, and the OAU's first and only peacekeeping mission.

The OAU intervention in Chad is significant because of the major role that Nigeria played in the process, including its failure. The 'civil war' was to some degree a regional war, involving troops from multiple factions in Chad, alongside Libyan and Nigerian troops supporting different factions. This experience would be influential on both the OAU's and Obasanjo's thinking throughout the 1990s, and the historical context sheds an important light on some of the views about peacekeeping operations on the continent as well. The failure of the OAU mission would lead to a reticence in the organisation towards engaging in other peacekeeping missions for the next decade.[4] However, because of the sensitivities involved with Libya, Chad, and Nigeria facing each other at future OAU deliberations, it was hardly mentioned, yet it provides a subtext for much of the later discussions at least until the 1990s.

The Chadian Civil War, 1966–1982

The Chadian Civil War started in 1966 with the formation of Frolinat (Front de Libération National du Tchad), a union of anti-government opposition groups. Capitalising on instability in the country, Libya occupied the Aouzou strip in 1973, ownership of which it disputed with Chad. By 1978, Felix Malloum, who had seized power in a coup, formed a government with Hissène Habré, formerly in Frolinat before falling out with its leader, Goukouni Oueddei.[5] However, following the renewed outbreak of violence between Habré's and Malloum's forces in February 1979, a conference was called in March in Kano, with Nigeria acting as mediator, though not all factions were present.

Following the Kano I accord, Nigerian troops were deployed in the country, both Malloum and Habré resigned, Goukouni was installed as leader of the transitional government (Gouvernement d'Union Nationale de Transition, GUNT), and remnant French forces promised to withdraw.[6] As tensions remained, a second Kano conference was called in April. Goukouni and Habré refused to cooperate with other factions this time (particularly those not present at Kano I, who had

---

[4] Naldi, *The Organization of African Unity*, 30–2.
[5] Mays, *Africa's First Peacekeeping Operation*, 29–30.   [6] Ibid., 36–7.

been unhappy with their sidelining), and reconstituted their own government after threatening to attack Nigerian troops. Mediation turned to Lagos as Libyan troops resumed attacks in the north around Aouzou, while also supporting a GUNT splinter faction, which was threatening to secede. However, the conference in Lagos was boycotted by the main GUNT factions, who rejected the communiqué from the conference and ordered Nigerian forces to leave.

Against this backdrop, the OAU discussed the creation of an OAU Defence Force that would be multinational but strictly a 'peacekeeping observer force'.[7] The OAU had endorsed the Nigerian mission at Monrovia in July 1979, giving the Nigerians more international legitimacy, but it was difficult to characterise the Nigerian force as 'neutral', with the Chadian factions viewing them as an 'occupation army',[8] and Nigeria (together with Libya) refusing Chad a seat at the Monrovia Summit. A faction led by Aboubakar Abderahmane (Forces Armées d'Ouest, FAO), a Kanembu, was favoured by Nigeria, and allegedly received private support from ethnic Kanembu in Nigeria with the Nigerian government's knowledge.[9] Nigeria issued an economic boycott against Chad, and with landlocked Chad's oil dependency on Nigeria, a second Lagos conference was promptly agreed in August. Lagos II again mandated a peacekeeping force, this time multinational and, importantly, stipulating that neighbouring countries would not participate, thus excluding both Libya and Nigeria. An OAU force comprising troops from the Republic of Congo, Guinea, and Benin was agreed, but only Congolese troops arrived in January 1980, and they refused to leave their barracks without the presence of the rest of the 'Pan-African' contingent. They departed just two months later in March, following a clash between Chadian factions that resulted in shelling of the Congolese barracks, killing one and injuring several more of the peacekeepers.

Goukouni meanwhile had agreed a treaty with Gaddafi, allowing Libyan troops into the country, including N'Djamena. Goukouni took advantage of this deployment to renew his offensive against Habré's Forces Armée du Nord (FAN), and he jointly announced with Gaddafi in January 1981 that the nations of Libya and Chad would be merging

---

[7] Ibid., 44.   [8] Ibid., 41.
[9] Azevedo, *Roots of Violence: a History of War in Chad* (London: Routledge, 1998; repr., 2004), 156.

at a future (undetermined) date.[10] Sudan and Egypt, both wary of Gaddafi, now openly turned to support Habré.[11] Stunned, Nigeria resumed its diplomatic initiatives, and the OAU ad hoc committee on Chad reconvened, reiterating that the Lagos II accord remained the basis of a peace deal in Chad. However, Nigeria began to lobby Libya for a way out, pressing it to accept, at least in principle, the idea of an OAU peacekeeping force as a replacement for Libyan troops.[12] Gaddafi's goal of becoming the next OAU president for 1982 was vehemently opposed by several African states, including Nigeria, which threatened to boycott a Tripoli summit unless Libyan troops were withdrawn. Goukouni also began to distrust the Libyan influence and, having secured a promise of French military aid and the OAU peacekeeping mission, requested Libya to leave in October 1981.[13] He then signed an agreement in Paris in November to accept the OAU peacekeeping mission. The Paris accord was envisaged by the French to replace the Lagos accord, but this move upset African leaders, who felt their diplomatic initiative was being hijacked, calling it 'the worst form of neo-colonialism'.[14] Nevertheless, a multinational contingent arrived, now including Nigeria, again, as well as Zairean and Senegalese troops.

Habré condemned the OAU mission, while Goukouni saw it 'as a total replacement for Libyan soldiers, meaning he expected them to fight Habré's forces as a peace enforcement mission and protect the [GUNT]'.[15] However, the OAU force maintained its neutrality, and thus failed to match the 'security' provided by the departing Libyan forces. The OAU mandate was now set by the meeting of the ad hoc committee in Nairobi (Nairobi accord), which freed it from the mandates of the politically charged Paris and Lagos accords. Militarily, Habré's FAN controlled most of Chad outside N'Djamena, which it avoided because of the presence of OAU forces. Facing funding shortfalls (most of the African states had failed to meet their promises to financially support the mission, and France withheld support for the OAU mission since the condemnation of the Paris accord), the third Nairobi meeting issued a short time-frame for an agreement between GUNT and FAN, which instead brought a rebuke from Goukouni. In

[10] Mays, *Africa's First Peacekeeping Operation*, 62-63.
[11] Azevedo, *Roots of Violence*, 160.
[12] Mays, *Africa's First Peacekeeping Operation*, 66.   [13] Ibid., 73.
[14] Ibid., 82.   [15] Ibid., 83.

April 1982, Nigeria announced the unilateral withdrawal of one of its contingents for 'economic' reasons, drawing condemnation from Goukouni, who returned to Libya for assistance, but this time was rebuffed by Gaddafi.[16] However, the OAU contingent continued to struggle for support, even as it was now clear that it was the only thing standing between Habré and total control of Chad. On 7 June 1982, Habré's FAN seized N'Djamena, forcing Goukouni to flee. The OAU then announced its withdrawal from Chad, ending its first peacekeeping operation in failure.

The Aftermath

Africa's first peacekeeping operation lacked virtually any of the requisites for a successful mission. The country that was most willing to provide troops and resources, Nigeria, was not an impartial actor and unilateral peacekeeping by Nigerian forces had been fraught with tension. Francophone African countries were unhappy with the operation, tensions over French forces in the country arose (some factions wished them to remain), and the Paris accord was regarded as neo-colonialism by several African states.[17] According to Mays, the force commander of the Nigerian mission, Colonel Magoro, reviewing the 1979 operation, recommended that 'Nigeria should never dispatch another unilateral peacekeeping contingent'.[18] Nevertheless, the OAU mission was hardly any better. The first deployment ended in total failure, with casualties incurred despite troops never leaving the barracks. The second deployment faced logistical and financial difficulties: attempts to secure funding from beyond the OAU failed, despite initial promises from France, and promised personnel never materialised (several countries failed to match their pledges for providing troops).[19] Without a clear normative framework, expectations were consistently mismatched, most fatally by Goukouni and GUNT, but also amongst supporting countries.

No interested external party could play an objective or impartial role, with Libya supporting various Frolinat groups and Goukouni, the French supporting Malloum and later Goukouni, Nigeria supporting the FAO while trying to play active mediator, and Sudan, Egypt, and the USA supporting Habré. It was difficult to characterise the various

[16] Ibid., 97–8.   [17] Ibid., 82.   [18] Ibid., 44.   [19] Ibid., 89.

peace summits as OAU decisions, such was the dominance of Nigeria in their proceedings.[20] The OAU's use of ad hoc committees to deal with the conflict was poorly thought out, and it never again embarked on a peacekeeping operation before its closure in 2000. When Libya (together with a Goukouni battalion) invaded Chad again in 1983, the OAU response was merely to try to broker mediation attempts (none succeeded until 1987, by which time Libyan troops had suffered several defeats). Intervention would be carried out solely by French troops, sidelining the OAU in the process.

Non-interference and diplomatic solutions were perhaps a better option to pursue if a peacekeeping force could not be financed and sustained. On the other hand, a clearer institutional structure and mandate, an agreement on costs and burden-sharing, and other operational stipulations would be required if the OAU were ever to embark on such operations again.[21]

The memory of this disastrous operation would influence Obasanjo and other important interlocutors on the continent. In 1980, Nigeria had blamed the presence of Libyan troops and the civil war in Chad, where Nigerian troops were deployed for peacekeeping operations, for causing major Muslim riots in Kano (the most important northern Nigerian city).[22] Obasanjo would repeatedly assert that instability in one country contributed to instability amongst its neighbours thereafter,[23] and began to search for more effective ways to deal with regional conflict. The experience of this war provides significant context in which even progressive diplomats were reticent to push continental machinery towards the provision of peacekeeping forces up to the 1990s.

The Africa Leadership Forum

The CSSDCA began through the Africa Leadership Forum. Obasanjo had stepped down as head of state in Nigeria in 1979, becoming the first military ruler to hand power to a democratically elected civilian administration. He then set up the Africa Leadership Forum (ALF) in 1988, officially non-governmental, but benefiting from his numerous

---

[20] Amoo, 'Frustrations of Regional Peacekeeping: the OAU in Chad, 1977–1982', *Carter Center Working Paper* 1, no. 1 (1991): 15–16.
[21] Ibid., 22–5. [22] Mays, *Africa's First Peacekeeping Operation*, 24.
[23] See, for instance, Africa Leadership Forum, *The Kampala Document*.

international networks. In search of a solution to Africa's conflicts, with the Chadian war central in his experience, he had studied the Helsinki Process in Europe, which provided opportunity for a détente between Cold War blocs. The sudden end of the Cold War in 1990 further led to a rethinking of Africa's problems. As Deng and Zartman note, the end of the Cold War had a paradoxical effect on Africa:

[It] created strong optimism about Africans' opportunity to solve their own problem. On the other hand, and perhaps paradoxically, the emergence of a new international system made Africans fear the consequences of the superpowers' abandonment and their increasing marginalisation. The CSSDCA process was strongly shaped by both these effects.[24]

Obasanjo was convinced that political cooperation and economic integration were necessary for Africa to fight its marginalisation, looking to Europe for a successful model at the time.[25] In 1990, the ALF convened a brainstorming meeting chaired by the head of the UN Economic Commission for Africa (UNECA), Adebayo Adedeji, the Secretary-General of the OAU, Salim Salim, and Obasanjo himself. Obasanjo called for 'a New Deal for Africa' and for 'an African instrument for security, stability and cooperation', which, echoing the Conference on Security and Cooperation in Europe (CSCE), he labelled the Conference on Security, Stability, and Co-operation in Africa.[26] By the end of the meeting, 'development' had been added alongside the other three functional areas, forming the Conference on Security, Stability, Development, and Cooperation in Africa (CSSDCA).

The meeting recommended the establishment of an OAU peacekeeping mechanism, and also reiterated several norms and processes as the 'Basic Ingredients for Democracy': pluralism, freedom of expression, an independent judiciary, political accountability, periodic elections, an independent civil service, promotion of literacy and political awareness, dangers of fundamentalism, compliance with human rights treaties, and, controversially, 'external constraining mechanisms', suggesting the CSSDCA could be one such instrument.[27]

---

[24] Deng and Zartman, *The Kampala Movement*, 109.   [25] Ibid., 110.
[26] Africa Leadership Forum, *Report on a Brainstorming Meeting for a Conference on Security, Stability, Development and Co-operation in Africa* (Addis Ababa: Africa Leadership Forum, 1990), 18.
[27] Ibid., 9–10.

In March 1991, the leading ALF figures, including Obasanjo, three African foreign ministers, and then-ANC foreign secretary, Thabo Mbeki, met in Cologne with senior officials who had participated in the Helsinki Process. They were inspired by the CSCE, which had begun as a private initiative before being embraced by governments to form the Organisation for Security and Co-operation in Europe (OSCE), and saw this as a possible route for the CSSDCA. However, they also saw a need to localise the process further. Following that meeting, a third conference involving African NGOs was held in Ota, Nigeria, and the NGOs were largely supportive, seeking to be invited to the following Kampala forum, given observer status in the OAU Abuja Summit, and consultative status with the OAU and UNECA.[28]

In May 1991, the next meeting was held, jointly chaired by the ALF, UNECA, and OAU Secretariat, in Kampala, Uganda. Five heads of state, three former heads of state (including Obasanjo), and about five hundred other participants including diplomats, scholars, business executives, and NGO members were present. The conference was notable for its unusual candour, in which Mozambique President Joaquim Chissano lamented the lack of African institutional mechanisms for participation in political life, Tanzanian former President Julius Nyerere complained about the democratic deficit, and UNECA's head, Adebayo Adedeji, who normally avoided political statements, argued that Africa's problems were due to 'poor governance, lack of public accountability and of popular participation'.[29] Dissenting views came from Zambian President Kenneth Kaunda and Sudanese President Omar al-Bashir – both blamed colonialism and structural inequalities with the rest of the world for Africa's problems.[30]

However, the final document was adopted 'in an atmosphere of consensus and enthusiasm'.[31] The Kampala Document asserted that 'The security, stability and development of every African country is inseparably linked with those of other African countries.'[32] Furthermore, it stated:

The interdependence of African States and the link between their security, stability and development demand a common African agenda based on a

---

[28] Deng and Zartman, *The Kampala Movement*, 115.   [29] Quoted in ibid., 116.
[30] Ibid., 116–17.   [31] Ibid., 117.
[32] Africa Leadership Forum, *The Kampala Document*, General Principles, II.

unity of purpose and a collective political consensus derived from a firm conviction that Africa cannot make any significant progress on any other front without collectively creating a lasting solution to its problems of security and stability.[33]

Squaring up directly against the OAU Charter's principle of non-interference, the Kampala Document called for a collective responsibility for regional security, whether within a state or crossing a state's borders. The four functional areas – security, stability, development, and cooperation – were now labelled 'calabashes' after the African gourd. Under the Security Calabash, it called for 'a framework for common and collective continental security', stating that African security 'must be a sacred and a primary responsibility of all African states as a whole ... which necessitates collective responsibility and action'.[34]

Finally, the Kampala Document outlined a two-year negotiation period, seeking a binding convention of OAU members under the CSSDCA.[35] The Kampala Document was then discussed by the Council of Ministers and the Heads of State at the following June 1991 OAU Summit, held in Abuja under the chairmanship of Nigerian President Ibrahim Babangida. Obasanjo, writing in 1991, claimed:

While no single African country opposed the Kampala Forum proposals at the Abuja meeting, procedural matters were at the heart of the agreement reached on the steps for the furtherance of the CSSDCA process in Africa. An overwhelming majority of African countries, having welcomed this initiative at an OAU Summit level, and in recognition of an increasingly precarious security situation and socio-economic crises on the continent, did not show any signs of wanting to delay the launching of the CSSDCA.[36]

However, his optimism would be short-lived. At the Abuja Summit, the decision was made that the Kampala Document should be distributed to all member states for comments, before being resubmitted to the Council of Ministers meeting in February 1992 and the following OAU Summit in June. None of the states had submitted any comments by February, or again in June of 1992. Postponing the deadline to 1993, whereupon no comments were submitted again, the OAU deferred the proposal indefinitely.[37]

---

[33] Ibid., General Principles, IV.   [34] Ibid., 9.   [35] Ibid., 26–7.   [36] Ibid., 5.
[37] Deng and Zartman, *The Kampala Movement*, 124.

Explaining the Kampala Rejection

At the close of the Cold War, and a time of US unipolar dominance, Obasanjo had thought that the timing was right for his proposal. Yet he failed to pass the proposal, nor, at least initially, did he manage to persuade African states that their norms were in need of rethinking following the great geopolitical shifts that had just occurred globally. Why did the Kampala Movement fail to achieve its objectives at the OAU?

I argue that Obasanjo did much right, but the failure is explainable on all the main factors of this model. Unlike the CSCE process, the norm circles he built had little relevance amidst the elite-driven dynamics in the OAU, and in any case were not as closely attuned to his thinking as he believed. He lost the initiative once the matter went to the OAU, failed to break through the solid resistance of the non-interference norm in the OAU, and failed to find any other opportunities for influence in order to get round his opponents. I first look at how the norm circles were distributed in the OAU, before analysing the three factors of (1) control of the initiative, (2) use of shared norms, and (3) metis in turn, to understand why the CSSDCA failed in 1991. This brings the case study to the next section, which will discuss the complete acceptance of the CSSDCA in 1999–2000, a marked contrast with the 1991 experience.

The Norm Circles

Whereas the ALF had garnered an impressive group of supporters, including some heads of state and the UNECA and OAU secretariats, there was clearly a lack of political will amongst others, even if the opposition was not voiced outright.[38] Felix Mosha, the head of the ALF in 1991, noted that the OAU members could be divided into four groups: (1) states genuinely in need of more time to review the proposal, (2) 'breakers' or states indifferent to the CSSDCA, (3) 'riders' who opposed the CSSDCA quietly, and (4) 'derailers', the states determined to stop the process.[39] There was almost no support if we

---

[38] Nathan, 'Towards a Conference on Security, Stability, Development and Co-operation in Africa', *Africa Insight* 22, no. 3 (1992).
[39] Deng and Zartman, *The Kampala Movement*, 125.

consider (1) and (2) as technically neutral, and (3) and (4) as comprising an opposing norm circle. To these groups, Deng adds 'brakers', who sought to simply slow it down.[40]

The utility of the proposal was hard to argue at the time when most African states were under military or one-party rule. The Kampala Document had asserted that democracy was fundamental for both security and stability,[41] but the lessons it could point to came largely from outside the continent – East European former communist countries – owing to the influence of the Helsinki Process on the framework. Multiparty democracy is clearly implied though not explicitly recommended in the Kampala Document, going only so far as to push 'plural political structures'.[42] Even this was seen as a threat to authoritarian regimes.

Even for the states that might have supported the idea in principle, what 'democracy' meant in an African context was not clear. Ugandan President Yoweri Museveni, while seen as a 'new breed' of African leader at the time, was nevertheless presiding over single-party rule in his country. Despite his support for the Kampala forum, he had reservations on what CSSDCA's 'democracy' should entail, stating that it could take 'many forms'.[43]

The Kampala Document also put forward the idea of 'mechanisms for mediation, conciliation and arbitration', and that 'Africa under CSSDCA, should institute a continental peace-keeping machinery'.[44] Cognisant of the failures in Chad, but without mentioning the problem as sitting heads of state were still active participants in the OAU, the CSSDCA suggested a more effective mechanism than the OAU's. The 1991 Cologne meeting had even led Obasanjo to conclude that 'Africa may need to make use of, or supplement, its existing regional organisation, the OAU, in advancing and implementing the process.'[45] Although, formally, the Kampala Document did not explicitly mention who would run such a force, the implication was that this might occur outside the OAU, given the OAU's strict stance on non-interference. However, this would put it potentially in conflict with the OAU Secretariat, with Salim Salim repeatedly calling for an avoidance of

---

[40] Ibid., 10–11.
[41] Africa Leadership Forum, *The Kampala Document*, 9–10, 13. [42] Ibid., 13.
[43] Deng and Zartman, *The Kampala Movement*, 126.
[44] Africa Leadership Forum, *The Kampala Document*, 10–11.
[45] Obasanjo, quoted in Deng and Zartman, *The Kampala Movement*, 114.

Explaining the Kampala Rejection 115

duplication and to strengthen existing mechanisms.[46] Without clearing up this ambiguity, at least one of the possible allies in the supporting norm circle was less than enthusiastic.

Civil society pressure proved to be less useful than it had been in the Helsinki Process. The OAU's then reputation as an elite club of African statesmen (or even 'dictators' club'[47]) was not undeserved, and there were few avenues for civil society groups to put pressure on the OAU or member states. Indeed, the very fact that the CSOs' main request at the Ota meeting was for access to OAU meetings and consultative status[48] suggested their influence would be limited.

Controlling the Initiative

Obasanjo's leading of the initiative from 1988 to 1991 was well managed and resourced, making consultative meetings around Africa, Western Europe, and the USA. At the Kampala meeting, he was keen to snowball earlier efforts into a true movement that would be irresistible. However, once it moved to the OAU, he lost control over what could be done as he was no longer in control of his government's machinery. His national head of state, General Ibrahim Babangida, was a military ruler who had taken over in a coup in 1985, and therefore unenthusiastic if not privately hostile. Yoweri Museveni too, at that time still presenting himself as a democratic reformist, 'was uncomfortable with the whole package, and did not come forward in Abuja'.[49] Other states may also have used informal channels to voice objections, pre-empting open support for the proposals.[50]

Yet Obasanjo at least had one card to play: as Deng and Zartman point out, 'In the conventional diplomacy of the OAU, if one head of state feels very strongly about an issue and speaks out loud, it is very difficult for others to counter him.'[51] This set up the official position in the OAU, in which Obasanjo noted 'no single African country opposed the Kampala Forum proposals',[52] but led instead to the referral to all member states for comments. However, this same norm of speaking

---

[46] Ibid., 112.
[47] Tieku, 'Explaining the Clash and Accommodation of Interests', 255.
[48] Deng and Zartman, *The Kampala Movement*, 115.
[49] Eloho Otobo, quoted in ibid., 128.   [50] Ibid., 125.   [51] Ibid.
[52] Africa Leadership Forum, *The Kampala Document*, 5.

strongly also applied the other way round: at the February 1992 Council of Ministers meeting, it was Libya and Sudan that vocally opposed the CSSDCA, and the emphasis on consensus made it hard for anyone to then support it openly.[53] However, the lack of state sponsors at the OAU level meant Obasanjo could not follow up and push the states for further support.

Finally, the pace at which Obasanjo worked from the Kampala Forum in late May to the OAU Summit at the start of June 1991 may have worked against him. With less than one and half months between the two meetings, there was insufficient time for supporters to debrief their governments or garner wider support. They also failed to produce the Kampala Document in all the four working languages of the OAU (English, French, Arabic, and Portuguese), which would later be held against them as some member states had not read the document.[54]

Use of Shared Norms

Arguably, the failure to successfully frame the CSSDCA around African norms was the Kampala Document's weakest point and greatest challenge. Whereas the cooperation and development calabashes were relatively uncontroversial, the CSSDCA challenged existing norms on the continent in three ways. First, it put democracy at the root of the solutions to stability and security of the continent. Second, it challenged the notion of sovereignty then held by the OAU, arguing that some of it must be ceded to solve African conflicts. Third, it emphasised collective responsibility for the provision of security on the continent, meaning all states would have to come up with a common framework and commitment to addressing these issues.

However, the first challenge to its ability to wield shared norms powerfully had nothing to do with its substantive content. Drawing on the Helsinki Process for inspiration led it to be viewed suspiciously by some as a Western initiative.[55] Conscious of this problem, where Helsinki had used 'baskets' for its three functional areas of security, economic development, and human rights, the CSSDCA had suggested four 'calabashes' for security, stability, development, and cooperation.

---

[53] Deng and Zartman, *The Kampala Movement*, 125.   [54] Ibid., 130.
[55] Ibid., 128–9.

But this was a superficial makeover that did not substantially change the misperceptions. Obasanjo had also repeatedly stressed that it was not adopting the Helsinki Process wholesale, or even adopting the norms that resulted from Helsinki, but rather looking at Helsinki as a template for addressing African challenges.[56]

As mentioned earlier, the emphasis on democracy as the basis of stability and development put the CSSDCA at odds with a host of African regimes. Moreover, the examples Obasanjo had to draw upon of collapsed authoritarian regimes were mostly East European. Virtually every African country after independence had started out democratic, before overthrow in military coups on account of poor governance, corruption, or economic performance. Few military regimes were unpopular at their outset and many maintained degrees of legitimacy for years.[57]

Obasanjo's own experience as a Nigerian military ruler handing power to a democratically elected civilian administration was a poor example. Nigeria's Second Republic had collapsed to another military coup just four years later amid allegations of corruption and poor economic performance. That regime had been overthrown by another coup less than a year later. The sitting president, Ibrahim Babangida, was liberalising the country to a limited degree but it was not democratic. Countries emerging from conflict and enjoying a period of stability, such as Uganda, were not democratic in the sense that Obasanjo advocated. Whereas democracy might be a good idea, there was little evidence in 1991 that the Western form would work well in Africa, a point raised by erstwhile supporter Yoweri Museveni.[58] Obasanjo failed to offer successful indigenous examples to counter this charge.

The surrender of sovereignty was perhaps the hardest sell. While not mentioned in the final Kampala Document, the preliminary Addis brainstorming session report had stated explicitly: 'For peacekeeping operations and peace-making activities to be effective, there will be the need for African governments to surrender some degree of sovereignty to the sub-regional or regional body involved.'[59] African states had

---

[56] Africa Leadership Forum, *Brainstorming Meeting for CSSDCA*, 28–9.
[57] Mazrui, 'Soldiers as Traditionalizers: Military Rule and the Re-Africanization of Africa', *World Politics* 28, no. 2 (1976).
[58] Deng and Zartman, *The Kampala Movement*, 126.
[59] Africa Leadership Forum, *Brainstorming Meeting for CSSDCA*, 7.

been formed out of the experience of colonialism, and sovereignty that was hard fought for would not be easily relinquished. Despite the end of the Cold War, with actors such as Libya funding insurgencies around the continent, there were very good reasons to continue to stress norms of non-interference, and suspicions that any delegation of authority might be captured by other states for their own advantage.[60] At this point, there were virtually no examples where the ceding of sovereignty could benefit Africa, in spite of much earlier debates about federalism that had dominated the original establishment of the OAU.

Collective responsibility for security was controversial. For Obasanjo, it stemmed from his frustration with the Chadian Civil War. African states had pledged either funding or troops, but had failed to deliver and Nigeria had taken the brunt of the peacekeeping task, but also the blame for its failure. Through the CSSDCA, the goal was to establish a permanent mechanism for peacekeeping operations. While details were not provided at this stage, it was clear that the central lessons of Chad – lack of neutrality of actors, unclear mandates and expectations, lack of funding, and lack of logistic capacity – needed to be overcome, and the CSSDCA process would deliberate on how this could occur.

Another of CSSDCA's supporters, the former Tanzanian President Julius Nyerere, had also once engaged in a foreign intervention – the invasion of Uganda in 1979. Like Obasanjo, he had also been frustrated by OAU 'mediation' attempts through 1978–9 when Uganda invaded Tanzania at the Kagera Salient.[61] However, the Tanzanian counterattack, with the assistance of Ugandan insurgents, led to the overthrow of Idi Amin in April 1979. Receiving no support from the OAU, Tanzania alone bore the estimated £250 million bill it was saddled with following the invasion.[62] Nyerere was thus one of the few who recognised and lamented the problem of a lack of collective responsibility for dealing with conflicts in the OAU.

---

[60] Deng and Zartman, *The Kampala Movement*, 127.
[61] Roberts, 'The Uganda–Tanzania War, the Fall of Idi Amin, and the Failure of African Diplomacy, 1978–1979', *Journal of Eastern African Studies* 8, no. 4 (2014): 695.
[62] Ibid., 705.

Explaining the Kampala Rejection

The aftermath of the invasion would lead to the OAU's first open debate about the nature of sovereignty and non-interference at the Monrovia Summit in June 1979. Nyerere had been an influential figure in the Pan-Africanist movement, a leader of the Monrovia sovereigntist norm circle, whose credentials as an African liberation leader were unquestioned. As the incident had clearly shown, the OAU Charter's norms had failed to effectively function, and OAU mechanisms had failed to resolve the conflict. Nyerere was thus unapologetic. As Roberts describes:

> Nyerere himself described the OAU as being a 'trade union' for African leaders, ring-fencing them from criticism. He had previously pointed out that Amin had killed more Africans than Smith's regime in Rhodesia or Vorster's in South Africa. 'Had Amin been white ... free Africa would have passed many resolutions condemning him. Being black is now becoming a certificate to kill fellow Africans'. In turning the same accusations levelled against racist white African leaders against the organisation that was supposedly the embodiment of African unity, Nyerere – the defiant pan-Africanist – implicitly called into question the credibility of the OAU's authority to mediate between the belligerents.[63]

The resultant debate led to the first revival of the idea of establishing an African peacekeeping force (somewhat different from Nkrumah's idea of a standing army, but with similar logistical requirements), and a draft human rights declaration was drafted.[64] However, this was as far as the debate would go at this point.

While a figure no less than Nyerere supported Obasanjo, neither managed to budge the OAU's position either in 1979 or in 1991. Other states held firm to Article III(2) of the OAU Charter that insisted on non-interference. In 1991, Obasanjo got as far as an acknowledgement that 'there is a link between security, stability, development and cooperation in Africa'[65] in the OAU final communiqué of the Abuja Summit. However, on the other norms, he would have to bide his time.

---

[63] Ibid., 703.
[64] Sturman and Hayatou, 'The Peace and Security Council of the African Union: From Design to Reality', in *Africa's New Peace and Security Architecture*, ed. Engel and Porto (Farnham: Ashgate, 2010), 59.
[65] Quoted in Africa Leadership Forum, *The Kampala Document*, 4.

The Adoption of the CSSDCA

With the odds seemingly completely stacked against the CSSDCA in 1991, the story of its acceptance at Sirte in 1999, and the OAU's adoption of the CSSDCA Solemn Declaration a year later at Lomé, seems highly improbable. After the stalling of the Kampala Movement, Obasanjo continued to speak out against human rights abuses in Nigeria. He was subsequently imprisoned by the next military ruler of Nigeria, Sani Abacha. Abacha died suddenly in 1998, and after a brief interim period, Obasanjo was elected president in February 1999, returning to power as a democratically elected head of state. Obasanjo wasted no time in putting CSSDCA back on the OAU agenda, preparing to relaunch it even before the Algiers Summit of June that year.[66]

Whereas the Chad conflict had been the guiding frame in 1991, by 1999 Nigerian forces were involved in peacekeeping operations in Guinea-Bissau, Sierra Leone, and Liberia through 1998–9, providing the core of the ECOWAS peacekeeping forces, the ECOWAS Monitoring Group (ECOMOG). Discovery that Nigeria was spending as much as US$1 million a day in Sierra Leone had created domestic opposition to its peacekeeping mission, and an urgency for other states to get involved.[67] As Obasanjo stated in an interview in 1999:

That [criticism that ECOMOG is a 'Nigerian show'] is part of the reason we want [a] genuine defence accord. To have an ECOMOG that is truly [an] ECOMOG force not a 'Nigerian-MOG' camouflaging as ECOMOG. That is one thing the defence accord can do and should do. ECOMOG ... cannot stay as it is. It can't go on having Nigeria foot the bill, Nigeria contributed about 95%, what sort of ECOMOG is that? The burden must be shared.[68]

Collective responsibility, a core part of CSSDCA, would remain a key foreign policy agenda for Nigeria, more so than in 1991 when its first ECOMOG missions were deployed. At the Algiers OAU Summit in 1999, Obasanjo pressed for the year 2000 to be named the Year of Peace, Security, and Solidarity, with the lofty goal of ending all conflicts in Africa that year. This was adopted by consensus, including a

---

[66] Tieku, *Governing Africa*, 91.
[67] Tieku, 'Explaining the Clash and Accommodation of Interests', 259.
[68] Obasanjo, 'Collective Security is the Answer', *Africa Forum* 3, nos. 2–3 (1999): 4–5.

The Adoption of the CSSDCA

reference to the Kampala Document and CSSDCA.[69] Muammar Gaddafi then called for the extraordinary summit at Sirte.

While the contest that ensued when Gaddafi unveiled his plan for a 'US of Africa' is covered in Chapter 3, Obasanjo succeeded in getting an agreement in the Sirte Declaration for the OAU to 'Convene an African Ministerial Conference on Security, Stability, Development and Cooperation in the Continent, as soon as possible'.[70] This would be held in May 2000, in Abuja, and was preceded by a meeting of experts a few days earlier. The outcome was a draft for the CSSDCA Solemn Declaration as well as a draft Declaration on the Framework for an OAU Response to Unconstitutional Changes of Government,[71] both following instructions from the Algiers Summit. Both declarations were then adopted by consensus at the following OAU Heads of State Summit in Lomé in June.

The CSSDCA Solemn Declaration represented the remarkable turnaround of a proposal that had been rejected just eight years earlier. The main precepts had not been watered down. Security was stated to be a collective responsibility of African states.[72] Democracy was still maintained as a prerequisite for stability, security, and development. While it did not explicitly urge the transfer of sovereignty as the 1990 Addis brainstorming meeting had suggested (this was omitted in the 1991 Kampala Document too), it pronounced collective responsibility for security provision for both Africans and their states, and noted that 'African countries will need to transfer certain responsibilities to continental or sub-regional institutions.'[73]

Finally, the administrative steps began, with the CSSDCA Solemn Declaration initiating a biennial Standing Conference, the CSSDCA Unit being established within the OAU Secretariat in 2002, and work beginning on a Memorandum of Understanding (MoU) to work with NEPAD and avoid duplication.[74] The MoU was adopted at the Durban Summit in 2002. What explains this turnaround from the

---

[69] OAU, 'Declaration of the Year 2000 as the Year of Peace, Security and Solidarity in Africa' (AHG/Decl.2 (XXXV)) (Algiers 1999),
[70] 'Sirte Declaration' (EAHG/Decl. (IV) Rev. 1) 1999,
[71] Khamis, *Promoting the African Union*, 120.
[72] OAU, 'CSSDCA Solemn Declaration' (AHG/Decl. 4 (XXXVI)) (Lomé 2000), 10 (c), (e).
[73] Ibid., 13(d).   [74] Khamis, *Promoting the African Union*, 133.

defeat of 1991? Once again, the norm circles and practices show their importance as explanatory parts of the process.

The Norm Circles

The norm circles did not coalesce the same way they had in 1991. It was noticeable in 1991 that the majority of backers of CSSDCA were non-state actors: Obasanjo and Salim in their personal capacities, the ALF, UNECA, Thabo Mbeki as foreign minister-in-exile for South Africa's ANC, and civil society groups formed the core of the 'Kampala Movement'. Only Julius Nyerere spoke as a state actor for Tanzania, while Obasanjo failed to persuade his own head of state, Ibrahim Babangida, or the host of the Kampala Movement, Yoweri Museveni, to openly back it. By 1999, however, Obasanjo was now back in power in Nigeria, Mbeki was now the leader of post-apartheid South Africa, and Salim had become an elder statesman of African regional politics, the longest serving Secretary-General of the OAU.

While Libya was a strong and vocal opponent in 1991, the utility calculation of open opposition had changed. Gaddafi had refashioned himself as a conflict mediator with his return to Africa,[75] offering to mediate in disputes across the continent (including conflicts involving groups he was funding,[76] such as Charles Taylor's Liberia). It was difficult for him to openly oppose Obasanjo when his own proposal for the 'US of Africa' was on the table: in the consensus-based decision-making structure of the OAU, if he opposed Obasanjo's CSSDCA, it could easily backfire with Obasanjo openly opposing the 'United States of Africa'.

This was not lost on either man: as one AU official described it, Obasanjo got CSSDCA approved 'as a compromise with Gaddafi'.[77] Without Gaddafi openly opposed, the imagined norm circle of opponents shrunk. Other opponents such as Sudan's Omar al-Bashir or Kenya's Daniel Arap Moi did not raise objections, so any other 'riders' (opponents who did not openly criticise the idea) from the previous contest evaporated. As Tieku has noted, the norm of Pan-African solidarity can be a powerful force if the opposing sides are greatly

---

[75] Huliaras, 'Qadhafi's Comeback', 17.
[76] Solomon and Swart, 'Libya's Foreign Policy in Flux', *African Affairs* 104, no. 416 (2005): 475–6.
[77] Interview with AU official, 22 February 2016.

The Adoption of the CSSDCA

mismatched: this brings pressure on the weaker norm circle to concede to allow the consensus to go ahead.[78]

Controlling the Initiative

One of the most significant changes was Obasanjo's return to power in Nigeria. As a sitting head of state, he now enjoyed real influence in the OAU, and could follow up matters, develop coalitions, or negotiate with opponents at a state-to-state level in ways he was unable to in 1991. Furthermore, he was much more patient in letting the process unfold, and by now the documents were well understood. While the Sirte decision tasked him with updating the Kampala Document, very little required changing and this was done well within the schedule. Twelve months passed between the Algiers and Lomé summits, in which the process moved from 'recalling' the Kampala Document (Algiers, June 1999), to calling for a ministerial conference on CSSDCA (Sirte, September 1999), to finalising the CSSDCA Solemn Declaration (Abuja, May 2000), and its final adoption at Lomé in June 2000.

Metis: Opportunities for Influence

There were, of course, some opportunities for Obasanjo to gain leverage to press his influence, but his options were limited, both by his own choice and by external factors. For example, Obasanjo did not want to weaken the proposal or introduce ambiguities to get a better chance of acceptance by the main vocal opponents, Libya, Kenya, and Sudan.[79] In any case, Libya, then a supporter of various insurgent armed groups in several other African countries, may have seen the CSSDCA as a direct threat to its actions on the continent and would not be convinced. Sam Iboke, then head of the OAU's Conflict Resolution Division, suggested that the CSSDCA was perceived to directly target the practices of governments like Libya and Sudan.[80] Some thus saw it as a 'take-it-or-leave-it' proposal, and chose to leave it.[81] Obasanjo also lacked state champions. Aside from Nyerere, Uganda's Yoweri

---

[78] Tieku, *Governing Africa*, 25.
[79] Deng and Zartman, *The Kampala Movement*, 125.   [80] Ibid.
[81] Ibid., 129.

Museveni – whose capital, Kampala, was most closely associated with the initiative – failed to speak up in support of the proposal at Abuja.

On the other hand, some opponents appeared to find novel and potentially spurious reasons to oppose Obasanjo. In 1991, the OAU had endorsed six African candidates for consideration for the post of UN Secretary-General (UNSG) to replace outgoing UNSG Javier Perez de Cuellar. The Egyptian diplomat Boutros Boutros Ghali was considered the favourite after lobbying London and Washington, but Obasanjo was probably the leading black African candidate,[82] and this may also have contributed to blocking the CSSDCA proposal. The CSSDCA was recast by opponents as Obasanjo's personal vehicle for the UNSG post, for if the CSSDCA had succeeded, he would have received enormous personal credit for his role in fundamentally reshaping African norms of non-interference and sovereignty and revitalising the institutional mechanisms for addressing African conflicts.

Obasanjo himself denied such rumours and held that the timing was uncomfortable for him,[83] but he was so closely associated with the project that he could not effectively counter the rumours. Hans d'Orville, then coordinator of the InterAction Council and the ALF, suggested personal rivalries between Salim Salim (who had been vetoed by the USA for the UNSG post in 1981[84]) and Ibrahim Babangida also served to scuttle Obasanjo's flagship project.[85] However, given Salim's role in the Kampala process and pushing through several ideas from the Kampala Document into the OAU after 1991 – which I argue below are essential to understanding the rapid acceptance of the CSSDCA at the second reckoning in 1999 – it is hard to accept that Salim directly undermined Obasanjo on the CSSDCA.

Use of Shared Norms

Despite the failure of 1991, and rumours of personal rivalry with Obasanjo, Salim Salim, the OAU Secretary-General, continued to work towards implementing many of the ideas of the Kampala forum

---

[82] Fleming, 'If an African Cannot Succeed Javier Perez De Cuellar', *UPI*, 15 September 1991.
[83] Deng and Zartman, *The Kampala Movement*, 132.
[84] Fleming, 'If an African Cannot Succeed Javier Perez De Cuellar.'
[85] Deng and Zartman, *The Kampala Movement*, 131.

The Adoption of the CSSDCA 125

within his ambit in the Secretariat. His efforts in supporting the CSSDCA at the second round of asking were not an exception. In 1992, the OAU agreed to explore a conflict resolution mechanism, a direct recommendation of the Kampala Document. Salim had argued that the OAU 'should be enabled to intervene swiftly in situations where tensions evolve to such a pitch that it becomes apparent that a conflict is in the making'.[86] The instrument was established the following year at Cairo as the Mechanism for Conflict Prevention, Management, and Resolution (MCPMR), albeit with reservations by Sudan and Eritrea.[87]

While the declaration establishing the mechanism neither made mention of the CSSDCA nor used any of its language (such as asserting the link between security, stability, and development), the structure had finally been set up. However, it was constrained by non-interference restrictions imposed by the OAU Charter, limiting it to mediatory initiatives in identified conflicts. This pushed it to focus on prevention through an early warning system, but at least incremental steps were made beyond the 1991 impasse. As van Walraven notes, 'Part of the success of these reforms, which were swiftly put into practice, was that they worked on the basis of *existing institutions* (the Bureau) as well as *past ideas* – speeding up response time and restricting member state membership in relevant organs.'[88] The 1998 Ouagadougou Declaration, which did not involve Obasanjo (then still in prison), had also determined 'to make the search for peace, security and stability our primary concern', a clarion call of the Kampala Movement, and evoking language found in the Kampala Document, committed to the 'establishment and consolidation of democratic systems', and 'strengthen[ing] the Central Organ of the OAU Conflict Prevention, Management and Resolution Mechanism'.[89] Even the engagement with civil society, part of the CSSDCA, was arguably a strategic rather than core component for Obasanjo, with the OAU holding its first civil society interface meeting

---

[86] Quoted in Sturman and Hayatou, 'The Peace and Security Council', 60.
[87] OAU, 'Declaration of the Assembly of Heads of State and Government on the Establishment within the OAU of a Mechanism for Conflict Prevention, Management and Resolution' (AHG/Decl.3 (XXIX)) (Cairo 1993).
[88] Van Walraven, 'Heritage and Transformation', 51, emphasis added.
[89] OAU, 'Ouagadougou Declaration' (AHG/Decl. I (XXXIV)) (Ouagadougou 1998).

on the sidelines of the Yaoundé Summit in 1996. From the Harare Summit in 1997 onwards, concept papers on formal civil society participation were being circulated and reviewed.[90]

Salim would thus state at the first ministerial CSSDCA, not unreasonably, that: 'The [CSSDCA] is therefore not a completely new project. It builds upon the foundation of frameworks, mechanisms, and joint activities that are already in place.'[91] Key components of the Kampala Document were no longer foreign ideas. The link between democracy and security, stability and development had been asserted several times in OAU declarations after 1991. The conflict resolution mechanism (MCPMR) had been established, albeit an imperfect one constrained by the OAU Charter. Civil society engagement was emerging from the nascent process at Yaoundé. Objections about copying from the Helsinki Process were not raised this time round, and it was hardly mentioned.

Finally, whereas in 1991 Obasanjo would have struggled to identify successful democracies on the continent, by 1999 his own country offered hope, although it paled in comparison to democratic post-apartheid South Africa, now a member of the OAU and Africa's most dynamic and largest economy at the time. Mandela's leadership and the South African Truth and Reconciliation Commission were widely lauded for their roles in successfully and peacefully lifting a country fraught with racial tensions.

The one remaining idea that may have been controversial was the implicit ceding of sovereignty. While explicit mention of transferring sovereignty, as in the Addis Ababa 1990 brainstorming meeting report, had never been part of the Kampala Document, the CSSDCA still implicitly supported it. As Tieku argues, the notion of interdependence between security and development 'not only implies that the maintenance of security anywhere in Africa is a collective responsibility of all African states, but also suggests that sovereignty no longer offers the protection behind which African leaders can conceal the abuse of their citizens'.[92] The CSSDCA's challenge to sovereignty was still present,

---

[90] Interview with AU official, 3 February 2016.
[91] Salim, 'Statement by Dr Salim Ahmed Salim, Secretary General of the OAU to the Ministerial Conference on Security, Stability, Development and Co-operation in Africa (CSSDCA), Abuja, Nigeria, 8th May 2000' (Abuja: OAU, 2000), 5.
[92] Tieku, 'Explaining the Clash and Accommodation of Interests', 256.

though less directly stated. However, the Gaddafi factors worked in its favour: with the much more ambitious 'United States' proposal on the table – a proposal to dissolve all the African countries by 2000 – the sovereignty concessions that the CSSDCA was suggesting seemed relatively slight.

Metis

There was virtually no opposition to the CSSDCA at the second round of asking, so there was little need for Obasanjo to look for further opportunities for influence. Perhaps the key factor removing Gaddafi's objections was that Gaddafi required Obasanjo not to openly oppose his own proposal for a US of Africa at Sirte. The deal struck between the two removed the most important obstacle for Obasanjo, though it did not preclude him from undermining Gaddafi's project in other ways. He also crucially got Thabo Mbeki, an early participant in the Kampala process, fully on board with the assurance that it would not threaten the democratisation components of NEPAD and vice versa.[93]

Finally, one perennial shortcoming in the OAU was the lack of finance (and therefore follow-through) for otherwise good ideas. Whereas such initiatives would typically seek out external donors (Obasanjo had done so himself, lobbying the USA for support for the Kampala process in 1991), this time he left nothing to chance. Nigeria pledged to fund 'any implications' related to the CSSDCA costs from the outset, though it also invited other countries to join in.[94] It was thus very difficult to raise any objections, procedural or normative, to the idea.

Conclusion

The failure and then success of the CSSDCA would be hard to explain without detailed understanding of the practices of the OAU and AU. The CSSDCA's impact on Africa's continental institutions is hard to overstate. From 2001, the CSSDCA began to split – the overlaps with

---

[93] Makinda and Okumu, *The African Union*, 31.
[94] Obasanjo, 'Address by His Excellency President Olusegun Obasanjo, on the Occasion of the OAU Ministerial Conference on Conference on Security, Stability, Development and Cooperation in Africa (CSSDCA), Abuja, 8 May 2000' (Abuja: OAU, 2000), 8.

NEPAD involved the development and cooperation pillars and were thus subsumed under NEPAD. Most prominently, the idea of the reporting and evaluation mechanism originally conceived in the 2001 CSSDCA conference developed self-evaluation performance benchmarks[95] that would go on to form the African Peer Review Mechanism (APRM), one of the key institutional mechanisms of NEPAD.[96] The other major ideas revolved around governance and security. Whereas the less controversial calabashes, such as development and cooperation, may not be solely credited to the CSSDCA, it is the AU's new norms that were contested that unmistakably trace their influence back to it. Thus understanding the contested norms first suggested at Kampala in 1991 allows one to appreciate the impact they would have in many of the documents and structures of the new African Union.

The core idea of the CSSDCA – collective responsibility for security – would be the central focus of a host of new structures in the AU. The idea of 'non-indifference' and distancing itself from the strict adherence to non-interference of the OAU became constitutive of the new identity of the AU.[97] The Constitutive Act's Art. 4(h) on the right to intervention could not have passed without the groundwork that supporters of the CSSDCA had done in the preceding eight years. The Peace and Security Council that would be established in 2003 following a series of debates about the defunct OAU Central Organ and Conflict Resolution Mechanism (MCMPR) draws heavily from the CSSDCA.[98]

The CSSDCA's emphasis on democratic governance resulted in the *Declaration on the Framework for an OAU Response to Unconstitutional Changes of Government* at Lomé. This would culminate in the 2007 *African Charter on Democracy, Elections and Governance*, which entered into force in 2012. Such a document would have been unthinkable in 1991 when the question of what role democracy even had to play in Africa was still debated by the heads of state.

---

[95] Khamis, *Promoting the African Union*, 135.
[96] Akinsaya, 'Nigeria at the African Union', 105.
[97] Williams, 'From Non-Intervention to Non-Indifference: the Origins and Development of the African Union's Security Culture', *African Affairs* 106, no. 423 (2006).
[98] Tieku, 'Explaining the Clash and Accommodation of Interests', 257.

Conclusion 129

Finally, civil society participation – even including the participation of diaspora African communities (such as in the Caribbean and Americas) – branched out of the CSSDCA into a permanent institution, the Citizens and Diaspora Directorate (CIDO). The CIDO is mandated to work on AU–civil society partnerships (or member state and civil society partnerships), promoting CSO participation in AU affairs. Part of the CIDO also serves as the Secretariat for the Economic, Social, and Cultural Council (ECOSOCC), formed in 2004 as an advisory organ of the AU composed of CSOs, represented by two CSOs per member state. The CSOs are organised into thematic clusters, including political affairs, economics, and so on, giving them formal input into the AU processes.[99]

The first African civil society conference was held in 2002, formally with a structure of two participants per country (one man and one woman). So successful was the CSSDCA that it was wrapped up by 2004, with only the CIDO as a visible institution left standing. Some officials described the CSSDCA as now being known as CIDO,[100] but this seems to understate the expansive scope of other issues it originally contained. Another stated, 'So all the components of CSSDCA were already split between CIDO, [Peace and Security Council], [and] governance under NEPAD and developed in to [the African Peer Review Mechanism]. That was how it "died," or you could say "internalized", as aspects [of the CSSDCA] went into every unit.'[101] The norms had all been integrated into the AU. The factors that were involved in its 1991 rejection and 1999 acceptance are listed in Table 4.1.

Could this be simply explained as an instance of a norm 'cascade'?[102] Three of the stages – initial denial, tactical concessions (such as the Conflict Resolution Mechanism), and reaching prescriptive status – are clearly part of the story. Obasanjo could also be classed as a 'norm entrepreneur', with his Kampala Movement a kind of transnational advocacy coalition. However, the model features a prominent role for international pressure in combination with transnational advocacy coalitions. These are absent from the story – Western influence was limited to serving as an inspiration through the 1970s Helsinki Process, and rather than helping, seemed to be

[99] Interview with AU official, 9 February 2016.
[100] Interview with AU official, 3 February 2016.
[101] Interview with AU official, 22 February 2016.
[102] Risse, Ropp, and Sikkink, *The Power of Human Rights*.

Table 4.1 *The rejection and acceptance of the CSSDCA*

Factors	Proposing norm circle	Opposing norm circle
Members	Obasanjo, Africa Leadership Forum, UNECA, Salim Salim, Tanzania (1991)	Libya, Sudan, Zambia, Nigeria, Uganda, Kenya (1991)
	Nigeria, South Africa, OAU Secretariat (1999)	No open opposition (1999)
Control of initiative	• Kampala meetings, failure to prepare adequately for Abuja (1991) • Acceptance at Sirte (1999) • First CSSDCA Ministerial Conference in Abuja (2000) • Establishment at Lomé (2000)	• Referring CSSDCA proposal for 'feedback' by member states after Abuja (1991) • No open opposition (1999)
Norms invoked	• Helsinki Process (for conflict management, 1991) • Challenge to OAU norms and practices on collective responsibility for security, democratic governance, and ceding sovereignty (1991) • OAU Conflict Mechanism (1999) • Ouagadougou and Algiers Declarations on collective security (1998/9)	• Non-interference, sovereignty, self-determination (1991 and 1999)
Metis	• Lack of OAU member state champions (1991) • Suggestion to bypass OAU mechanisms (1991, failed) • Nigerian financing of initiative (1999)	• Aspersions against personal motivations of Obasanjo (1991) • Withdrawal of Libyan objection (quid pro quo over 'United States of Africa', 1999)
Outcome	Rejected (1991); accepted (1999)	

Conclusion 131

hindering the 1991 attempt, when the CSSDCA was painted as a 'Western' initiative. The key proponents in 1991 were non-state actors: the ALF, UNECA, OAU Secretary-General, Thabo Mbeki while ANC shadow foreign minister, and Obasanjo as an ex-head of state. Nigeria and South Africa returning in 1999 as new democracies changed the key dynamic.

The Kampala Movement dissipated after the 1991 defeat, and the few incremental steps to smuggle CSSDCA ideas into OAU structures are largely down to the role of Salim working within the OAU Secretariat. Other civil society groups that Obasanjo promoted and sought legitimacy from had virtually no influence in OAU decision-making in 1999, when the CSSDCA was accepted. CSOs had only just achieved their first OAU interface meeting in 1996, in which no demands for a CSSDCA-type reform were requested, and much of the work of the CSSDCA from 2000 onwards was indeed to create those very avenues for their participation and potentially future influence – much the way the Helsinki Process served to start that journey for Eastern Europe. The transition to the AU remained an elite-driven process, but was transformed by the roles played by several new actors, such as the leaders of Nigeria, Senegal, and South Africa.

A second alternative hypothesis is that one could simply point to the coming to power of Obasanjo as head of state in Nigeria, one of the 'big five' contributors to the OAU, who thereby easily achieved his objectives – a more realist or materialist explanation. Yet Obasanjo faced a consensus-oriented organisation where any single state could have blocked his proposal (and several had done so the previous time – voting, while institutionally possible, is virtually never used[103]); while Libya's opposition may have been muted by what Gaddafi was seeking, Sudan's or Kenya's potential opposition was not. It is only through understanding the shared practices and norms within the organisation that this puzzling lack of opposition can be explained. Furthermore, a wholly materialist explanation begs another question as to why such events – big states pushing through whatever pet project they desire – don't happen *all* the time given the AU's unequal allocation of funding contributions, and when the process was so seemingly effortless for Obasanjo the second time around. The material aspect might partially

[103] Interview with AU official, 3 February 2016.

explain some facts, but also clearly is an insufficient explanation in the overall outcome.

Finally, whereas Obasanjo seems to be a central figure in the entire process, this is not to suggest a 'big man' theory of how he succeeded. Indeed, part of the resistance to his initiative in 1991 involved the personalisation of his role and his being so closely associated with the proposal that it was used against him. He did use the means available to him to push the idea consistently over several years. But other factors are undoubtedly influential. The pushing through of various initiatives in the intervening years between 1991 and 1999, much of which while Obasanjo was in prison, allowed there to be numerous precedents or shared norms from which to draw– a particular failing in 1991 – before the CSSDCA was pitched again. As one AU official recounted:

The [OAU] Secretariat is powerful in shaping norms. Same with the [AU] Commission. They are the custodian of decisions. Some [member states] forget what was decided, but we remind them. You cannot agree to decide on something if first you have to cancel a previous decision. Increasingly, members don't want to touch old decisions. Policy compliance is becoming a norm – a self-imposed one.[104]

This encapsulates the central notion of the power of 'competence' – comprising controlling the initiatives, the mastery of shared norms, and seeking opportunities for influence. Knowing how the OAU worked, the incremental pushing of initiatives to create path dependencies became possible and a vital factor in realising the core ideas of the CSSDCA. Thus Salim's quiet lobbying around the Central Organ and MCPMR must be understood against a longer timespan against which the reforms could eventually take place. While these instruments were criticised in the 1990s as ineffectual, they played a crucial role in framing the collective security debate later: they existed, so one could no longer criticise the mechanism of the CSSDCA as a foreign idea, but the mechanisms were ineffectual, which entailed new powers written into the AU Constitutive Act to make them work.

---

[104] Interview with AU official, 3 February 2016.

5 | *The Pan-African Parliament*

In order to ensure that the peoples of Africa are fully involved in the economic development and integration of the Continent, there shall be established a Pan-African Parliament.
Treaty Establishing the African Economic Community

Introduction

The Pan-African Parliament (PAP) was established in 2004, part of a series of structural changes that exemplified the new African Union as more progressive, democratic, and participatory. Initially, it would only have advisory powers, but it was envisioned to eventually become the full legislature of the AU. Yet, if democratising the continent's regional institution was a major goal of the newly formed democratic powers such as South Africa and Nigeria, and if the transition to the AU provided the perfect opportunity to do so, why did the PAP come into being with mere advisory powers, and why were these powers never further bolstered as it progressed? Why, moreover, was it South Africa and Nigeria that proved the most resistant to the expansion of PAP powers? More than a decade into its existence, its strength as an institution has not changed, and it appears even further away from becoming the legislative body it was originally envisaged to be.

The formation of the PAP was one of the essential contests between the federalist vision of Muammar Gaddafi and the more progressive views of the new democracies. Moreover, the pretext for opposition to the United States of Africa was that the union had to be for the African people. As quoted earlier, one AU official who witnessed the debate stated:

However, on the union government, we said there should be greater consultation with the African people before we can form this union government.

The opinion that led – became the dominant position – was that we should not create a union of governments or leaders, but of citizens.[1]

Ironically, for an institution that was originally a cornerstone of Nigeria's regional economic integration plans, it was curtailed because of the plans put forward by Gaddafi to merge African states as a single union government, and it could not be risked that the PAP would have the legislative powers it was originally intended to have. The PAP protocol thus also took a longer time to be accepted, but the skilful use of the OAU/AU procedures was needed to ensure that it did not emerge with powers over the heads of state assembly or to create new laws for the continent. Even then, the first protocol included a provision for its eventual role to include 'full legislative powers'[2] and reviews after five and then ten years.[3] Yet, when the ten-year review came up, while accepting the PAP to be the 'legislative organ' of the AU, it was decided that its functions and powers would be determined by the Assembly of the Heads of State and Government, who would decide on the areas in which the PAP could draft laws.[4] Although this protocol has yet to be ratified, it will shape the direction of the PAP and make it unlikely for a more participatory or democratic institutional form to take its place.

Far from being an additional pillar to 'represent all the peoples of Africa',[5] the PAP's subordination under the Assembly would prevent it from going beyond a technical or advisory role. This case study exemplifies a 'qualification' of a proposal in which its initial intentions were watered down through the process of contestation, with neither side decisively able to 'defeat' the other and from which an uneasy compromise resulted. It also demonstrates how its prospects as an institution will depend on the competence of respective norm circles as they try to push the functions they desire within the regional grouping.

---

[1] Interview with AU official, 9 February 2016.
[2] African Union, 'Protocol to the Treaty Establishing the African Economic Community Relating to the Pan-African Parliament' (Sirte 2001), Art. 2(3).
[3] Ibid., Art. 25.
[4] 'Protocol to the Constitutive Act of the African Union Relating to the Pan-African Parliament' (Malabo 2014), Art. 8(1).
[5] 'Protocol to the Treaty Establishing the African Economic Community Relating to the Pan-African Parliament', 2001, Art. 2(2).

Historically, the PAP has its origins in the 1980 Final Act of Lagos, an OAU declaration which instituted the Lagos Plan of Action.[6] Faced with economic decline in the 1970s and the failure of its members to seriously address poverty, the OAU sought ways in which to drive self-reliant economic development. Part of this involved the establishment of an economic community to drive regional integration, hoping that the comparative advantages of trade could promote endogenous growth. In 1990, an Arusha Summit organised by the UN Economic Commission for Africa (UNECA), the influential thinktank driving regional integration efforts, adopted the African Charter for Popular Participation in Development and Transformation, which implored greater participation in development processes.[7]

The Treaty Establishing the African Economic Community

The Treaty Establishing the African Economic Community (hereafter the Abuja Treaty) was finally adopted by OAU member states in 1991. It entailed the establishment of an African Economic Community (AEC), with many of the structures inspired by the European Economic Community at the time. The Abuja Treaty provided for a Pan-African Parliament under Arts. 7(1)(c) and 14, stating: 'In order to ensure that the peoples of Africa are fully involved in the economic development and integration of the Continent, there shall be established a Pan-African Parliament.'[8] Moreover, it ambitiously proposed that the PAP would be constituted by the 'election of its members by continental universal suffrage'.[9] UNECA, the drafters of the Abuja Treaty, lamented the lack of national parliaments' discussion of economic integration issues.[10] It therefore suggested that an African Commission, which would 'make policies in the interest of the African Union', needed to be established, which then ideally ought to report to the PAP:

---

[6] Nzewi, *The Role of the Pan African Parliament in African Regionalism: Institutional Perspectives and Lessons for Africa* (Saarbruecken: Verlag Dr Mueller, 2011), 135.
[7] Ibid., 139–40.
[8] OAU, 'Treaty Establishing the African Economic Community' (Abuja 1991), Art. 14(1).
[9] Ibid., Art. 6(2)(f)(iv).
[10] UNECA, *Report on Status of Regional Integration in Africa: Progress, Problems and Perspective* (Addis Ababa: UNECA, 2003), 9–10.

[The Commission] will have to act independently as a body for the collective interest of the AU. Hence, they will first and foremost be there to advance the goals of the African Union, and not national representatives defending their individual national interests. Such a Commission would normally have reported to the African Parliament, which, in principle, is a representative body of the people. But in the absence of this pan-African institution, the African Commission will have to report to the Assembly of Heads of State through the Executive Council. It may be possible to empower the Commission of the AU (the secretariat) to perform this role if member States so wish, but this will require transforming the secretariat structure and functions to act as such.[11]

Thus, in UNECA's view, the original function of the Pan-African Parliament was to review and legitimise decisions or policies of an independent commission tasked with driving regional economic integration. Even where it had to work with existing structures such as the Assembly of the Heads of State, the ideal roadmap pointed to it being situated within an independent cluster of institutions promoting supranational interests first and foremost, with a democratically elected Pan-African Parliament at its apex. The PAP, part of the sixth and final stage of establishing the AEC, had a proposed timeline of five years from the date of ratification. However, while the Abuja Treaty was ratified in 1994, a protocol for the PAP, alongside numerous other protocols required for the Abuja Treaty,[12] had not yet been agreed by 1999.

Indeed, the first stage – the establishment and rationalisation of RECs for each part of Africa – had barely progressed in the first five years after ratification. The Abuja Treaty did not contain formal rules on the relations between the regional economic communities such as ECOWAS, SADC, and EAC, and the AEC proper. The AEC was also technically separate from the OAU as a legal entity, and this created difficulties in the crossover of plans and even potentially the legitimacy of actions presented. The draft protocol on relations between the AEC and RECs had only been endorsed in November 1996, five years after Abuja, and there were not enough ratifications for the treaty to enter into force by 1999.

Aside from the PAP, the Abuja Treaty also entailed several other specific institutions, namely, the African Central Bank, the African

---

[11] Ibid., 12.   [12] Khamis, *Promoting the African Union*, 39–41.

Monetary Union, and the African Court of Justice.[13] However, none of these had yet had any legal protocols to establish them. On parliamentary participation, the OAU had only got as far as deciding to convene a consultative forum for African parliamentarians in 1998, in anticipation of establishing the PAP.[14] When this had not yet occurred by the 1999 Algiers Summit, the Council of Ministers had to remind member states that decisions were binding and urged them to organise it urgently.[15] The Pan-African Parliament, sitting at the sixth stage of the AEC plan, was low on virtually everyone's priorities prior to the Sirte Summit.

Nigeria's Role

Nigeria's attachment of the cities of Lagos and Abuja to the two economic integration plans for the continent was not coincidental – it had been a major driver of these initiatives, hosting Lagos as an extraordinary summit and using the 1991 Abuja annual summit to adopt the treaty establishing the AEC. It had thus strongly backed their acceleration and development wherever possible and was closely linked with the developments over twenty years.

By 1999, it was clear that the stages of the Abuja Treaty were not moving according to the original planned timeline, and it was necessary to revitalise the process. Whereas the 1980 Final Act of Lagos had planned to set up the AEC by 2000, it was clear that, the Abuja Treaty notwithstanding, any form of economic community was not going to be meaningful given the regional conditions at the time.

Olusegun Obasanjo, returning to power in 1999, worked quickly to set up units in Nigerian ministries to promote integration, immediately creating a Ministry for Cooperation and Integration in Africa that year that would serve as the focal point for both ECOWAS and OAU matters.[16] The depth of commitment to the Abuja Treaty, its new democratic credentials, and strong emphasis on participation (a core

---

[13] 'Sirte Declaration' (EAHG/Decl. (IV) Rev. 1) 1999, para. 8(ii)(b).
[14] OAU, 'Decision on African Economic Community' (AHG/OAU/AEC/Decl. I (II)) (Ouagadougou 1998), Decision 4. Consultative Forum for African Parliamentarians.
[15] Khamis, *Promoting the African Union*, 60.
[16] Alli, *The Role of Nigeria in Regional Security Policy* (Abuja: Friedrich Ebert Stiftung, 2012), 16–17.

part of Obasanjo's CSSDCA) therefore makes Nigeria's opposition to expanding the role of the PAP puzzling on normative grounds.

At a broader level, the 'good governance' agenda in the 1990s had pushed for higher standards of participation and accountability,[17] and this thinking had spread to many international organisations such as the World Bank and United Nations. While the OAU formally did not make any institutional changes in response, both internal and external pressure had begun to be exerted to improve its standards in this direction. A draft charter on participation in development had been prepared as far back as 1989.[18] 'Good governance' thinking on participation and accountability was also visibly present in the texts of the Kampala Document[19] and the Conference on Security, Stability, Development, and Cooperation in Africa.[20]

However, the defeat of the Kampala Movement in 1991 had stalled efforts to democratise the regional organisation or make it more participatory in the meantime. Yet, in the intervening period, the rise of new democracies in South Africa and Nigeria, two of Africa's 'big five' donors to the OAU, raised the prospects that the continental body could also open itself to more inclusive participation, departing from its derisory nickname as a 'club of dictators'. The opportunity was then reopened in 1999 following the Sirte Summit and agreement for the establishment of the AU.

The Contest over the Pan-African Parliament

As noted in earlier chapters, the original response to Gaddafi's plan for a United States of Africa was that it should go back for 'greater consultation with the African people'[21] on the formation of a union, which prevented an immediate and inflexible decision. Given Obasanjo's appeal for the acceleration of the steps towards the AEC, it also introduced a path dependency.

The problem that arose from using the AEC as the alternative to the US of Africa was that the Abuja Treaty entailed the creation of a Pan-

---

[17] Woods, 'Good Governance in International Organizations', *Global Governance* 5, no. 1 (1999).
[18] Tieku, *Governing Africa*, 76.
[19] Africa Leadership Forum, *The Kampala Document*.
[20] 'CSSDCA Solemn Declaration' (AHG/Decl. 4 (XXXVI)) 2000,
[21] Interview with AU official, 9 February 2016.

African Parliament (PAP).[22] While not prescribing what powers the PAP would have, it was clear from the functions expected of it that these would include real legislative powers to draft laws and accelerate ratification processes. The PAP, as conceived in the Abuja Treaty, was a means to introduce proposed trade laws earlier to national legislators, who could hopefully debate and then domesticate them more quickly.[23] It could also potentially raise the legitimacy of such laws as they passed through a more democratic review process.[24]

In comparison, Gaddafi's original proposal suggested an 'African Congress', which was structurally more akin to the OAU's Assembly of the Heads of State, with one member chosen per state for a four-year term.[25] However, according to this proposal, the Congress would function as the 'legislative authority concerning all issues that fall within the competence of the United States of Africa',[26] including decisions on drafting of laws, budgets, taxes, trade relations, appointment of the judiciary, property rights, foreign policy, and political appointments of the US of Africa.[27]

Gaddafi was fixated not on the text of his proposal,[28] but on the substance, and he saw the PAP as his opening to create the supranational legislature he sought.[29] Dropping the nomenclature of the 'African Congress' from his original proposal (which, in any case, originally subordinated the heads of state to lawmakers under an individual president), he now began to push the PAP as a central, defining institution of the new African Union.[30] This put it higher on

---

[22] 'Treaty Establishing the African Economic Community', 1991, Art. 14.
[23] Khamis, *Promoting the African Union*, 55.
[24] Nzewi, 'Influence and Legitimacy in African Regional Parliamentary Assemblies: the Case of the Pan-African Parliament's Search for Legislative Powers', *Journal of Asian and African Studies* 49, no. 4 (2014).
[25] OAU, 'Draft of the Establishment of a State of the United States of Africa', Art. 13.
[26] Ibid., Art. 18.   [27] Ibid., Arts. 17–18.
[28] Libyan Arab Jamahiriya, 'Explanatory Notes on the Libyan Proposal for Amendment of the Constitutive Act of the African Union'.
[29] It was originally labelled the 'African Congress' in Gaddafi's US of Africa proposal, but by the following year, he was strongly advocating the 'Pan-African Parliament', which he noted was mentioned in the Abuja Treaty. Gaddafi, 'Address of the Leader of the Al-Fatah Revolution, Brother Muammar Gaddafi, at the Opening Ceremony of the OAU Ministerial Meeting on the Establishment of the African Union and the Pan-African Parliament' (Tripoli: Libyan Arab Jamahiriya, 2000), 15.
[30] Ibid.

the priority list than even the AEC had it, in which UNECA had revised the timeline for the sixth stage (wherein the PAP would be established) to 2023–8.[31]

Obasanjo, meanwhile, having claimed to make the acceleration of the AEC the central focus of the AU, committed the AU circle to also accepting an institution that could arguably promote the more ambitious target of a union government. Moreover, if Obasanjo argued that he was not in principle against the idea of establishing the political union, only that Africa was not yet ready,[32] then he could not simultaneously object to the establishment of one of the structures proposed for this purpose. The struggle was now about how to shape and define the PAP – which, as far as the Abuja Treaty was concerned, had not yet defined any functions or powers – according to the competing goals of both norm circles. This dispute between maximalists, who wanted the broadest interpretation of the PAP's powers, and minimalists, who saw it as primarily an AEC instrument, would thus mark the contestation over the PAP, with significant implications for the norm – democratisation in the AU – that it was intended to embody.

Whereas the Constitutive Act would be agreed quickly at the very first Heads of State Summit in Lomé, the protocol on the Pan-African Parliament would continue to go through several rounds of deferrals. At Lomé, it was decided the PAP would not have supranational powers, at least during the interim period,[33] though the compromise text in the final protocol agreed it would eventually obtain these. Other future functions, such as parliamentary confirmation of AU Commission officials, appeared still to be included in plans as late as December 2001.[34]

However, as the contest unfolded, the PAP was gradually relegated to a subordinate position below the Assembly, finally having only consultative and advisory powers. The compromise granted in its 2001 protocol was that it would eventually 'evolve into an institution with full legislative powers'.[35] Although the plan to evolve it into a

---

[31] UNECA, *Status of Regional Integration in Africa*, 2.
[32] Akinsaya, 'Nigeria at the African Union', 106–7.
[33] Khamis, *Promoting the African Union*, 93.
[34] OAU, *Report of the Secretary General on the Implementation of the Lusaka Summit on the Texts Relating to the Key Organs of the African Union*, 22.
[35] 'Protocol to the Treaty Establishing the African Economic Community Relating to the Pan-African Parliament', 2001, Art. 2(3).

Controlling the Initiative: From Sirte to Lomé

legislature was enthusiastically taken up by the first plenary group of the PAP, they never achieved this task, and when review of the Protocol came up after ten years, as stipulated in the original Protocol[36] (another compromise sought to placate the federalists), the contest again arose over the eventual functions and powers of the PAP, this time in Art. 8 of the new draft Protocol. That new protocol was eventually adopted in 2014 but with the PAP subordinate to the Assembly, unlike the original vision where it was as an equal institution, with all its powers to be defined by the Assembly when needed. However, the protocol has not been ratified and sits with a mere twelve ratifications of a required twenty-eight as of January 2021.

While the goal of greater national participation in continental affairs was achieved, the extent and scope of that participation was significantly curtailed, resulting in a qualifying of the original goals of virtually all the original norm circles, whether from the viewpoint of the AEC-acceleration proponents or the US of Africa union government circle. The contest also was significant in degrading the ability of the institution to play a significant role in the new AU, watched warily by both sides for potential breaches of the compromise.

Controlling the Initiative: From Sirte to Lomé

Given the 'surprise' at Sirte, control of the initiative was very important at this first stage. As events would later play out, the Sirte Declaration would come to be seen as the guiding document for the African Union and the stakes were thus high in what was included or not within the summit's concluding declaration.

Positioning the Pan-African Parliament

The Sirte Declaration in 1999, while open on the final structures the AU would take, nevertheless reserved a special place for the Pan-African Parliament. In Gaddafi's draft text of the Sirte Declaration, when it came to recalling the Abuja Treaty, only the Pan-African Parliament, amongst more than a dozen other institutions entailed by the Abuja Treaty, obtained special mention:

---

[36] Ibid., Art. 25(2).

In that regard, we have provided our Continent with an adequate framework for the orderly and sustained development of our countries in the social and economic fields by having adopted and ratified the Abuja Treaty Establishing the African Economic Community. We, hereby, rededicate ourselves to the key provisions and objectives of the Treaty, including, in particular, the establishment of an African Parliament which will make it a Community of Peoples.[37]

Given the appeal to the AEC, Gaddafi's opponents could not also object overtly to the PAP, and thus even in the heavily redacted final version of the Sirte Declaration that omitted seventeen paragraphs of Gaddafi's text, the PAP retained its special mention:

We aim to establish that [Pan-African] Parliament by the year 2000, to provide a common platform for our peoples and their grass-root organisations to be more involved in discussions and decision-making on the problems and challenges facing our continent.[38]

With the Sirte Declaration giving the AU and PAP specific mentions, it implied that the two institutions should receive equal billing, and this was the initial interpretation. The OAU Secretary-General, Salim Salim, referred to the AU and PAP as 'twin-objectives',[39] while Algerian President Abdelaziz Bouteflika described the process as 'the project establishing the African Union and the Pan African Parliament'.[40] A consultants' draft of the new structures of the AU, while removing the controversial 'president' suggested by Gaddafi's original proposal, also had the three-armed structure of Pan-African Parliament, Assembly of the Union (Heads of State), and Court of Justice at least till 2002. (See Figure 5.1.)

Gaddafi, keen to keep the momentum going on this institutional structure, ensured it was the only specific item to have its own deadline for completion, independent of the establishment of the AU. Indeed, in his opinion, 'The Sirte Declaration talks about a congress with

---

[37] 'Draft Sirte Declaration', para. 17.
[38] 'Sirte Declaration' (EAHG/Decl. (IV) Rev. 1) 1999, para. 8(ii)(b).
[39] Salim, 'Statement at the Experts Meeting on the AU and PAP', 8.
[40] Bouteflika, 'Discours de Son Excellence Abdelaziz Bouteflika, Président de la République Algérienne Démocratique et Populair et Président en Exercice de l'Organisation de l'Unité Africaine à la 36ème Session Ordinaire de la Conférence des Chefs d'Etat et de Gouvernement de l'Organisation de l'Unite Africaine, Lomé 10–12 Juillet 2000' (Lomé: Democratic and Popular Republic of Algeria, 2000), 18.

Controlling the Initiative: From Sirte to Lomé

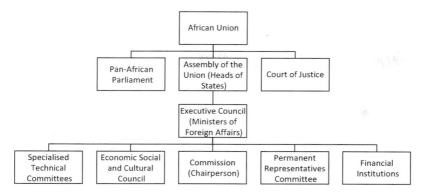

Figure 5.1 Consultants' proposed organisation chart of the African Union (source: OAU, 'Transition of the OAU to the African Union: Institutional Capacity Building Needs and Interim Arrangements: Report of the Consultants, June 14, 2002'
(Addis Ababa: OAU Archives, 2002), Annex II).

mandates like those of the American congress. The African peoples should be allowed to exercise their rights.'[41] Thus, while Gaddafi held the advantage, he ensured great prominence for the PAP in the founding plans for the AU, and this would take years to unravel; finally, it was only possible to dilute it to a certain degree without omitting it.

Drafting the Treaties

After Sirte, the task of the technical consultation on establishing the relevant organs and structures, as well as the drafting of the various treaties required for the AU, would be managed by the OAU Secretariat. This gave the initiative back to the Secretariat, which had rather different ambitions from those of Gaddafi. Although Gaddafi hosted several of the meetings, the way they were set up (including who participated), their timing, and the manner in which problems were framed were determined by the Secretariat, and this gave them unusual control over the initiative. Libya mistakenly believed that hosting meetings 'would allow them to use the privileges usually given to the

---

[41] Gaddafi, 'Address at the OAU Ministerial Meeting, Tripoli 2000', 15.

host state to influence the experts to revise the Expert Text',[42] but instead this met firm opposition from the opposing norm circle. Providing a way out of the deadlock permitted the Secretariat to strategically manage some of the various rivalries between norm circles to effect the changes they sought.[43]

The initial draft of the new Constitutive Act would be created by consultants, tasked with rationalising the separate structures of the OAU and the AEC.[44] However, they were possibly unaware of and did not understand the nature of the debate that had gone before, regarding the 'United States of Africa' proposal and the 'African Union' counter-proposal, and had difficulties in rationalising these structures. They proposed a pyramidal structure with the OAU atop the AU and AEC (as paired institutions). Within the AU, the PAP sat as one of three institutional branches of the union (see Figure 5.1), and would be governed by a separate protocol.

The Secretariat was unhappy with the resultant proposal, particularly the suggestion that the AU would coexist with the AEC and OAU,[45] and they therefore edited it heavily, including a provision to explicitly supersede the AEC and OAU treaties, thereby dissolving both institutions.[46] Salim argued that this was necessary to incorporate the views of the Secretariat as well as numerous member states they had consulted.[47] These changes would therefore leave the AU as the sole continental body, regardless of whether it was an intergovernmental, confederal, or federal organisation.

The new draft was then reviewed by a meeting of experts and parliamentarians in April 2000. While the experts reviewed both the draft Constitutive Act and the PAP protocol article by article, agreement could not be reached on the substantive matters, particularly the powers and functions of the parliament. Many of the divisions fell along minimalist/maximalist lines (some proposed it should function exactly as a national parliament, with supranational powers to enforce laws created), but the experts group also disagreed on administrative and procedural issues, such as financing and the numbers of delegates each member state would have (whether in equal numbers or as a ratio

---

[42] Tieku, *Governing Africa*, 111.   [43] Ibid., 75.
[44] Khamis, *Promoting the African Union*, 84–5.
[45] Tieku, *Governing Africa*, 105.
[46] Khamis, *Promoting the African Union*, 88.
[47] Salim, 'Statement at the Experts Meeting on the AU and PAP', 3.

based on population).⁴⁸ These would need to be referred to a higher level body for clarification.

The impasse was seized by Gaddafi as an opportunity to throw the entire project out, and return to his original 'United States of Africa' as the working document. Libya offered to host the preparatory meeting necessitated by the experts' impasse, and this gave Gaddafi a chance to regain the initiative. At Tripoli, ostensibly a ministerial-level conference, Gaddafi brought in the heads of state of the most supportive members of his norm circle: Omar al-Bashir of Sudan, Konaré of Mali, Jerry Rawlings of Ghana, Charles Taylor of Liberia, Wade of Senegal, Idris Deby of Chad, and Bakili Muluzi of Malawi. Al-Bashir, Konaré, Wade, Taylor, and Rawlings each gave speeches in support of Gaddafi's agenda.⁴⁹ Addressing the ministers, Gaddafi argued that recent developments were unsatisfactory and not done according to the Sirte Declaration.

However, Gaddafi's berating of delegates at the ministerial meeting in Tripoli may have backfired, demeaning them as if they did not 'know what they were doing'.⁵⁰ This was implicitly acknowledged later in Konaré's speech in Lomé, where he pleaded that delegates 'appreciate that certain countries, or group of countries, may play a leading and driving role without individual domination and without exclusivity or exclusion (*concevoir que certains pays, ou groupes de pays, puissent jouer le rôle d'avant-garde et de locomotive sans domination particulière et sans exclusive, ni exclusion*)'.⁵¹ Other states were simply unprepared to discuss the Libyan counter-proposal, including Nigeria, South Africa, Algeria, Guinea, and Uganda.⁵² It was agreed then that the proposed PAP would not have supranational powers, and this was the working principle going into the Lomé Summit.

At Lomé, the debate resumed with positions similar to the divide in Tripoli as to the powers of the AU structures. Mali President Alpha Konaré, ostensibly a supporter of Gaddafi but more pragmatic and seeking a compromise, suggested that an agreement could still be reached if the supranational powers of the PAP were dropped,⁵³ and this sealed its fate. The PAP protocol was once again

---

⁴⁸ Khamis, *Promoting the African Union*, 90–1.   ⁴⁹ Ibid., 91.
⁵⁰ Tieku, *Governing Africa*, 112.   ⁵¹ Konaré, 'Allocution à Lomé, 2000', 10.
⁵² Tieku, *Governing Africa*, 112.   ⁵³ Konaré, 'Allocution à Lomé, 2000', 10.

referred to committee for further review, which would be held in Pretoria in November.

At the Pretoria meeting, now once again far from Gaddafi's gaze, the decision at Lomé to defer supranational powers made consensus far easier to obtain. Discussion centred on technical matters such as the composition, terms of references, diplomatic status, funding, and even the question of representation by African diaspora.[54] The PAP's powers were to be decided by the heads of state, as the committee agreed these would be beyond their power to decide. However, in reaching consensus on the rest of the protocol on the PAP, the committee sent an important signal that the deliberation was finished. Thus the Council of Ministers accepted their proposed draft protocol at the next meeting in Tripoli in March 2001, and recommended the Assembly to also adopt the protocol at the same summit.[55]

Shared Norms: the Sirte Declaration vs the AEC Treaty

Arguably, this entire contest over the Pan-African Parliament was a contest over the meaning of a shared norm – the institution entailed by the AEC, or by the Sirte Declaration (which invoked, but arguably superseded, the Abuja Treaty's PAP). However, both texts left relatively open the interpretation of the necessary functions. Thus, smaller aspects of the proposal contributed agreed norms that could be interpreted differently in order to bolster the cases of different norm circles. The only authoritative text was the Sirte Declaration, but here past decisions of the OAU were applied as guiding the thinking for the PAP. The role of the OAU Secretariat and its Secretary-General, which could inform different groups as to what decisions were made, thus became elevated during this period.

The final Sirte Declaration, changed as it was from Gaddafi's text, was now the key site of struggle: the new 'African Union' would have to be based on the declaration, even inasmuch as the Declaration was derided as a 'blank cheque' by critics. Implicitly, Gaddafi also read into the Declaration his own assessment of the outcome of Sirte: his conviction that African leaders had broadly agreed with him on the need for a

---

[54] Khamis, *Promoting the African Union*, 90.
[55] OAU, 'Decision on the Draft Protocol to the Treaty Establishing the African Economic Community Relating to the Pan-African Parliament' (CM/Dec.566 (LXXIII), Tripoli, 1–2 March 2001.

Controlling the Initiative: From Sirte to Lomé

union government, and therefore his licence to micro-manage the drafting process. The draft Constitutive Act for the AU and the draft Protocol on the Pan-African Parliament thus began to be developed in twinned processes, though the PAP protocol would eventually take much longer to be adopted.

The Sirte Declaration was often used as a pretext by the maximalist circle to reject proposals it did not like. For example, at Tripoli in 2000, Gaddafi suggested that the experts meeting had departed from the spirit and intentions of the Sirte Declaration, coming up with a structure that was not acceptable to him. Further, he charged that they had no directions from their heads of state, which undermined any decisions they made:

> It seemed that all the African leaders had no idea about the Experts Meeting ... The Experts came to Tripoli a few days ago and had their meeting here. I saw them and thanked them for coming. I also asked them about the instructions they had received from their governments. No one gave me the answer.[56]

The experts' authority, he argued, could only come with the approval of their heads of state, who had adopted the Sirte Declaration (and whom Gaddafi therefore tried to depict as coming to share his point of view regarding the new AU). Yet he was also cognisant that the experts were operating based on shared norms, except that in his view those norms (stemming from the OAU and Abuja treaties) were no longer relevant:

> The Experts came without knowing the details and without any instructions from their respective countries ... For the Experts, it was just a routine meeting in Addis Ababa. They could not transcend the sacred documents – the OAU Charter and the Abuja Treaty. They could not do anything about the Union.[57]

The shared norms could also be used in other directions. The OAU Secretary-General Salim Salim appealed to the Sirte Declaration when he espoused quite a different view of the necessary functions of the PAP. Rather than painting the Sirte Declaration as a break with the past, he instead depicted it as a continuation of the OAU. In his opening address to the experts group, Salim stated:

[56] Gaddafi, 'Address at the OAU Ministerial Meeting, Tripoli 2000', 14.
[57] Ibid., 13–14.

> [T]he Sirte Declaration is a collective commitment by the Heads of State and Government for reinvigorating our quest for attaining the vision espoused by the Founding Fathers of our Continental Organisation in forging closer unity among African countries. The Declaration derives inspiration from the Charter of the Organisation of African Unity and from the subsequent landmark decisions that we have collectively made, and adds into these a strategic consideration of the challenges facing the African Continent as we enter the new millennium.[58]

This offered Salim the authority to take small inductive steps to frame a PAP closer to his own ideas. Gaddafi had been trying to use a tight deadline to prevent vacillation on his proposal for a Pan-African Parliament as a key institution constituting the United States of Africa. Instead, Salim turned this into a more liberal argument regarding the imperative for popular participation in continental affairs:

> Quite clearly, by underlining the urgency and importance of creating the Pan-African Parliament, our leaders recognised that the task of promoting the unity of our Continent is not simply a restrictive preoccupation of the Governments of our Member States, but that it involves the whole spectrum of our societies.[59]

Finally, he used the Sirte Declaration's openness on specifics to read a particular set of views into what the AU and PAP should entail:

> The [Sirte] Declaration does not spell out any particular model or models for either the Union or the Parliament. However, the leaders have emphatically underlined that the proposed Union should take us a major step further from where we are now. It should be endowed with sufficient powers and authority to act with vigour and dynamism in pursuing our collective interests and in advancing our national endeavours.
>
> Similarly, the Pan-African Parliament to be established needs to be adequately empowered to represent, articulate, and pursue the collective desires and concerns of the peoples of our Continent and in consolidating African unity. It is important that the new institutions should not simply be a rubber stamp mechanism that does not express the collective authority and aspirations of the African people.[60]

---

[58] Salim, 'Statement at the Experts Meeting on the AU and PAP', 1. [59] Ibid., 2.
[60] Ibid., 5.

Whereas Gaddafi's interpretation of the AU's 'collective interests' was to challenge Western powers, Salim's views were simply on making the OAU a more effective institution in addressing the continent's problems. This can be seen in the Secretariat's revisions of the consultants' original proposal, where strengthening of the Mechanism on Conflict Prevention, Management, and Resolution (MCMPR) and the Banjul Charter on human rights were central.[61] Finally, Salim framed the PAP as a democratic institution, far from simply being a congress of heads of state as Gaddafi initially suggested or an AEC implementation tool as others would have it, but something that could potentially check the authority of the Assembly.

AEC as Shared Norm

Shared norms did not only constrain the AEC proponents. The AEC also provided an opportunity to distance the PAP from the AU, despite its equal billing in earlier drafts of the AU plans. Initially, the draft protocol for the PAP was simply titled, 'Draft Protocol on the Establishment of the Pan-African Parliament'. Yet, for the opponents of Gaddafi's vision, this was not removed enough. At the experts meeting in Addis Ababa in April 2000, the group confusingly decided to rename the draft as the 'Draft Protocol to the Treaty Establishing the African Economic Community relating to the Pan-African Parliament'. Unlike the consultants' organisation chart that put it on equal footing with the Assembly of the Heads of State,[62] this relegated the PAP to being under the AEC, which was also hierarchically under either the OAU or AU in the transition plan. This seemingly semantic change can only be explained as part of the contestation to put distance between the PAP and the AU, particularly the heads of state assembly. At the same time, delegates were attempting to use the shared norm, the AEC – which constrained their resistance to the PAP – to thereby also relegate the PAP from its initial prominence that Gaddafi had fought for.

However, this raised a contradiction in terms because the AEC was intended to be dissolved through the creation of the AU, which would

---

[61] Tieku, *Governing Africa*, 105.
[62] OAU, 'Transition of the OAU to the African Union: Institutional Capacity Building Needs and Interim Arrangements: Report of the Consultants, June 14, 2002', Annex II.

merge the OAU and AEC.[63] Instead, here was a protocol that reiterated what was intended to be a superseded treaty and body under the new Constitutive Act.[64] This added to the confusion in the relationship between the AEC and AU as it could be inferred that the AEC was the sub-organ under which the PAP existed, rather than an integral part of the AU (bearing in mind that the two structures had once had equal billing, as discussed above). Nevertheless, in Art. 5 of the Constitutive Act mention of the AEC is omitted from the organs of the AU, whereas the PAP is the third organ listed (Art. 5(1)(c)). However, confusion remained over whether the AEC continued to exist or not thereafter.[65] Tussling over the shared norm of the AEC provided opportunities to position the PAP, but could also be used to weaken it.

Metis

The constraints created by the debate at Sirte actually gave the two opposing camps relatively little room to manoeuvre to persuade the other side. The PAP as a structure was agreed, but not its functions, and this could have been deadlocked if both sides decided to dig in their positions. The opportunities for 'metis' then came from elsewhere. Thomas Tieku has argued convincingly that this opportunity fell in the laps of 'Africrats', the bureaucrats working in the OAU Secretariat and later the AU Commission. He states that Africrats 'used their entrepreneurial skills, the OAU's institutional mechanisms, informal channels, and arguments to persuade representatives of states to select ambitious principles, rules, institutional structures, and decision-making procedures for the AU'.[66] According to Tieku, Africrats were not always successful in convincing everyone, but if they could persuade sufficient numbers and a sizeable consensus emerged, the Pan-African norms of solidarity could take over and isolated leaders were likely to conform with the majority – a principle seen, for example, in Obasanjo's second attempt at the CSSDCA proposal (discussed in Chapter 4). Some of the Africrats' strategies in the context of the Pan-African Parliament have already been discussed above, such as Salim's appeal to shared norms to push his vision of the role of the Pan-

---

[63] Konaré, 'Allocution à Lomé, 2000'.
[64] 'The Constitutive Act of the African Union', 2000, Art. 33(2).
[65] Interview with AU official, 22 February 2016.
[66] Tieku, *Governing Africa*, 25.

African Parliament,[67] despite having no formal decision-making power (since this belongs to the member states). Africrats also tried to build norm circles out of the member states through their extensive consultations. Not only did they secure support for certain ideas in advance, they could also gauge reactions of certain members and attempt to tailor amendments more agreeable to the those who were holding out.[68] Consultations with civil society groups added further legitimacy to their texts, given both Gaddafi's and his opponents' appeals to the 'African people' as significant actors and ostensible beneficiaries of their proposals.

However, specific to 'metis', or the art of invention, is the use of the contingent circumstances to engineer advantageous positions for their desired outcome. The Africrats masterfully did this by framing the division to be between 'statists' and 'continental unionism' as the two extreme ends. They suggested the statist view was the cause of the inability of the OAU to address many of the current challenges and it therefore needed more powers. The federal demands from the other side were not helpful given that conditions could not support such a federal union at that time. The logical conclusion, which they did not overtly state, was that their solution in the middle was the correct compromise.[69]

This was interesting because, seen from a norm circle perspective, it potentially positioned the same figures against themselves. The 'statists' who argued for non-interference were typically authoritarians, uninterested in any kind of external meddling in their internal affairs. The 'unionists' were often from the same boat: Burkina Faso, the Central African Republic, Chad, Liberia, Libya, Niger, Sudan, and Togo, eight of the ten states[70] broadly supporting federalism, were authoritarian at the time of the debate and would have certainly argued against any form of external intervention in their own states (such as their original opposition to the liberal CSSDCA in 1991). Those holding out against Gaddafi's plan who were staunch non-interventionists, such as Kenya and Zimbabwe, were normally close to Gaddafi's position on other matters. Arguably, if the federal idea were not on the table, the same federalist states would have fallen into

---

[67] Salim, 'Statement at the Experts Meeting on the AU and PAP'.
[68] Tieku, *Governing Africa*, 106.   [69] Ibid., 109.
[70] The other two states were Mali and Senegal, which had democratic leadership.

the 'statist' camp together with the likes of Kenya and Zimbabwe, opposed to the limited humanitarian interventions under grave circumstances suggested by more liberal states.

The actual opponents to Gaddafi's US of Africa, such as Nigeria and South Africa, did not take the extreme view of statism that Salim suggested was the opposite pole. Instead, they believed that in order to accelerate the AEC, a delegation of some sovereignty was indeed necessary to promote economic integration and trade. Even on security, Obasanjo had long been arguing for collective responsibilities, stemming from growing interdependence and the spill-over of conflicts across borders.[71] Thus the structures that resulted, including the PAP, had the potential to be more in line with their views as a 'compromise' position between two poles that featured the same authoritarian tendencies. The final AU decision on the PAP situated it in an organisational position equal to several other AU organs that came under the oversight of the Executive Council, without legislative powers (see Figure 5.2).

The Review of the Pan-African Parliament Protocol

The maximalist proponents did secure some concessions, but not nearly as many as they had conceded. Primarily, the line that they had been promised was that the PAP would eventually 'evolve into an institution with full legislative powers'.[72] This acknowledged the broad agreement that all sides eventually desired a continental union, though they differed on the timeline or indeed the strategy to get there.

With the entry into force of the Constitutive Act in 2000, the transition period from the OAU to the AU began. Gaddafi was further assured that the issues he was concerned with would be clarified and resolved before the end of this transition period. Meanwhile, the final Protocol provided for reviews of the act after five and ten years, during which time the effectiveness would be reassessed.[73]

The parliament was formally launched in 2004, though members of parliament (MPs) may not have been aware of the contest that preceded it. The first strategic plan of the new parliament, running from

---

[71] Africa Leadership Forum, *The Kampala Document*, 9.
[72] 'Protocol to the Treaty Establishing the African Economic Community Relating to the Pan-African Parliament', 2001, Art. 2(3).
[73] Ibid., Art. 25.

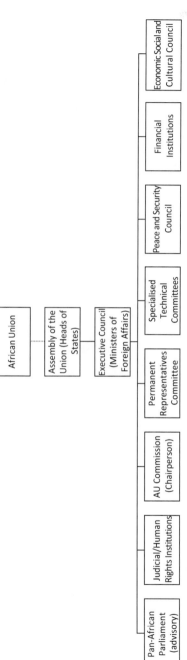

Figure 5.2 The position of the PAP in present AU organisational structure

2006 to 2010, boldly accepted the challenge to 'transform from an advisory and consultative body to a full legislative organ'.[74] Unlike their states' formal positions, PAP MPs attempted to take independent views from their member states.[75] Support for full legislative powers has been virtually unanimous within the PAP since its inception.[76]

However, in 2009, when the first review period came up, a revised protocol – put forward by the AUC, examined by legal experts, and approved by Ministers of Justice – was rejected by the Assembly in May 2012.[77] The contest played out as the model predicts: division over the utility of the protocol, appeals to shared norms, and creative initiatives to try to reconfigure the norm circles more in favour of the proposal, or metis.

The rejection in 2012 was over the functions and powers of the PAP in Art. 8, which the new protocol had presumed would be fully extended after the transition period of the 2001 protocol. However, the creation of the institution had introduced a new set of actors – the PAP MPs – and they attempted to leverage their governments independently for more powers, irrespective of the sovereignty contest that had developed at the Assembly. However, the Assembly still functioned by consensus and had authority over the PAP, so the PAP MPs and AU Commission had to find other means to pass their proposal.

The revised version in 2013 diluted Art. 8(1) to stipulate that the functions and powers of the PAP would be determined by the Assembly of the Heads of State. The president of the PAP, Bethel Amadi of Nigeria, noted that they had watered down the original proposed protocol:

The draft protocol only gave the PAP legislative functions and not legislative powers as understood in the sense of the powers of National Parliaments. Thus, the PAP with legislative functions will not possess the legal capacity to make laws binding member States without specific adoption by the Assembly of Heads of States and subsequent ratification and domestication by

---

[74] Pan African Parliament, 'Strategic Plan, 2006–2010: "One Africa, One Voice"' (Midrand, South Africa: African Union, 2005), Section 10.6.
[75] Touray, *The African Union*, 177.
[76] Sheku Dumbuya, PAP MP of Sierra Leone, quoted in Pan African Parliament, 'Pan-African Parliament Hansard Report, Second Session – Third Parliament' (Midrand, South Africa: African Union, 2013), 91.
[77] Touray, *The African Union*, 178.

National Governments. In fact, Article 8(1)(a) clearly states that the Assembly of Heads of States shall have the power to determine the subject areas on which the PAP may legislate or propose model laws and such draft model laws shall be submitted to the Assembly of Heads of States for its consideration and approval. This means that the PAP cannot even embark on any legislative process without the approval of the Assembly of Heads of States.[78]

Moreover, he argued that the oversight functions in Art. 8(2) were already provided for in the existing 2001 Protocol Arts. 11(1), (2), and (5).[79] In other words, the PAP took two important steps to get its new proposal accepted: it weakened the text to reduce its powers (thereby removing objections or potential sovereignty costs and thus increasing potential utility of the protocol, thereby enlarging the potential norm circle in support of it), and it argued that its other functions were already established in previously shared norms. This alone, however, was not sufficient, and it also used other opportunities for influence.

At the Second Session of the Third Parliament on 6 May 2013, members spoke vocally in support of the transition to full legislative powers, and complained about the refusal by African heads of state to move on this issue. In addition, they got leaders of the regional parliaments – the East African Legislative Assembly, the ECOWAS Parliament, and the SADC Parliamentary Forum, together with President John Mahama of Ghana and the AUC Chairperson, Nkosazana Dlamini-Zuma – to support the proposal for full legislative powers.[80]

The president and his committee also pursued advocacy missions to various member states and embassies to persuade them of the necessity of the changes, as well as to assuage concerns that the new protocol would threaten their sovereignty. In Amadi's view, the advocacy paid off, where the countries that they managed to visit then began to support their views. Some of these heads of state even openly spoke in support of the PAP's extension of powers, such as John Dramani Mahama of Ghana.[81] However, where they were unable to meet heads of state of hold-out countries, there was no opportunity to change their

---

[78] Bethel Amadi (Nigeria), President of the PAP, quoted in Pan African Parliament, 'Pan-African Parliament Hansard Report, Second Session – Third Parliament', 53.
[79] Amadi, quoted in ibid. [80] Ibid. [81] Amadi, quoted in ibid., 93.

minds. This was especially so in southern Africa, where the negative experience of the SADC tribunal made heads of state hostile to supranational bodies.[82]

This text was finally accepted in 2014, now as the 'Protocol to the Constitutive Act of the African Union relating to the Pan-African Parliament'. However, the trade-off to these compromises was that the underlying norms – the democratisation of regional processes – were not strengthened as much as was desired by the MPs.

Finally, the 2014 protocol removed mention of its aim 'to evolve into an institution with full legislative powers',[83] and while deeming the PAP the 'legislative organ of the African Union', it also requires the Assembly of the Heads of State to determine what areas the PAP can draft model laws on and to approve any submissions by the PAP,[84] which effectively retains the advisory/consultative status of the PAP without stating it explicitly. The PAP thus may have legislative functions, but not legislative *powers*. The elaboration of other specific functions of the PAP in Art. 8(2) are also all advisory in nature, while Art. 8(5) states that these powers do not apply to the AU's assembly, court, or council. Nevertheless, as with many legal agreements, it will be some years before its entry into force. As of January 2021, this new protocol had twenty-one signatures just twelve ratifications.[85]

Conclusion

The PAP created a dilemma for the opponents of the US of Africa, as it implied they must transfer more sovereignty to the AU than they were prepared to. Without overtly opposing it, the only solution Gaddafi's opponents could muster was to send it continuously back to subcommittees for further examination.[86] However, the deadlock on the

---

[82] Amadi, quoted in ibid., 94.
[83] 'Protocol to the Treaty Establishing the African Economic Community Relating to the Pan-African Parliament', 2001, Art. 2(3).
[84] 'Protocol to the Constitutive Act of the African Union Relating to the Pan-African Parliament', 2014, Art. 8(1).
[85] African Union, 'List of Countries that Have Signed, Ratified/Acceded to the Protocol to the Constitutive Act of the African Union Relating to the Pan-African Parliament', African Union Commission, www.au.int/web/en/treaties/protocol-constitutive-act-african-union-relating-pan-african-parliament.
[86] AHG/Decl. 143 (XXXVI), 'Decision on the Establishment of the African Union and the Pan-African Parliament', para. 5.

matter was also used by Gaddafi to argue that they should therefore revert to the original proposal (the 'United States of Africa' draft constitution) that he had presented at Sirte. This suggestion was referred to committees and therefore rebuffed indirectly.[87]

As Gaddafi's attempts at a more maximalist AU were rebuffed, he increasingly turned to appeals to the 'people', arguing that these arrangements needed to 'ensure full involvement of the people from the beginning of the process'.[88] This turn to the implicit legitimacy of the institution he was proposing must be read in the context of the strong but understated rebuffing of his grand federal schemes by other member states. Despite his continued reservations over the Constitutive Act as it was drafted, he conceded to drop the matter at Lomé, noting that they would defer proposed amendments 'in order not to stymie the coming into force of the Constitutive Act'.[89] The concession Konaré suggested at Lomé also sealed the fate of the PAP as an advisory body, despite it being the structure that Gaddafi was closest to achieving as part of his federal vision.

Ultimately, despite the manoeuvres of the Secretariat, an interim period as an advisory body was all that could be agreed upon, and even when the review came after the allotted five years, its powers were not fundamentally strengthened. While path dependencies clearly influenced the original coming into being of the PAP, they will also affect it going forward. Efforts to reform the PAP[90] must be understood in the light of its historical development, an accident of the convergence of two competing visions of African integration that were irreconcilable – the AEC and the United States of Africa. The factors affecting the contest are listed in Table 5.1.

The lack of desire to reopen the debates around Gaddafi's federal vision will prove a hindrance to the ability to affect change in the PAP in the future. The Protocol to the Constitutive Act of the African Union relating to the Pan-African Parliament has just twelve ratifications. The

---

[87] Khamis, *Promoting the African Union*, 91.   [88] Ibid., 93.

[89] Libyan Arab Jamahiriya, 'Explanatory Notes on the Libyan Proposal for Amendment of the Constitutive Act of the African Union', 1.

[90] See, for example, Navarro, 'The Creation and Transformation of Regional Parliamentary Assemblies: Lessons from the Pan-African Parliament', *Journal of Legislative Studies* 16, no. 2 (2010); cf. Magliveras and Huliaras, 'Understanding Success and Failure in the Quest for Peace: the Pan-African Parliament and the Amani Forum', *The Hague Journal of Diplomacy* 11(2016).

Table 5.1 *The contestation over the Pan-African Parliament*

Factors	Proposing norm circle	Opposing norm circle
Members	OAU, UNECA, Libya, Senegal, Mali, Ghana, Liberia, Chad, Malawi, Burkina Faso, the Central African Republic, Niger, Sudan, Togo	Nigeria, South Africa, Algeria, Guinea, Uganda
Control of initiative	• Long genesis as key institution in AEC • Sirte extraordinary summit • Hosting (and monitoring) of preparatory expert group meetings	• Rush to adopt Constitutive Act at Lomé • Stipulation as advisory body with eventual intention to become full legislative organ in Constitutive Act (2000)
Norms invoked	• AEC's 'Pan-African Parliament' • Agreement to form the 'African Union', including popular participation in the Sirte Declaration	• Rhetorical entrapment of AEC to avert United States of Africa (no ideational/ discursive opposition)
Metis	• Personal intervention and appeals by Gaddafi • Union is intended for the 'citizens' of Africa, making regional parliament essential	• Framing the contest as opposition between 'statists' and 'unionists' rather than between democrats and authoritarians • Concession of Mali to non-supranationality
Outcome	Advisory body (qualified)	

Protocol on Amendments to the Constitutive Act of the African Union also has not entered into force as of January 2021, with heavyweights such as Algeria, Nigeria, and Ethiopia still yet to ratify. While the former document was only adopted in 2014, both documents must be understood as byproducts of the contestation period when Gaddafi actively and forcefully tried to impress his vision of a continental state on to the African Union. While he failed, not all structures could be avoided, and some reflect norms that would otherwise be desirable, such as democratic participation and representation, and these protocols reflect that.

An external observer expecting great things from the Pan-African Parliament, perhaps unhelpfully hailed by Thabo Mbeki as 'a sign of democratic maturity in Africa',[91] would find themselves disappointed in this regard. African reforms will be incremental and issue-specific, and unlikely to repeat the *carte blanche* period provoked by Gaddafi, and accepted only as far as to include other powerful states' interests, as Thomas Tieku has argued.[92] Prospects for reform of the Pan-African Parliament are unlikely to improve, unless facts on the ground change that significantly change the utility calculus of the opposing states. A new and significant crisis of legitimacy or a critical mass of states to push forward a reinterpretation of participatory regional integration will be needed to effect real and lasting institutional change, and give the PAP the powers it needs to fill the input legitimacy gap in the AU.

This case is a puzzling fit for liberal constructivist theories. At first glance, countries like Nigeria, with its strong association with the AEC and Obasanjo's personal association with the CSSDCA encouraging wider participation in regional affairs, and South Africa, with its overtly liberal foreign policy, should have been the strongest proponents of this project, aligning with their broader aims of encouraging democratisation on the continent. Instead, associated as it was with Gaddafi's US of Africa, they became its major opponents. Even with the demise of Gaddafi in 2011, this position has not changed, and they once again opposed the proposed amendments in 2012, even when, by now, the major supporters of the move were the PAP MPs themselves, many of whose democratic credentials were unimpeachable.

Finally, attempts to read into the creation of the Pan-African Parliament some form of institutional mimicry are likely to be disappointed. While the name and its genesis within the AEC could certainly point to European models, its development was not an outcome of following the logics of regional integration and/or input legitimacy that

---

[91] Quoted in Mbete, 'The Pan-African Parliament: Progress and Prospects', in *The African Union and its Institutions*, ed. Akokpari, Ndinga-Muvumba, and Murithi (Auckland Park, South Africa: Fanele, 2008), 307.

[92] Tieku, 'Explaining the Clash and Accommodation of Interests'.

creates a potential for institutional isomorphism. PAP MPs have since argued strongly for a role in promoting integration and ratification of treaties, but this has not moved enough of the heads of state. The gap between its actual functions and the functions required to perform the required role will remain a continuing puzzle if the view persists that it was created because of institutional isomorphism. Instead, the leaders who debated the institution were concerned mostly by the prospect of continental federalism, which they were not prepared to accept. The PAP was an accident of their diversion of Gaddafi's larger proposal, being an overlapping part of the AEC as well as the United States of Africa.

Thus, the practices of the OAU and AU are intractably part of the explanation of how and why the PAP emerged in the shape it did. The norm circles were split – not on ideational lines but on contingent ones based on their support for or opposition to the federal idea, which again blurred lines because those opposed to federalism could nevertheless strongly support economic integration and some concessions on sovereignty. Power and interests-based explanations might go furthest in explaining the contest, but they falter on the result that anything at all was achieved, given that as a consensus-favouring organisation every member state had a potential veto, and there were opportunities to wield it at several points. Furthermore, the final institution agreed was incapable of serving *any* of the Assembly members' interests, simply functioning as an advisory body in which its recommendations and reports show little sign of being noticed by the Executive Council or Assembly.[93]

The nature of its development, however, is well accounted by the norm circle contestation outlined. Two competing groups emerged contingently, in spite of past preferences (such as Nigeria strongly backing the AEC Treaty, from which the PAP originated), and contested the functions and powers of the proposed institution. Whenever the initiative was controlled by the Secretariat, they were able to extract more progressive functions in the protocol, but these were periodically set back by interventions led by Libya, who sought a full legislature, and used their hosting of meetings to check for departures from their position. Unfortunately for the opponents of federalism, the PAP had been part of the shared norms on regional integration to

---

[93] Touray, *The African Union*, 180.

Conclusion 161

which they had appealed, in order to deflect the union government proposal. This elevated the institution to an unusually prominent position initially, from which the opposing norm circle would have to work extremely hard to avert the suggested organ.

With the sides deadlocked, the only solution that could be reached was that the PAP be watered down into an advisory body, with reviews to be undertaken later. The contest then resumed right where it had left off at that later date, though the PAP MPs themselves had started to form a core set of actors – a new norm circle, distinct from the member states they originated from – because of their different view of the utility of the institution. This made them firm supporters of strengthening the legislative powers of the PAP, even against the stances of their governments. Up to the present time, however, they have only succeeded in introducing legislative functions for the body, but not any powers, which are reserved in the domain of the Assembly.

Whether this new configuration of democratic actors can reform the institution to promote the norms it was originally intended to promote, I would suggest, will come only if new facts or conditions are able to enter the utility calculus of the opposing norm circle. It will not be a technocratic reform, but a new normative contest. The demise of Gaddafi and retirement of some of the other major actors has not been sufficient to shift national positions, and some may be reverting to statist positions. Thus, when a new contest develops, a significant degree of metis is likely to be needed to effect a change. Regardless of the motivations, the resultant contest will have significant effects on how far one can judge the new AU to have incorporated democratisation within its own workings. As it remains, the elite-driven nature of the AU has not substantially changed, and for all the talk of incorporating the African people into its workings, it failed to substantially do so during the best opportunity it had.

PART III

The Association of Southeast Asian Nations

The support for sovereignty in ASEAN was 'one of the strongest unifying principles among the disparate countries that came together in 1967 to form ASEAN'.[1] As in Africa, colonialism had been considered the most egregious violation of sovereignty and non-interference, and this was a precious right for the newly independent states. With the Cold War providing the general overlay for regional cooperation, ASEAN spent its first three decades as a relatively informal grouping. However, an 'ASEAN Way' developed that established procedural norms out of its practices. Its few established rules committed to non-interference and the upholding of individual member sovereignty, and despite some challenges in the 1990s, remained virtually unchanged until debates began on the creation of an ASEAN Charter in the early 2000s.

The need for an ASEAN Charter had first been discussed in 1974 but ultimately rejected,[2] and it would take thirty years to return to the idea. The Philippines, followed by Malaysia, had been lone voices pushing for a charter in the 1980s and 1990s, but when Singapore came on board in the early 2000s, the critical mass for the charter began to coalesce.[3] Whereas the idea of a formalisation of the grouping had generally been mooted over the years, what changed was the need for legalisation prompted by changes in the 1990s, particularly the EU's institutionalisation and suggestions that the post-Cold War order was going to be organised by regional blocs.

While Southeast Asia did not suffer the kind of insecurity Africa did in the 1990s, it was tumultuous in a different sense. The 1997–8 East Asian financial crisis hit the original ASEAN members particularly hard. Economic instability proved the catalyst in unseating an

[1] Natalegawa, *Does ASEAN Matter? A View from within* (Singapore: ISEAS-Yusof Ishak Institute, 2018), 178.
[2] Woon, *The ASEAN Charter*, 14–19.
[3] Interview with ASEAN official, 9 October 2017.

authoritarian leader such as Indonesia's Suharto, while other ASEAN states faced the financial pains of billions of dollars being withdrawn or wiped from their economies overnight. ASEAN's expansion to include Cambodia, Laos, Myanmar, and Vietnam (collectively known as the 'CLMV' countries) in the 1990s had led to a serious test of its norms, particularly how ASEAN's rigid stance on 'non-interference' could be interpreted and upheld, especially over the entries of Myanmar and Cambodia.[4] These experiences had led Southeast Asian states to take a more qualified view of sovereignty, even if they were still committed to non-interference formally.[5]

By the early 2000s, China was also on the ascent, swallowing the bulk of new foreign direct investment to the region, and its rapid growth was competing with ASEAN just as its economies had begun to recover.[6] Economic integration needed to be accelerated, but this was complicated by ASEAN's recent expansion, which had widened the diversity of economic forms and levels of development within the grouping. It thus became apparent that a legal framework was needed to support ASEAN decisions and conventions and grant the organisation a legal personality.[7] The legal personality in turn would allow it to make multilateral agreements with non-ASEAN states and other multilateral organisations. As early as January 2003, the newly installed Secretary-General, Ong Keng Yong, had been presented with the idea of a charter via senior staff at the Secretariat, and he endorsed it 'enthusiastically'.[8] Because of the development gap between the newer and older members, flexibility was needed for the newer members to come up to speed with ASEAN agreements, yet at the same time, it could not be so flexible that there were no rules at all.[9] This was

---

[4] Acharya, *Constructing a Security Community*, 111–14.
[5] Tan, 'Whither Sovereignty in Southeast Asia Today?' in *Re-Envisioning Sovereignty: the End of Westphalia?*, ed. Jacobsen, Sampford, and Thakur (Aldershot: Ashgate, 2008).
[6] Jones and Smith, 'Making Process, not Progress: ASEAN and the Evolving East Asian Regional Order', *International Security* 32, no. 1 (2007).
[7] Acharya, *Constructing a Security Community*, 234.
[8] Chalermpalanupap, 'In Defence of the ASEAN Charter', in *The Making of the ASEAN Charter*, ed. Koh, Manalo, and Woon (Singapore: World Scientific, 2009), 121.
[9] Koh, Manalo, and Woon, *The Making of the ASEAN Charter* (Singapore: World Scientific, 2009), 85.

essential if ASEAN were to develop a 'community', as suggested in the ASEAN planning documents.

An ASEAN Charter was officially suggested by Malaysia in 2004[10] and then formally accepted in the Vientiane Action Programme (VAP), even though that was only a framework for *economic* integration. Nevertheless, ASEAN then agreed to begin the task of developing a charter at the 2005 Kuala Lumpur Summit. From the initially slow acceptance of the idea, the process moved quickly once the decision was made. An Eminent Persons Group (EPG) was formed to make recommendations for the charter, and their report was endorsed by ASEAN in January 2007. The High Level Task Force (HLTF) on the Drafting of the ASEAN Charter was then formed and it began its work, presenting the charter text by the end of the year, and therefore ready to be adopted at the ASEAN Summit in Singapore in November 2007. The contention over human rights norms would continue, some of the questions having been deferred during the EPG and HLTF processes. Additional committees would eventually determine the scope and functions of a human rights body, eventually forming the ASEAN Intergovernmental Commission on Human Rights (AICHR) in 2009, and the AICHR would be responsible ultimately for the creation of the ASEAN Human Rights Declaration (AHRD) in 2012.

This section looks at the status of human rights in the charter drafting process – where human rights were finally accepted as a normative value in ASEAN – and then the extended process between the formation of the AICHR and the creation of the AHRD – where its scope and applicability were circumscribed to conform with ASEAN procedural norms.

In parallel with these direct questions on the regional grouping's role to limit the sovereign powers of their members on human rights, there was a question about the decision-making process within ASEAN that was called the 'ASEAN minus X' formula. Unlike consensus decision-making, ASEAN had begun to occasionally make decisions without some countries that were unwilling to agree to a particular decision. It was a workaround for pushing through decisions that were deemed necessary by most of the members, but impossible to attain through consensus. As such, it threatened to bypass at least one member's

---

[10] Caballero-Anthony, 'The ASEAN Charter: an Opportunity Missed or One that Cannot be Missed?' *Southeast Asian Affairs* (2008): 71–2.

sovereign interests, and this led to a debate between separate functional groups within governments in contrast with the more ideological divide between liberal and authoritarian states over human rights. The major events of the case study periods are listed in Table III.1.

Table III.1 *Timeline of ASEAN charter processes*

Date	Event	Notable developments
January 1992	4th ASEAN Summit	Framework Agreement on Enhancing ASEAN Economic Cooperation adopted, referring to a '2 plus X' formula
July 1993	26th ASEAN Ministerial Meeting (foreign minister level)	ASEAN commits to respect universal human rights as set out in the Vienna Declaration and Programme of Action, superseding the earlier Bangkok Declaration that had set out an exceptional 'Asian values' position
1995–9		Vietnam, Laos, Myanmar, and Cambodia successively attain ASEAN membership Initiative from human rights groups establishes the Working Group for the Establishment of an ASEAN Human Rights Mechanism
November 2002	8th ASEAN Summit, Phnom Penh, Cambodia	Agreement to develop an 'ASEAN Economic Community' High Level Task Force on Economic Integration appointed
October 2003	9th ASEAN Summit, Bali, Indonesia	Declaration of ASEAN Concord II adopted Agreement to develop an 'ASEAN Community', expanding the earlier Economic Community to include security and socio-cultural dimensions Economic HLTF recommends acceleration of liberalisation using 'ASEAN minus X' formula

Table III.1 (*cont.*)

Date	Event	Notable developments
November 2004	10th ASEAN Summit, Vientiane, Laos	Vientiane Action Programme (VAP) adopted, fleshing out ASEAN's three pillars: economic, political-security, and socio-cultural ASEAN Charter proposed by Malaysia
December 2005	11th ASEAN Summit, Kuala Lumpur, Malaysia	Eminent Persons Group on the ASEAN Charter established
January 2007	12th ASEAN Summit, Mandaue (Cebu), Philippines	EPG Report on the ASEAN Charter presented and endorsed by ASEAN High Level Task Force for the Drafting of the ASEAN Charter established, meeting thirteen times between February and October 2007
November 2007	13th ASEAN Summit, Singapore	ASEAN Charter signed, including provision for an ASEAN human rights body High Level Panel (HLP) on an ASEAN Human Rights Body set up
2008–9		HLP meets eight times to agree the terms of reference for the ASEAN Intergovernmental Commission on Human Rights
October 2009	15th ASEAN Summit, Cha-am and Hua Hin, Thailand	Cha-Am Hua Hin Statement on the Intergovernmental Commission on Human Rights and ToR for AICHR adopted
February 2011		Guidelines on the Operations of AICHR adopted
July 2011		AICHR appoints the Drafting Group on the ASEAN Human Rights Declaration

Table III.1 (*cont.*)

Date	Event	Notable developments
January 2012		AICHR takes over the drafting process from their Drafting Group; drops Drafting Group's text entirely to start afresh; completes final draft by June
November 2012	21st ASEAN Summit, Phnom Penh, Cambodia	ASEAN Human Rights Declaration and Phnom Penh Statement on the AHRD adopted

6 | *Human Rights 'Protection' in the ASEAN Charter*

The Purposes of ASEAN are ... To strengthen democracy, enhance good governance and the rule of law, and to promote and protect human rights and fundamental freedoms, with due regards to the rights and responsibilities of the Member States of ASEAN.

The ASEAN Charter[1]

Introduction

Given ASEAN's motivations for drafting its charter (strengthening economic integration) and having omitted any mention of human rights in regional agreements as recently as the Bali Concord II, it is surprising that human rights were mentioned at all. Furthermore, in both the VAP[2] and the Kuala Lumpur Declaration,[3] the mandate for human rights included only promotion, and not protection, and so the commitment then was weak at best. How then did the *protection* of human rights along with a human rights body also make it into the ASEAN Charter in 2007? And why, contrary to a norm cascade theory, would little further be done to elaborate the regional protection instruments (however weak) following this small victory of sorts?

Diffusion theories, relying on a causal pathway from the EU to ASEAN, inevitably find that they cannot explain behavioural characteristics (i.e. ASEAN states do not tend to behave more like EU states), though at times some institutional isomorphic features are

---

[1] 'Charter of the Association of Southeast Asian Nations', 2007, Art. 1(7).
[2] See Davies, 'Explaining the Vientiane Action Programme: ASEAN and the Institutionalisation of Human Rights', *Pacific Review* 26, no. 4 (2013). However, by his account, the influence of the Track III working group for a human rights mechanism had faded by 2006, as ASEAN governments took control of the process.
[3] ASEAN, '2005 Kuala Lumpur Declaration on the Establishment of the ASEAN Charter' (Kuala Lumpur: ASEAN, 2005).

observed,[4] leaving much of the puzzle unsolved. Realist explanations would look for a coercive mechanism from strong to weak states, but in a situation when every state has a veto, it should predict no change, or no charter. Others have pointed out that these developments counterintuitively occurred at a time when the EU was actually decreasing human rights pressure on ASEAN, having failed to block the entry of Myanmar.[5] Finally, more specific constructivist accounts such as norm localisation would rely on the action of norm entrepreneurs framing an external norm according to local 'cognitive priors', but there are precious few 'cognitive priors' relevant to the elites that one can argue were applicable in this scenario, nor were the key decision-making circles – the Eminent Persons Group (EPG) and High Level Task Force (HLTF) on the ASEAN Charter, and ASEAN Foreign Ministers – 'norm entrepreneurs' in the sense of committed normative agents seeking change.

I argue that the successful approval of the human rights body in the charter comes down to the same dynamics argued throughout this book: the contestation that played out at the regional level, featuring the interplay of utility, norm circles, and power, determined the outcome.

There were two main norm circles that were particularly instrumental at different stages of the process as these provided the genesis of the fundamental characteristics of the body. They were both committed to following the 'ASEAN Way' and included a representative from each member state. First, there was the EPG on the ASEAN Charter, which was established after Kuala Lumpur in 2005 with a mandate to outline the parameters for a charter. Following ASEAN's endorsement of the EPG report on the ASEAN Charter, in January 2007[6] a second group was set up, the High Level Task Force (HLTF) for the Drafting of the

---

[4] See, for example, Jetschke and Murray, 'Diffusing Regional Integration'; Munro, 'The Relationship between the Origins and Regime Design of the ASEAN Intergovernmental Commission on Human Rights (AICHR)', *International Journal of Human Rights* 15, no. 8 (2011). In favour of mimetic adoption is Katsumata, 'Mimetic Adoption and Norm Diffusion: "Western" Security Cooperation in Southeast Asia?', *Review of International Studies* 37, no. 2 (2010). However, this is insufficient to account for the key features of the agreements, according to Davies, 'Explaining the Vientiane Action Programme'.

[5] Davies, 'Explaining the Vientiane Action Programme', 390.

[6] ASEAN, 'Cebu Declaration on the Blueprint of the ASEAN Charter' (Cebu, Philippines: ASEAN Secretariat, 2007).

ASEAN Charter, which was mandated to begin the actual work of drafting. They would then present drafts to be 'ready for signature' at the November 2007 ASEAN Summit in Singapore,[7] or on the fortieth anniversary of ASEAN's founding.

Authoritarian and Liberal Norm Circles

The newly accepted group of CLMV countries (Cambodia, Laos, Myanmar, and Vietnam) were cognisant of human rights pressures on the grouping that had complicated negotiations with the European Union over an ASEAN–EU free trade agreement. The EU had been adamantly opposed to Myanmar, then under international sanctions, joining ASEAN. Conversely, ASEAN was affronted by what it considered undue meddling in its internal affairs, and thus EU pressure may have ironically increased Myanmar's chance of acceptance in the grouping. Cambodia had faced similar difficulties in entering the grouping, owing to Hun Sen's coup against Prince Norodom Rannaridh in 1997 that jeopardised the Paris Peace Agreement. Nevertheless, after considerable debate within ASEAN, it had been accepted in 1999.[8]

Thus, while the CLMV countries were relatively new to the grouping, they were not prepared to allow the goalposts to be shifted such that the grouping would create rules inimical to their national interests.[9] Indeed, for them, the relatively tepid wordings on human rights had far more significance than they did for the other countries, given Myanmar's experience with Western pressure. Nevertheless, some countries such as Vietnam also sought improvement in their human rights standards as part of their efforts to normalise relations with the United States.[10]

The core liberal group of Indonesia, Thailand, and the Philippines had antithetical interests. The Philippines had become a democracy in Southeast Asia following its overthrow of Ferdinand Marcos in a

---

[7] Koh, Manalo, and Woon, *The Making of the ASEAN Charter*, xix.
[8] Acharya, *Constructing a Security Community*, 108–10.
[9] Nguyen, 'The Making of the ASEAN Charter in my Fresh Memories', in *The Making of the ASEAN Charter*, ed. Koh, Manalo, and Woon, 102–3.
[10] Ong, 'ASEAN: Managing Egos and National Interests', in *50 Years of ASEAN and Singapore*, ed. Koh, Seah, and Chang (Hackensack: World Scientific, 2017), 295.

popular revolt in 1986. Thailand, never having been colonised, had a democratic government, though this was complicated by frequent military coups as well as the symbolic but significant authority of the Thai monarchy. Indonesia was the latest to join the fray following the removal of Suharto in 1998. A series of governments later, and having recovered from the worst of the East Asian financial crisis, Indonesia under Susilo Yudhoyono was keen to project a positive international image,[11] taking a proactive stance to promote human rights regionally, despite lingering issues in Timor-Leste, Aceh, and Papua.

Given their fledgling experiences with democracy, these countries were keen to promote a form of democratic lock-in: encouraging and promoting democratisation and liberalisation in the region, particularly through cooperation amongst the national human rights commissions.[12] Prominent civil society groups had arisen among members particularly from this grouping, and sustained human rights considerations in the foreign policy calculus of their respective governments. Chief among these was the Working Group for the Establishment of an ASEAN Human Rights Mechanism. Unlike most civil society organisations or NGOs, this was quasi-governmental at its founding, comprising leaders of human rights commissions or committees from Thailand, the Philippines, and Indonesia. In 2001, it was chaired by Marzuki Darusman, a senior figure in Suharto's Golkar Party, and former attorney-general of Indonesia.

This unusual degree of access also made the Working Group influential in these three countries.[13] However, such influence was contingent on the government's relationship with its human rights commissions: Malaysia, too, had a human rights commission (SUHAKAM), and its members were active in the Working Group. However, the ruling UMNO government, whose leader Mahathir Mohamed had railed against human rights forcefully during the 'Asian values' debate, resisted influence from SUHAKAM,[14] and consequently there was little pressure to support human rights development for the Malaysian representative in the EPG or the HLTF. And whereas formal cooperation between the human rights commissions peaked in

---

[11] Tan, *The ASEAN Intergovernmental Commission on Human Rights*, 87.
[12] Ibid., 193. [13] Davies, 'Explaining the Vientiane Action Programme', 386.
[14] Tan, *The ASEAN Intergovernmental Commission on Human Rights*, 117–18, 201.

2006–7,[15] their influence with ASEAN-level circles had begun to wane by 2006.[16] This interestingly correlated with developments from the ASEAN Charter (under deliberation from 2005 to 2007) through to the terms of reference (ToR) of the ASEAN Intergovernmental Commission on Human Rights (discussed 2007–8) and the ASEAN Human Rights Declaration (discussed 2009–12).

The Eminent Persons Group on the ASEAN Charter

Following Vientiane, the task was now to develop a broad framework in which the future ASEAN Charter would be situated. However, this idea was met sceptically by the CLMV countries. Having joined ASEAN when it was a loose and informal organisation, the timing of the charter and ensuing legalisation was viewed suspiciously, especially if one of the stated goals was for ASEAN's external partners to treat the organisation more seriously: this could be interpreted as an alternative way for the external partners, particularly the EU, to leverage pressure on the grouping over Myanmar, as it had done earlier through the ASEAN–EU free trade agreement. Interim steps were needed to socialise these members and gain their trust through having them participate in the process.[17]

An Eminent Persons Group was therefore formed to study this issue, with representatives from each of the ten member states. It included one former head of state, three deputy prime ministers, and two foreign ministers. (See Table 6.1.) Each was extremely well-versed on their governments' positions and putative national interests. However, officially, they served in their private capacities rather than as representatives of their respective governments to 'enable them to think out of the box and to make radical recommendations on how to strengthen ASEAN and for the Charter'.[18]

The EPG held consultations beyond the member state governments, including the ASEAN Interparliamentary Organisation (AIPO), the Working Group for an ASEAN Human Rights Mechanism, think-tanks, other business and civil society organisations, and at the EU headquarters.

---

[15] Ibid., 193. [16] Davies, 'Explaining the Vientiane Action Programme', 402.
[17] Interview with ASEAN official, 9 October 2017.
[18] Koh, Manalo, and Woon, *The Making of the ASEAN Charter*, 50.

Table 6.1 *Members of the Eminent Persons Group on the ASEAN Charter*

Name	Country	Position or former senior position(s)
Lim Jock Seng	Brunei	Minister of Foreign Affairs and Trade II
Dr Aun Porn Moniroth	Cambodia	Chairman, Supreme National Economic Council of Cambodia
Ali Alatas	Indonesia	Former Minister of Foreign Affairs
Khamphan Simmalavong	Laos	Former Deputy Minister of Commerce
Musa Hitam	Malaysia	Chairman, EPG Former Deputy Prime Minister, Malaysia
Dr Than Nyun	Myanmar	Chairman of the Civil Service Selection and Training Board
Fidel V. Ramos	Philippines	Former President
Prof. S. Jayakumar	Singapore	Deputy Prime Minister, Coordinating Minister for National Security, and Minister for Law
Kasem S. Kasemsri	Thailand	Former Deputy Prime Minister and Minister of Foreign Affairs
Nguyen Manh Cam	Vietnam	Former Deputy Prime Minister and Minister of Foreign Affairs

Source: ASEAN, 'List of Members of the Eminent Persons Group (EPG) on the ASEAN Charter', ASEAN Secretariat, www.asean.org/storage/images/archive/ACP-EPGMember.pdf.

Ali Alatas (Indonesia) suggested that the EPG itself draft the charter (a version of which he produced at the second meeting), but other members disagreed.[19] Fidel Ramos (Philippines) went as far as proposing a full-fledged ASEAN Union, including parliament, legislature, and court, but this did not get much traction.[20] While the EPG report finally contained numerous recommendations designed to strengthen ASEAN unity, some of these were deemed to encroach too far in the direction of a supranational body, and were rejected, particularly

---

[19] Woon, *The ASEAN Charter*, 19.
[20] Jayakumar, *Be at the Table or Be on the Menu: a Singapore Memoir* (Singapore: Straits Times Press, 2015), 90.

mention of potential sanctions against members.[21] Thus the term 'ASEAN Summit' was retained in place of the 'ASEAN Council' (even though their composition and functions were identical), and mention of an 'ASEAN Union' was removed, while the Secretariat was not given as extensive powers as the EPG recommended.[22]

Nevertheless, the EPG's recommendations were not always watered-down: in one key area, human rights, ASEAN would go beyond what they recommended. The EPG report concluded that ASEAN should more forthrightly express its norms in the charter:

> The Charter should include, among ASEAN's objectives, the strengthening of democratic values, ensuring good governance, upholding the rule of law, respect for human rights and international humanitarian law, and achieving sustainable development.[23]

It also mentioned the idea of an actual human rights mechanism that could effect the protection of human rights, but stopped short of explicitly recommending it:

> The EPG discussed the possibility of setting up of an ASEAN human rights mechanism, and noted that this worthy idea should be pursued further, especially in clarifying how such a regional mechanism can contribute to ensuring the respect for and protection of human rights of every individual in every Member State.[24]

If the Philippines, Indonesia, and Thailand were at the forefront of promoting human rights in ASEAN, the delegates they sent to the EPG – Fidel Ramos,[25] Ali Alatas,[26] and Kasem S. Kasemsri[27] – were less beholden to proactive support for human rights and less likely to be influenced by civil society groups, and did not push it. As Termsak Chalermpalanupap recounts, 'The EPG members found the issue too

---

[21] Caballero-Anthony, 'The ASEAN Charter', 74.
[22] Manalo, 'Drafting Asean's Tomorrow: the EPG and the ASEAN Charter', in *The Making of the ASEAN Charter*, ed. Koh, Manalo, and Woon, 44.
[23] ASEAN, *Report of the Eminent Persons Group on the ASEAN Charter*, para. 27.
[24] Ibid., para. 47.   [25] Former President of the Philippines.
[26] Former foreign minister in Suharto's cabinet.
[27] Former deputy prime minister in the transitional government of Anand Panyarachun. Panyarachun took over from a military regime in 1992, and was criticised for failing to investigate human rights abuses of the military.

hot to handle and thus did not attempt to work out any specific recommendation.'[28]

At this stage of the process, the default ASEAN position on human rights – that the subject was less important than non-interference and member sovereignty – thus held, in spite of the EPG's mandate to be 'bold and visionary'.[29] The idea of a protection mechanism was nevertheless pursued by the Philippines, particularly. Gloria Arroyo, then President of the Philippines, urged the ASEAN foreign ministers to establish a human rights body, which then began the debate in the HLTF.[30]

The High Level Task Force for the Drafting of the ASEAN Charter

The process now moved to its most crucial stage, the actual drafting of the charter. Reflecting ASEAN norms, each representative of the HLTF was a senior government official from one member country, though they now had a narrower mandate than that of the EPG, and time was limited if they were to make the deadline of completion before ASEAN's fortieth anniversary.

While the EPG report was endorsed by the ASEAN heads of state in January 2007, the HLTF did not view their task as simply fleshing out the EPG's recommendations. External influence was also limited by design. For example, the HLTF was not required to meet any particular group, though it did so as a courtesy when invited.[31] It was also under the direct supervision of the ASEAN foreign ministers, who met as a group when giving the HLTF instructions and clarifications.[32] The HLTF did not engage the media,[33] and even the liberal members considered them a potential nuisance.[34]

---

[28] Chalermpalanupap, 'In Defence of the ASEAN Charter', 126–7.
[29] ASEAN, *Report of the Eminent Persons Group on the ASEAN Charter*, 2.
[30] Bwa, 'The Jewel in my Crown', in *The Making of the ASEAN Charter*, ed. Koh, Manalo, and Woon, 32.
[31] Koh, Manalo, and Woon, *The Making of the ASEAN Charter*, 50.
[32] Ibid., 51.
[33] Ong, 'At Close Quarters with the Drafting of the ASEAN Charter', in *The Making of the ASEAN Charter*, ed. Koh, Manalo, and Woon, 112.
[34] Pibulsonggram, 'The Thai Perspective', in *The Making of the ASEAN Charter*, ed. Koh, Manalo, and Woon, 86.

Unlike the EPG, which simply dropped discussion of human rights, the HLTF members were not so disposed. The fault lines thus tended to fall along more recognisable normative lines as discussed above: those countries with national human rights commissions (Malaysia, Thailand, the Philippines, and Indonesia) were more forceful in pushing for an ASEAN human rights commission (although Malaysia was the least committed of the four[35]), while the more authoritarian countries (Cambodia, Laos, Myanmar, Vietnam) were against a commission and would only accept a consultative body. Those 'in between' did not have national human rights commissions, though on paper they comprised the absolute monarchy of Brunei (wherein rights are fully derogable in its constitution[36]) and 'soft authoritarian' Singapore, which ex ante normative predictions would have suggested should be against a human rights commission. As it turned out, Singapore played broker between the two norm circles, assisted at times by Brunei.[37]

Moving from the officially endorsed EPG report to the HLTF drafting process should not have raised further contentions, if member states were coherent normative entities. However, the pathways of influence were also different, as the EPG was a relatively closed group, while in the HLTF process, some countries had representatives from civil society organisations involved, while others only had government representatives without external consultations.[38] How each HLTF member interpreted their role and relationship with other actors was determined by their national governments. It implied not only uneven sources of influence, but also uneven degrees of legitimacy.

This therefore made the normative complexion in these new norm circles different (even if the drafters shared some views of their EPG counterparts), which in turn changed the dynamics. The utility of various statements in the EPG report would come to be reassessed, while more precise language in the drafting process began to clarify implications, several of which became apparently unpalatable to different norm circles.

---

[35] Poole, '"The World is Outraged": Legitimacy in the Making of the ASEAN Human Rights Body', *Contemporary Southeast Asia* 37, no. 3 (2015): 361.
[36] Ng, 'The State of Brunei Darussalam', in *Rule of Law for Human Rights in the ASEAN Region: a Base-Line Study*, ed. Cohen, Tan, and Mohan (Jakarta: Human Rights Resource Centre, 2011), 36.
[37] Woon, *The ASEAN Charter*, 139.
[38] Chalermpalanupap, 'In Defence of the ASEAN Charter', 129.

Table 6.2 *Members of the High Level Task Force for the Drafting of the ASEAN Charter*

Name	Country	Position
Osman Patra	Brunei	Permanent Secretary, Ministry of Foreign Affairs and Trade
Dr Kao Kim Hourn	Cambodia	Secretary of State, Ministry of Foreign Affairs and International Cooperation
Dian Triansyah Djani	Indonesia	Director-General, ASEAN–Indonesia Department of Foreign Affairs
Bounkeut Sangsomak	Laos	Deputy Minister of Foreign Affairs
Ahmad Fuzi bin Abdul Razak	Malaysia	Ambassador-at-large, Ministry of Foreign Affairs
U Aung Bwa	Myanmar	Director-General, ASEAN–Myanmar Ministry of Foreign Affairs
Rosario G. Manalo	Philippines	Special Envoy for the Drafting of the ASEAN Charter
Prof. Tommy Koh	Singapore	Ambassador-at-large, Ministry of Foreign Affairs
Prof. Walter Woon		Solicitor-General, Attorney-General's Chambers
Pradap Pibulsonggram	Thailand	Deputy Permanent Secretary, Ministry of Foreign Affairs
Nguyen Trung Thanh	Vietnam	Assistant Minister, Ministry of Foreign Affairs
Pham Quang Vinh		ASEAN SOM Leader, Ministry of Foreign Affairs

Source: Koh, Manalo, and Woon, *The Making of the ASEAN Charter*, 209–10.

On Utility and Norm Circles

Given the governmental composition of the HLTF, some areas of agreement were relatively straightforward, and these were the areas they started working on first.[39] Regardless of the human rights mandate, none of the members were keen for the body to be a 'finger-pointing' instrument (i.e. it would not have an investigative or

---

[39] Nguyen, 'The Making of the ASEAN Charter in my Fresh Memories', 98.

advocacy role), preferring it to have an advisory role.[40] Beyond that, however, contestation was inevitable with such diverse political orientations in the room.

A 'liberal' norm circle comprising Indonesia, Thailand, and the Philippines outlined their interests for a strong human rights mechanism from the outset. For this set of countries, for 'protection' to have any weight, it would have to entail a body capable of acting: presumably with a monitoring role at a minimum (though none was interested in more ambitious institutional features such as a court). What a norm of human rights 'protection' implied was therefore an institutional feature that would be contested amidst various proposals.

Some of this circle stated their interest in normative terms. For Indonesia, the charter had to resonate with its public, meaning that 'the principle of democracy, good governance, fundamental freedoms, rule of law and constitutional government as well as the promotion and protection of human rights, were imperative'.[41] Thailand argued from a more instrumental position that 'the ASEAN Community must not only provide the peoples of ASEAN with the opportunity to prosper, but closer ASEAN integration must also secure an improvement in the quality of life and human security for the ASEAN peoples. Moreover, ASEAN has to give prominence to the promotion of democracy, good governance, human rights and fundamental freedoms as shared values.'[42] Malaysia was not as committed as the others to having a commission, in spite of having its own national human rights commission, occasionally occupying the middle ground.[43]

The CLMV countries, despite their relatively lower levels of economic development and recent entry into ASEAN, were not timid but actively opposed the commission. They would not allow themselves to be coerced into an agreement against their national interests. As Ong relates:

They pushed for their respective formulation of words, cajoled other member states' representatives to accept their concern about the unbridled future direction of ASEAN, and handled the reactions to their negotiation tactics

---

[40] Pibulsonggram, 'The Thai Perspective', 90.
[41] Djani, 'A Long Journey', in *The Making of the ASEAN Charter*, ed. Koh, Manalo, and Woon, 141–2.
[42] Pibulsonggram, 'The Thai Perspective', 84–5.
[43] Koh, Manalo, and Woon, *The Making of the ASEAN Charter*, 58.

in a manner reminiscent of the Ramayana drama on stage: slow and steady, and unyielding on the fundamentals.[44]

Indeed, there was a sense of asymmetry at times, with older ASEAN states having 'to counter the notion of being seen to be too "generous" in conceding to the CLMV states on various critical and sensitive issues in the Charter'.[45] Regardless of other differences in the material 'power' of the various ASEAN member states, within the domain of the HLTF meetings, these were equal and competent representatives, cognisant of their ability to use ASEAN norms and member equality to not be cowed.

The most contentious meetings of the HLTF were the eighth and tenth meetings, where the human rights body was being discussed.[46] At the eighth HLTF meeting, Koh describes the norm circles as divided into three groups: the CLMV states were opposed to the creation of an ASEAN human rights commission, the Philippines, Indonesia, and Thailand were in favour, and the remainder 'occupied the middle ground'. A compromise text stating that a human rights body would be established 'at a time acceptable to all ASEAN member states' was adopted at the meeting, but then promptly rejected by the governments of the Philippines, Indonesia, Malaysia, and Singapore. The Philippines proposed to establish the commission on an 'ASEAN minus X' formula (allowing other members to join when they were ready), which was supported by Indonesia, Malaysia, and Thailand, but rejected by the CLMV countries. Here Koh states that ASEAN Secretary-General Ong Keng Yong 'saved the day' by putting forward an 'innocuous text' indicating the members would 'cooperate to establish an ASEAN human rights body'.[47]

The preceding dispute subsequently resulted in the clarification that the 'ASEAN minus X' principle applied only to economic matters (and not social or political norms), according to the HLTF's Second Meeting with Foreign Ministers.[48] That meeting also decided that a human rights body would indeed be established under the charter,

---

[44] Ong, 'At Close Quarters with the Drafting of the ASEAN Charter', 113.
[45] Abdul Razak, 'Facing Unfair Criticisms', in *The Making of the ASEAN Charter*, ed. Koh, Manalo, and Woon, 21.
[46] Woon, *The ASEAN Charter*, 25–6.
[47] Koh, Manalo, and Woon, *The Making of the ASEAN Charter*, 59.
[48] Ibid., 60.

against the CLMV HLTF members' earlier opposition. The battle would then move to its functions.

The tenth HLTF meeting, which returned to the subject of human rights, 'proved to be the most contentious'.[49] In Koh's account, disagreements continued over (1) the function of the human rights body, (2) whether the HLTF was to draft the human rights body's terms of reference (ToR), and (3) whether it should be completed before the signing of the charter.[50] The CLMV grouping was adamant that the HLTF should finish the terms of reference alongside the charter, but that body would only have consultative status. Opposing them, Indonesia, Malaysia, the Philippines, and Thailand argued that the ToR were not in the HLTF's mandate, although Manalo (Philippines) argued that the body's function and powers should include monitoring.

The following day, the two factions occupied separate floors of their hotel, with the CLMV in one, and Indonesia, Malaysia, the Philippines, Thailand, and newly added Brunei in the other, with Singapore as go-between.[51] Finally, the compromise text deferred the question on the ToR to the ASEAN foreign ministers, and also tasked the ASEAN Secretariat to hold an informal discussion on the elements for inclusion in the ToR, in order to update its non-paper on the subject.[52] Ultimately, the ASEAN foreign ministers agreed that the ToR need not be resolved before the signing of the charter,[53] deferring that argument to a future high level panel (see Chapter 7).

These episodes plainly demonstrate the function of perceived utility in dividing groups into opposing norm circles. To tip the balance for consensus, 'innocuous' wording that widened the perceived utility (or else appeared less threatening to national interests) was necessary to gain agreement. When functions were specified (e.g. a 'monitoring' function for the human rights body), these were plainly rejected. Pressure from the outside (particularly from human rights groups)

---

[49] Woon, *The ASEAN Charter*, 26.
[50] Koh, Manalo, and Woon, *The Making of the ASEAN Charter*, 62.
[51] Singapore had taken over the chair from the Philippines, but Singapore's attempt to separate the chair (Tommy Koh) from the national representative (Walter Woon) was apparently unsuccessful as both of them eventually shuttled between the two norm circles. They were also supported in part by Brunei. See Woon, *The ASEAN Charter*, 139.
[52] Koh, Manalo, and Woon, *The Making of the ASEAN Charter*, 62-3.
[53] Woon, *The ASEAN Charter*, 139.

was such that the HLTF realised 'that the inclusion or otherwise of a reference to an ASEAN Human Rights mechanism was looked upon as a measure of the relevance and significance of the Charter itself'.[54]

Yet contestation only applied in the specific circumstances of this domain: the norm circles within the HLTF, interacting with that of their foreign ministers (who might be able to resolve an impasse). Moving back to the heads of state could also entail a resumption of contestation.

Controlling the Initiative

In contrast to the much more combative struggle over the initiative as witnessed in the AU over the 'US of Africa', in this process, the initiative was largely constrained by time, and during the key disputes, managed by a relatively neutral actor, Singapore. The Philippines had originally begun the process, as Philippines President Gloria Arroyo had initiated calling for a provision for a human rights commission as an ASEAN organ, which ASEAN leaders instructed the HLTF to draft for their examination in March 2007 at their first meeting.[55] The Philippine HLTF representative, Rosario Manalo, was the first chair. While Manalo was commonly referred to as the 'Iron Lady', she was considerably invested in the process and said to have let emotion get the better of her at times.[56] Moreover, as chair she was sometimes required to take a neutral position, and was frequently asked whether she was saying things in her role as chair or as Philippines representative. The 'chair' role may have hobbled her ability to push certain ideas, a complication Singapore was aware of: they later sent two representatives – one to hold the chair and the other to argue the country position where applicable.[57]

Between the first HLTF meeting in February 2007 and the last one in October 2007, it was always apparent to the HLTF members that time was short, and that agreements over quite fundamental areas would need to be resolved in some form. Each HLTF member took turns hosting meetings, and the 'informal' approach favoured by the 'ASEAN Way' was used throughout.[58]

[54] Abdul Razak, 'Facing Unfair Criticisms', 21.
[55] Koh, Manalo, and Woon, *The Making of the ASEAN Charter*, 54.
[56] Ibid., 63.   [57] Interview with ASEAN official, 30 August 2017.
[58] Bwa, 'The Jewel in my Crown', 34.

The HLTF for Drafting the ASEAN Charter

The guiding principles for approaching the charter were themselves debated, but it was agreed that it should be visionary, brief, but comprehensive, an 'enabling instrument of ASEAN that will be used in a legal framework', and be both 'flexible' and 'enduring'.[59] This was in accordance with the original goal for the charter to support ASEAN community-building and integration. The nine principles were accepted and provided working guidelines on which the HLTF members based their deliberations.[60]

On the final day of the thirteenth and final HLTF meeting, with time severely constrained, the drafters adopted a new ground rule that any single objection would lead to the HLTF dropping the idea.[61] The need to complete the draft by 22 October 2007 in time for the presentation to the Thai cabinet, before impending Thai elections in December, meant this was a hard deadline that could otherwise thwart the completion of the drafting. This accelerated the process, but also prevented cleaning up the draft charter for repetition and awkward phrasing.[62]

The Philippines began the process, and the chair was passed to Singapore after the eighth meeting, which covered the most crucial meetings regarding the potential functions of the human rights body. Singapore, a relatively neutral actor, then controlled the initiative at the crucial stages, acting as a go-between during the most polarised stages of the process. Perhaps learning from the Philippines' experience, Tommy Koh brought in the Solicitor-General Walter Woon to take the national position for Singapore, so that he could maintain a neutral position. As it was, neither of the norm circles could wholly control the initiative in the process, while consensus requirements made it impossible to move ahead without others on board.

Shared Norms

Virtually all the shared norms involved in the process were found in the 'ASEAN Way': informality, respect for sovereignty, and the need for consensus. These norms were procedural (informality and consensus-building) or ambiguous (i.e. respect for sovereignty), and thus offered few normative guidelines as to how to proceed on human rights. There

---

[59] Nguyen, 'The Making of the ASEAN Charter in my Fresh Memories', 98.
[60] Ibid.   [61] Koh, Manalo, and Woon, *The Making of the ASEAN Charter*, 65.
[62] Woon, *The ASEAN Charter*, 21.

was little in the ASEAN Way that indicated any promotion of human rights, and indeed part of the role of the ASEAN Charter was to depart from strict informality to develop a more rules-based organisation. While various members enunciate several rights in their respective constitutions, there is no consistent trend or universal commitment across all members.[63] However, all the member states had at least signed the Convention on the Rights of the Child (CRC) and the Convention on the Elimination of All Forms of Discrimination against Women (CEDAW), but a general human rights stance had to go beyond such a narrow set of norms.

The EPG had also avoided the discussion of human rights, albeit mentioning it as a 'worthy idea'.[64] There was thus little leverage either side could obtain in exploiting cognitive priors or shared norms. As Abdul Razak recounts, 'Persuasion and the power of arguments were recognised as the basis for compromise and final agreement.'[65] Despite this, deadlocks required three meetings with their foreign ministers to resolve multiple core issues relating to the function of the human rights body.

There were few agreed ASEAN norms on human rights to draw upon at this point to use as reference. The NGO Working Group had compiled a book on all ASEAN statements from the official records (e.g. summits, communiqués, reports, etc.) that referred to human rights and might imply what positions had been taken in ASEAN.[66] However, none was binding, few mentioned human rights directly (these had to be inferred), and there was no commentary that might provide guidance as to how ASEAN could proceed or build upon whatever putative precedents these statements provided.

Conversely, the CLMV members of either task force could not claim authority from ASEAN norms, which had no positions on authoritarian predilections. While the CLMV states had a common position,

---

[63] Wahyuningrum, *The ASEAN Intergovernmental Commission on Human Rights: Origins, Evolution and the Way Forward* (Stockholm: International IDEA, 2014), 7–10.
[64] ASEAN, *Report of the Eminent Persons Group on the ASEAN Charter*, para. 47.
[65] Abdul Razak, 'Facing Unfair Criticisms', 20.
[66] Working Group for an ASEAN Human Rights Mechanism, *ASEAN and Human Rights: a Compilation of ASEAN Statements on Human Rights* (Makati City, Philippines: Working Group for an ASEAN Human Rights Mechanism, 2003).

The HLTF for Drafting the ASEAN Charter

these were viewed as shared national positions, rather than having any precedence in ASEAN norms. They were also the youngest members of ASEAN, and just taking a unified, proactive stance was unusual for the grouping at that point in time.[67] As Nguyen, the Vietnam representative of the HLTF recounted, 'There were three bases for the HLTF to work on, namely the ASEAN Leaders' instructions, the EPG Report and relevant ASEAN Documents, but these were too broad to build on.'[68] In these uncharted waters, neither side had much basis to leverage against the other.

Metis

Perhaps the most contentious question was that of whether to have the body mentioned in the charter or not. The deadlock within the HLTF could not be resolved amongst themselves, so this had to be referred to the ASEAN foreign ministers. As Tommy Koh recounts:

> The ministers met by themselves, without their staffers. Only the chairman of HLTF and the ASEAN Secretary-General were present. When the meeting was over, the Secretary-General provided the HLTF with a summary of the ministers' decisions. The decision to establish an ASEAN human rights body was greeted by some of my colleagues with disbelief. I remember that my colleague from Vietnam demanded to see his minister. Ong Keng Yong had the unpleasant duty of informing us that our ministers did not want to see any of us![69]

Within the closed doors of the foreign ministers' meeting, it was not possible for the HLTF to predict what the outcome would be. However, the dynamics between the two sets of competing norm circles were different and, cognisant of certain bottom lines by the respective governments, it may have been possible to establish what the outcome would be, and then seek an authoritative decision that could not be disputed, rather than attempt to come up with a weak decision within the grouping that would then be scrutinised by the higher-level meeting. ASEAN foreign ministers were less likely to have

---

[67] Ong, 'At Close Quarters with the Drafting of the ASEAN Charter', 113.
[68] Nguyen, 'The Making of the ASEAN Charter in my Fresh Memories', 97.
[69] Koh, 'The ASEAN Charter at 10: Prospects and Retrospect', *Myanmar Times* (Yangon, 2017).

big debates as implementation did not concern them[70] – this was handled at the Senior Officials Meeting (SOM), a level below them.

Given the closed nature of the HLTF, with consensus-based decision-making in ASEAN that granted equal structural power, exerting additional influence above their internal debates was difficult. Part of the unintended consequence of being so well socialised with one another was that they were familiar with any attempts to wield undue influence.[71] As one HLTF member put it,

> Members of the HLTF took great pains to preserve the principle of equality within ASEAN in the course of tediously negotiating the 55 articles contained in the Charter. No undue pressure of one or more states by other member states was tolerated. ... The absence of 'undue pressure' did not mean the complete absence of 'threats' exhibited by some members from time to time.[72]

Aware of the need for consensus, it was possible for any single actor to stall the process. However, there were social pressures not to do so, because that would then turn that actor into playing a 'dominant role', which was not encouraged.[73] The ASEAN Secretary-General Ong lamented the Indonesian and Philippine delegates' 'unrestrained ways', which may have worked against them when it came to persuasion.[74]

Accounts vary but are surprisingly frank in their description of the means by which deadlocked situations were addressed. Attempts were made at various points to use 'spa diplomacy',[75] wherein delegates were treated to extensive hospitality by various hosts so as to make consensus easier to reach. However, it did not appear to have any effect on the ability of representatives to stand by their national positions,[76] though it did contribute to the informality. As Koh describes, following the dispute in the tenth HLTF meeting:

> In the hope of breaking the impasse, the Chair [i.e. Koh himself] organised a working dinner ... hoping that colleagues would feel more relaxed in a

---

[70] Interview with ASEAN official, 14 November 2017.
[71] For example, Bwa, 'The Jewel in my Crown', 33; Ong, 'At Close Quarters with the Drafting of the ASEAN Charter'.
[72] Abdul Razak, 'Facing Unfair Criticisms', 20, 21.   [73] Ibid., 20.
[74] Ong, 'ASEAN: Managing Egos and National Interests', 295.
[75] Bwa, 'The Jewel in my Crown', 34.
[76] Pibulsonggram, 'The Thai Perspective', 88.

dinner setting. This was not the case. Strong words were exchanged, with one colleague threatening to pack his bag and go home.[77]

In this close-knit environment, there were occasional threats to walk out (which would have stalled discussion), but there was a social cost to doing so. Ultimately, referral to ASEAN leaders or foreign ministers was used to break deadlocks, but because these were in themselves further discussions between the ASEAN member states at a higher level, neither side could use the method with certainty that it would be to their advantage.

Ratification

As can be seen from the differences between the EPG report and the final ASEAN Charter,[78] the two groups differed on several key respects. Moreover, while the original impetus for the charter was to deepen economic integration (as stated in the VAP), for unrelated reasons (perhaps 'domestic reasons', per Koh[79]), the HLTF rebuffed approaches from a separate possible source of influence, the ASEAN Economic Ministers. Surprisingly, the group with the wider mandate (the EPG) failed to support human rights, while the group with the narrower mandate (the HLTF) under close supervision did ultimately effect it.

Finally, the ASEAN Charter emerged by 2007, stating that the purpose of ASEAN, inter alia, is 'to promote and protect human rights and fundamental freedoms' (Art. 1(7)). It is again repeated in Art. 2(2)(i) that ASEAN members shall act in accordance with 'respect for fundamental freedoms, the promotion and protection of human rights, and the promotion of social justice'. As Woon describes, 'The constant repetition of these themes may not be elegant drafting but it was a conscious decision on the part of the HLTF to do so.'[80] At this stage, while the ToR for a future human rights body were yet to be determined, both promotion and protection were reiterated twice, intended as a strong signal to the future High Level Panel (HLP) working on the ToR for the AICHR on what might be included.

The argument that appears to have swayed the CLMV circle comes from the Vietnamese account: 'A common understanding was agreed

---

[77] Koh, Manalo, and Woon, *The Making of the ASEAN Charter*, 63.
[78] Ibid., 11.   [79] Ibid., 65.   [80] Woon, *The ASEAN Charter*, 37.

that ASEAN needs to establish its own standards of human rights protection and promotion, and that human rights should not be left as an excuse for outsiders to intervene into ASEAN's own affairs.'[81] This is a utility argument, not a normative one, in that it appeals to the self-interest of the sceptical countries without requiring normative buy-in. With all the contestation, Chalermpalanupap's summation was clear: 'The Charter is certainly imperfect. None of the drafters is completely satisfied with the outcome. Anything done by consensus would certainly not be the most desirable. But this is how ASEAN keeps every member state on board, moving together at a pace comfortable to all.'[82]

An ASEAN Charter was not a new idea,[83] but it had been rejected in a much earlier round of debates in the 1970s, as it was considered then to violate the informal and flexible approach favoured by the grouping. At that time, the agreement reached was simply the Treaty of Amity and Cooperation (TAC) and the Declaration of ASEAN Concord I (Bali Concord I) both in 1976, rather than a formal charter. The perceived utility of a charter was much stronger when it was reproposed by Malaysia, in the light of discussions about how to forge the ASEAN community, but even then it still faced opposition.[84] As Ong Keng Yong, the ASEAN Secretary-General at the time of the drafting of the charter, described it: 'The decisive moment of action came when the forces of globalisation eroded the competitive edge of the ASEAN economies and weakened ASEAN's ability to remain centre-stage of regional affairs and development.'[85] This imperative was still broad, but it did require ASEAN to have a holding position on several norms, especially with respect to human rights. Whereas the general need for a charter was agreed, contestation around the extent of human rights protection was the most contentious area. Here, with an ambiguous conception of protection, the pro-human rights norm circle narrowly managed to edge out their authoritarian opponents.

Even with adoption, the contestation was not over. As Tan recounts, when Myanmar presented its instrument of ratification in July 2008, it qualified it with a statement that there could be no interference in the internal affairs of member states by the yet-to-be-established human

---

[81] Nguyen, 'The Making of the ASEAN Charter in my Fresh Memories', 103.
[82] Chalermpalanupap, 'In Defence of the ASEAN Charter', 128. [83] Ibid., 119.
[84] Desker, 'Is the ASEAN Charter Necessary?', *RSIS Commentaries* 77 (2008).
[85] Ong, 'At Close Quarters with the Drafting of the ASEAN Charter', 108.

rights body. At the opposite end, the Philippines had threatened not to ratify the charter until Aung San Suu Kyi was released, though it eventually did so on 7 October 2008. The counter-argument made was that it could not hold Myanmar to an 'ASEAN standard' until the charter was ratified and therefore constituted as an ASEAN standard.[86] Indonesia, likewise, protested that the human rights body would be ineffectual, and institutionalisation of human rights had to be strengthened. However, it too finally ratified the charter on 21 October 2008.[87]

Conclusion

What was agreed was not a new normative stance for ASEAN; rather 'they negotiated and agreed upon a normative *statement*, in an environment of normative contestation'.[88] The actors in the EPG and HLTF were all familiar with one another, and this perhaps negated any attempts to spring surprises. Deadlocks were frequent and relied on referrals to the foreign ministers to be resolved.

This was a victory for getting human rights supported by official ASEAN agreements for the first time, but a narrow victory. It only narrowly avoids classification as a 'qualified' success because the norms *inferred* were not changed, even though a compliance mechanism could not be included. Bound by ASEAN norms, neither of the norm circles had decisively wielded the initiative, been able to identify 'shared' norms with which to frame their position, or been able to use other assets for influence. Utility then proved to be the only separating factor, which required a very ambiguous commitment to tip the norm circles in favour.

As Tommy Koh, the chairperson of the charter drafting team pointed out, it was a 'miracle' that ASEAN even got a human rights body, as only four of the ten members had national human rights commissions at the time, and this in effect was a case of the minority (of four) leading the majority (of six).[89] The hopes for a stronger

---

[86] Yeo, 'Remarks by Minister for Foreign Affairs George Yeo and his Reply to Supplementary Questions in Parliament during Cos Debate (MFA) on 28 February 2008' (Singapore: Ministry of Foreign Affairs, 2008).
[87] Tan, *The ASEAN Intergovernmental Commission on Human Rights*, 156–7.
[88] Poole, 'The World is Outraged', 360, emphasis in the original.
[89] Koh, 'The ASEAN Charter at 10: Prospects and Retrospect'.

human rights body would have to be deferred to the next round of debate over the terms of reference, but at least ASEAN had now stated its position in favour of both promotion *and* protection of human rights, and at least there would be a human rights body rather than none at all. As it stands, the charter is open to amendments under Art. 48, but this option has not been exercised since.

In this case study, the utility of the 'human rights body' was ambiguous enough to avoid objection from member states, but attempts to specify it further (to a 'commission', with monitoring powers) were rejected. When the next round of debate took place (on the terms of reference for the ASEAN human rights mechanism, which eventually became the ASEAN Intergovernmental Commission for Human Rights), featuring different levels of each variable, the 'protection' element could not be successfully introduced. The analysis of the case and key factors is summarised in Table 6.3.

In this instance, the norm circles did not always feature states, but eminent groups and individuals, who behaved in ways that are not reducible to the states they represented. Indeed, their dynamics featured norm circles within norm circles, having the hallmarks of the state preferences which they represented, yet bearing emergent properties from their personal interactions with one another and their mandates to be 'bold and visionary',[90] as well as the drive towards consensus. Each circle would then interact with its own member states' political leaders, resulting in the formation of the ASEAN Charter. Unlike in liberal democracies, wider civil society had little impact on ASEAN decision-making.[91] However, unlike the OAU, where singular leaders dominated their foreign policy interactions, bureaucracies in ASEAN were more influential than individuals in setting foreign policy.

The ASEAN Secretary-General Ong Keng Yong, who acted as a resource person for both the EPG and HLTF, reflected:

We were told to honour the past (in other words, not to forget those time-tested principles and norms used by ASEAN to date), celebrate the present (that is, implement those activities and programmes already agreed to in various agreements and treaties), and innovate for the future (meaning to introduce new ideas and mechanism to institutionalise and modernise

---

[90] ASEAN, *Report of the Eminent Persons Group on the ASEAN Charter*, 2.
[91] Collins, 'A People-Oriented ASEAN: a Door Ajar or Closed for Civil Society Organizations?' *Contemporary Southeast Asia* 30, no. 2 (2008).

Table 6.3 *Human rights 'protection' in the ASEAN Charter*

Factors	Proposing norm circle	Opposing norm circle
Members	Indonesia, Philippines, Thailand, Malaysia	Cambodia, Laos, Myanmar, Vietnam
Control of initiative	• Philippines (Arroyo) had decided human rights must be part of new charter • Philippines initial chairmanship	• Delaying tactics • Lack of time for new amendments
Norms invoked	• Universal Declaration of Human Rights • Vienna Declaration • Convention on the Rights of the Child (CRC) and Convention on the Elimination of All Forms of Discrimination against Women (CEDAW)	• Non-interference, sovereignty • 'ASEAN Way': informality, pragmatism, consultation, and consensus
Metis	• Foreign ministers' decision to create an ASEAN human rights body (AHRB) • 'Spa diplomacy'	• Threats to walk out
Outcome	Accepted	

ASEAN). Our assignment was to do all that without upsetting the balance ASEAN has constructed to take care of the multitudes of national interests and sensitivities. This is notwithstanding the [EPG report] wherein sacred cows, like the principle of non-interference in domestic affairs, were qualified. The EPG Report provided the starting point for the drafting of the Charter. At the same time, it was a constant source of dilemma. What the EPG recommended was not what [the HLTF] could include in the ASEAN Charter without contention. When the HLTF members debated those issues, more questions and even outright reservations on what should go into the Charter arose.[92]

---

[92] Ong, 'At Close Quarters with the Drafting of the ASEAN Charter', 110.

One way to read this statement is to map it on to the variables used in this model. The 'multitudes of national interests and sensitivities' are good proxies for the imagined and proximal norm circles[93] that HLTF members were working from, based on utility estimations. The shared norms are explicitly invoked as 'time-tested principles' and 'activities and programmes already agreed' in ASEAN. And contestation is fundamental in the interaction of all these factors, which Ong describes as the reopening of 'contention' and 'outright reservations'.

This case study has shown how the interplay between interests and practices such as leading the initiative, using shared norms, and using external sources of influence were key factors in explaining the insertion of human rights promotion and protection into the ASEAN Charter. The EPG recommendations on a human rights protection mechanism were more limited than what was introduced in the eventual ASEAN Charter, drafted by the HLTF. This may in part be explained by a heavier emphasis on reaching consensus without hard national positions drawn out, and overt contestation was avoided.

For the HLTF, however, there was more overt contestation. The Philippines controlled the initiative initially, being determined that human rights would be part of the charter's values. Initially the chair, Rosario Manalo, the Philippines' representative on the HLTF, was the only outright human rights advocate, and extremely experienced in the drafting of human rights legislation. However, the process then moved to a very tight deadline, and the Philippines gave up the chair at the eighth meeting, before the most heated debates occurred. Having put the notion of human rights on the table, it became impossible to avoid it thereafter, even as the opposing norm circle sought to downplay the significance and refused to accept a substantive protection mechanism, at least in the charter.

The 'ASEAN Way' of consensual decision-making neutralised a lot of potential power differentials, requiring the actors to reach compromises on situations or else seek referrals from the foreign ministers, who also met and decided by consensus. The liberal circle could not appeal to external human rights conventions as sources of legitimacy: in both the EPG and HLTF, they downplayed visits to Europe, and arguably, alluding to European values would have

---

[93] See the discussion in Elder-Vass, *The Causal Power of Social Structures*, chapter 2.

been counter-productive for the liberal norm circle. Instead, they had to argue for human rights in an instrumentalist fashion, i.e. that this was good for the countries opposed to it, because they could not find other shared values to appeal to in support of human rights, when ASEAN had never explicitly taken a formal stance on human rights.

Finally, the ability to identify opportunities for further influence were limited. 'Spa diplomacy' was geared towards getting actors to reach consensus positions, but it did not successfully change any actors' national positions, or reconfigure the norm circles. Materialist accounts would have great difficulty explaining any of these features at all, given the strict structural equality imposed within ASEAN, and the at-best equal division of states on the matter, particularly with the need for consensus to obtain results. Arguably, they would simply point out that none of this really mattered at all, since nothing was binding and nothing tangible was at stake. But this would beg several questions and ignore the path dependency created that would lead to the next two cases, involving more negotiating and increasing the constitutive potential of the norms in question for ASEAN's future identity as an organisation.

Constructivist accounts of a norm cascade that might follow would probably be rather disappointed with the tepid increments that did eventually occur. This stage would be classed as stage 3 of the cascade, a tactical concession,[94] which under their model, reduces the room for manoeuvre of human-rights violating regimes, but there is no evidence ten years later that ASEAN's decision to institute human rights as a shared value in its charter changed any of these states' behaviours substantively. Furthermore, such normative changes are expected to eventually empower transnational advocacy networks, yet ASEAN's decision-making structures remain remote from activists. Thus, the practice of diplomacy in the region continued to hold far greater influence on normative outcomes than ideational factors or even growing interdependence, and the cascade, if it exists at all, is at best a trickle.

---

[94] Risse, Ropp, and Sikkink, *The Power of Human Rights*, 20.

7 | The ASEAN Human Rights Mechanism

The Foreign Ministers reviewed with satisfaction the considerable and continuing progress of ASEAN in freeing its peoples from fear and want, enabling them to live in dignity ... In this regard, and in support of the Vienna Declaration and Programme of Action of 25 June 1993, they agreed that ASEAN should also consider the establishment of an appropriate regional mechanism on human rights.

ASEAN Foreign Ministers Joint Communiqué, 1993[1]

Introduction

The failure to reach consensus in the charter drafting process meant that the contestation over human rights would continue into the next phase of negotiation. While it was agreed that the terms of reference (ToR) for the as-yet unnamed 'ASEAN human rights body' (AHRB) could take place after the drafting of the charter, the boundaries had already been established for the contest, given the debate over the functions of the body within the relatively broad notions of 'promotion' and 'protection' of human rights.

With the acknowledgement that human rights were a value of ASEAN, the next question was the degree to which ASEAN was prepared to institutionalise human rights principles into its structures. This chapter follows the process from the discussion of the establishment of an ASEAN human rights mechanism. This involved two integral components: the AHRB, which would be the implementing body in ASEAN, and the planned ASEAN Human Rights Declaration (AHRD), which would outline the norms guiding ASEAN, and through which the AHRB would operate. The AHRB would also

---

[1] ASEAN, 'Joint Communique of the 26th ASEAN Ministerial Meeting, Singapore, 23–24 July 1993' (Singapore: ASEAN Secretariat, 1993).

Introduction

initially be responsible for coming up with the declaration, even though the charter left unresolved what the nature of this body would be.

This chapter therefore traces the two phases, each of which involved contestation. First, there was the negotiation over the ToR of the human rights body, including the designation of its name as the 'ASEAN Intergovernmental Commission on Human Rights' (AICHR), which had been a residual conflict from the charter debate. The eventual ToR would be released alongside a political statement, the Cha-Am Hua Hin Declaration on the Intergovernmental Commission on Human Rights (hereafter the Cha-Am Hua Hin Declaration). This chapter then turns to the drafting process of the AHRD, which also came out alongside its own political statement, the Phnom Penh Statement on the Adoption of the ASEAN Human Rights Declaration (hereafter the Phnom Penh Statement). In both cases the political declarations were the result of the contestation, and an attempt to ensure there was no dilution of international human rights norms, having made concessions on the texts to assuage the opposing norm circle. I treat the two together as a single case because the body and its guiding norms together constitute a single 'mechanism' by which regional cooperation around human rights could be endorsed and enacted.

The accompanying political statements with clarificatory remarks in both cases illustrate the qualified nature of the results, which meant no side could successfully claim to have achieved their goals of unambiguously asserting their desired norms in the process. However, these processes were marked by considerable secrecy, even by ASEAN standards, and very little has been written about the actual process,[2] nor are ASEAN records open for public perusal. This chapter is therefore more reliant on interviews with officials in ASEAN who were first-hand witnesses and participants in the process. All claims were triangulated with at least one or more other source before being used. ASEAN also

---

[2] None of the accounts of the formation of the AICHR cover the negotiation process in detail. See Tan, *The ASEAN Intergovernmental Commission on Human Rights*; Munro, 'The Origins and Regime Design of AICHR'; Asplund, 'ASEAN Intergovernmental Commission on Human Rights: Civil Society Organizations' Limited Influence on ASEAN', *Journal of Asian Public Policy* 7, no. 2 (2014); Ryu and Ortuoste, 'Democratization, Regional Integration, and Human Rights: the Case of the ASEAN Intergovernmental Commission on Human Rights', *Pacific Review* 27, no. 3 (2014).

operates with a much smaller bureaucracy than other ROs, revolving around intergovernmental meetings, and as such, fewer officials took part in these processes, even as the weight of their statements and actions was consequently higher.

The ToR was a negotiated compromise. First, ASEAN did create a 'commission' analogous to the national human rights commissions in several of its member states. The issue had been too contentious for both the EPG and HLTF (see previous chapter), in which even naming the body a 'commission' had been disputed during the charter process. Second, it was not granted monitoring or investigative powers, though an unspecified notion of 'protection' was included in its mandate; how 'protection' would be instituted was left for the AICHR to determine. Third, it was created with an intergovernmental structure, following ASEAN norms of a government-appointed representative for each member state. If human rights are a check on sovereignty and the extent of the powers of the state, an intergovernmental commission was unlikely to promote such a function as intergovernmentalism preserves sovereign authority within their respective territories.

On the AHRD, ASEAN was divided on several fronts as well. First, it was committed to a human rights declaration, but attempts were made to insert 'duties' and 'obligations' by the authoritarian norm circle, as well as appeals to regional 'particularities'. The declaration was in such a state of compromise that at the eleventh hour, the Philippines and Indonesia threatened to walk out on it. In the end, the Phnom Penh Declaration was appended to its release, reasserting ASEAN's commitment to universal values of human rights and committing itself that nothing in the AHRD would go below existing international standards. While human rights groups condemned it, it was undeniable that ASEAN now had a set of human rights standards that had achieved buy-in from all member states.[3] This represented progress for ASEAN, given its consensus principle which results in lowest common denominator norms and the fact that several ASEAN member states had no human rights protections in their national laws.[4]

---

[3] Ng, 'ASEAN Human Rights Declaration: a Pragmatic Compromise', *RSIS Commentaries* 211 (2012).

[4] Ng, 'The ASEAN Human Rights Declaration: Establishing a Common Framework'.

Establishing the AICHR

A regional human rights body had been discussed as far back as 1993 during the debates around the Bangkok and Vienna declarations on human rights.[5] Then comprising only six members,[6] it was felt at the time that ASEAN could go forward with establishing the body. Although there had been long discussions leading up to the Bangkok Declaration, the ASEAN foreign ministers' joint communiqué of the July 1993 summit stated that ASEAN was committed to respect human rights as set out in the Vienna Declaration, and that 'human rights are interrelated and indivisible comprising civil, political, economic, social and cultural rights. These rights are of equal importance.'[7]

However, the entry of Vietnam into the grouping in 1995 and the difficulty in bringing it up to speed with the various ASEAN trade agreements left the idea of a human rights body forgotten.[8] Gradually, the decade following that witnessed a softening on the stance towards human rights, notably with the Thai Foreign Minister Surin Pitsuwan trying to encourage the grouping towards a more 'flexible engagement' with countries having poor human rights records.[9] Civil society advocates for a human rights body tried especially in the 2000s to frame it as consistent with existing ASEAN norms, giving it the independent capacity to investigate its own human rights issues and therefore preclude external interference.[10]

The contest over the implications in the charter had shown that various states' red lines were still difficult to budge. As the previous chapter shows, while human rights 'promotion and protection' were included in the charter, the HLTF could not agree on what that meant in the tight one-year timeframe they had to complete the draft. The 'liberal' norm circle of Indonesia, Thailand, and the Philippines, together with Malaysia, which had a national human rights commission, had argued that the body should include a monitoring function,

---

[5] ASEAN, 'Joint Communiqué of the 26th ASEAN Ministerial Meeting, Singapore, 23–24 July 1993'; Tan, *The ASEAN Intergovernmental Commission on Human Rights*, 151.
[6] Brunei, Indonesia, Malaysia, Philippines, Singapore, and Thailand.
[7] ASEAN, 'Joint Communiqué of the 26th ASEAN Ministerial Meeting, Singapore, 23–24 July 1993'.
[8] Interview with ASEAN official, 14 November 2017.
[9] Acharya, *Constructing a Security Community*, 176–7.
[10] Munro, 'The Origins and Regime Design of AICHR', 1197.

after conceding that its ToR could not be included in the charter.[11] This was therefore left to the next round of debate, with the High Level Panel on the Terms of Reference for an ASEAN Human Rights Body[12] (HLP on the ToR for an AHRB) established to discuss the scope and mandate of this new regional institution.

Hassan Wirajuda, the Indonesian foreign minister from 2001 to 2009, had also been responsible for setting up Indonesia's national human rights commission, Komnas-HAM, in the 1990s. Extending this to ASEAN under his ministerial term was a personal project of his.[13] Indonesia believed that a regional commission similar to that which had been established nationally was needed, as this would credibly allow ASEAN to address issues on which it faced criticism. It also felt that a regional human rights declaration should be aspirational and therefore contain values exceeding those of the national legislations, which put it at loggerheads with ASEAN, following a 'lowest common denominator' approach.[14] On the other side, the CLMV countries continued to worry that the body might be used as an instrument for interference in their domestic politics, and would resist any attempts to give it robust powers.

Prior to this debate, the ASEAN Secretary-General, Ong Keng Yong, had initiated a civil society interface with ASEAN leaders. It was hoped that this would allow the more authoritarian regimes to become more comfortable with civil society interactions, to demonstrate they need not be afraid. However, when it was hosted by Thailand in 2008, a Cambodian youth leader and prominent opposition activist was invited. When he confronted the Cambodian leader, Hun Sen, Hun Sen walked out and refused to be associated with the interface any longer. The following year, Vietnam decided against hosting it and the civil society interface petered out, with civil society groups establishing a parallel 'ASEAN Peoples Forum' which did not interact with ASEAN leaders.[15] The episode appeared to 'prove' the worst fears of the authoritarian regimes, that ASEAN mechanisms would be used for

---

[11] Poole, 'The World is Outraged', 359.
[12] The 'ASEAN human rights body' (AHRB) was the placeholder name for the body until it was officially designated as the 'ASEAN Intergovernmental Commission on Human Rights' (AICHR) later in the ToR process.
[13] Interviews with ASEAN officials, 16 and 31 October 2017.
[14] Interview with ASEAN official, 31 October 2017.
[15] Interview with ASEAN official, 9 October 2017.

political purposes – such as a confrontation with an opposition leader – and rightly or wrongly, this set the stage for deep mistrust at the start of the negotiations for the AHRB.

The Terms of Reference for a Human Rights Body

The ToR process began in 2008, with the expectation of a draft before the end of the year, and the ToR expected to be completed in the early part of 2009. Four of the delegates, from Laos, Malaysia, the Philippines, and Vietnam, continued as country representatives from the Charter HLTF process. The HLP met eight times between 2008 and 2009, charged with determining the mandate, membership, and functions of the AHRB.[16] They also met civil society groups during their third meeting in Manila in September 2008.

The HLP was drawn from functional Senior Officials Meetings (SOMs) in ASEAN. (See Table 7.1.) Because of the intergovernmental nature of ASEAN, SOMs are held regularly in functional areas in preparation for summits but also to work on the implementation of agreements and decisions by the leaders. With ASEAN hosting more than a thousand meetings annually, SOM officials were extremely familiar with each other as well as with ASEAN processes, collectively understood as the 'ASEAN Way'.

According to one perspective, the 'core group' in the HLP comprised Singapore, Thailand, Vietnam, Laos, and Brunei, to which Malaysia was added.[17] These officials all knew each other very well through SOM interactions, and 'the atmosphere was good throughout'.[18] While some disagreements carried over from the charter process, the fresh start with new officials enabled a less contentious process. Whereas Indonesia and the Philippines had been strong advocates for a human rights body with strong powers, and Rosario Manalo had returned in her role from the Charter HLTF, the decision was to follow ASEAN norms of intergovernmentalism and create a body that would

---

[16] ASEAN, 'Terms of Reference for the High Level Panel on an ASEAN Human Rights Body' (Singapore: ASEAN, 2008).
[17] Interview with ASEAN official, 5 September 2017.
[18] Muntarbhorn, *Unity in Connectivity? Evolving Human Rights Mechanisms in the ASEAN Region* (Leiden: Brill, 2014), 125.

Table 7.1 *Members of the High Level Panel for the Terms of Reference of the ASEAN human rights body*

Name	Country	Position
Shofry Abdul Ghafor	Brunei	Permanent Secretary, Ministry of Foreign Affairs and Trade
Om Yentieng	Cambodia	President, Human Rights Committee of Cambodia
Rachmat Budiman	Indonesia	Director of Political, Security, and Territorial Treaties, Department of Foreign Affairs
Bounkeut Sangsomak	Laos	Deputy Minister of Foreign Affairs
Ahmad Fuzi bin Abdul Razak	Malaysia	Ambassador-at-large, Ministry of Foreign Affairs
U Myat Ko	Myanmar	Secretary, Myanmar Human Rights Group Director-General, General Administration Department, Ministry of Home Affairs
Rosario G. Manalo	Philippines	Special Envoy, Department of Foreign Affairs
Bilahari Kausikan	Singapore	Second Permanent Secretary, Ministry of Foreign Affairs
Sihasak Phuangketkeow	Thailand (Chair)	Permanent Representative of Thailand to the UN Office in Geneva
Pham Quang Vinh	Vietnam	Assistant Minister, Ministry of Foreign Affairs

Source: 'List of Members of the High Level Panel on an ASEAN Human Rights Body (HLP)', ASEAN Intergovernmental Commission on Human Rights, http://aichr.org/about/hpl/.

reflect the ASEAN Way,[19] a proposal that was difficult to argue against as it built on the region's shared norms.

There was considerable debate about the naming of the body. As Termsak Chalermpalanupap describes:

So far, the following have been mentioned as possible choices: ASEAN Human Rights Mechanism (too passive and mechanical); ASEAN Human

---
[19] Interview with ASEAN official, 5 September 2017.

Establishing the AICHR 201

Rights Body (because it is now well-known); ASEAN Human Rights Commission (it conveys some mission by experts); ASEAN Human Rights Council (it gives the impression of being a policy decision-making entity); ASEAN Human Rights Consultative Council (no policy decision-making, just consultations); ASEAN Human Rights Forum (just a venue for discussion), etc.[20]

Each of these names was finally rejected, though the name 'commission' was argued by the Philippines to be the correct term as the AHRB had been established with a 'commission', that is, a specific mandate and purpose.[21] However, Myanmar insisted that it must be an interstate body, rather than one with potential representation from human rights groups.[22] This was recognised in the eventual naming of the AHRB as the 'ASEAN Intergovernmental Commission on Human Rights'. The delegates were therefore named 'representatives' rather than 'commissioners', as the AICHR members were the ASEAN countries, not the individual participants.

However, more ambitious ideas were not possible. Indonesia again attempted to put forward a human rights commission that would be able to perform the functions familiar to the national institutions. Hassan Wirajuda followed the negotiations as this was a personal interest of his. He leant heavily on his representative in the HLP, Rachmat Budiman, who in turn consulted closely with civil society representatives during the establishment of the body.[23] However, the nature of ASEAN norms meant there were limitations to what they could argue for, especially since the impasse during the charter process.

Indonesia finally accepted that the full human rights commission envisaged along the lines of the Indonesian institution that Wirajuda established was premature in ASEAN. It therefore conceded it would not have the terms for a complaints mechanism, an investigation protocol, and country visits. In short, there were no tangible 'protection' mechanisms granted for the body, despite its mandate to protect human rights. Indonesia was reportedly ready to walk out of the negotiations, but the Philippines persuaded it to cede these points on the condition that a separate statement be made that guaranteed no

---

[20] Chalermpalanupap, 'Ten Facts about ASEAN Human Rights Cooperation' (Jakarta: ASEAN, 2009).
[21] Interview with ASEAN officials, 16 October and 14 November 2017.
[22] Interview with ASEAN official, 5 September 2017.
[23] Interview with ASEAN official, 16 October 2017.

retreat from international human rights commitments,[24] and this emerged as the Cha-Am Hua Hin Statement on the Intergovernmental Commission on Human Rights, adopted on 23 October 2009 together with the ToR.

The Hua Hin Statement declared that the AICHR would be 'a vehicle for progressive social development and justice', and also added that the ToR would 'be reviewed every five years after entry into force to strengthen the mandate and functions of the AICHR in order to further develop mechanisms on both the protection and promotion of human rights'.[25] This, it was hoped, would keep the door open to more progressive mandates being implemented as ASEAN members became more comfortable with the functions of the commission. In the meantime, it was agreed that AICHR would start with promotional activities while ASEAN's conception of 'protection' was defined or operationalised.[26] The Singapore foreign minister, George Yeo, described it to the Singapore parliament as 'a body which, while lacking in teeth, will at least have a tongue and a tongue will have its uses'.[27] The inability to narrowly define its 'protection' mandate therefore meant it would be a political body, with a potentially politicised mandate.

The Drafting the ASEAN Human Rights Declaration

The ASEAN Intergovernmental Commission on Human Rights (AICHR) was therefore established with representatives from each of the ten ASEAN member states. While explicitly intergovernmental, representative selection was left to member states to decide.[28] Some countries, such as Indonesia and Thailand, put in civil society representatives. The representatives from Cambodia, Laos, and the Philippines moved seamlessly from the HLP into the AICHR – meaning that the Laos and Philippines representatives had been constants in the process since the Charter HLTF. Cambodia, Malaysia, and

---

[24] Interview with ASEAN officials, 16 and 31 October 2017.
[25] ASEAN, 'Cha-Am Hua Hin Declaration on the Intergovernmental Commission on Human Rights' (Cha-Am Hua Hin, Thailand: ASEAN, 2009), paras. 4 and 6.
[26] Interview with ASEAN officials, 9 October and 14 November 2017.
[27] Yeo, 'Remarks by Minister for Foreign Affairs George Yeo'.
[28] ASEAN, *ASEAN Intergovernmental Commission on Human Rights (Terms of Reference)* (Jakarta: ASEAN Secretariat, 2009), Art. 5.

Drafting the ASEAN Human Rights Declaration 203

Myanmar sent representatives from their national human rights commissions. Brunei and Singapore nominated a minister and senior magistrate respectively, but they were unconnected with their ministries of foreign affairs.

The dynamics of the group therefore started differently from those of the HLP, which had been very personal and familiar with ASEAN processes. Whereas Laos and the Philippines were the most familiar with the 'ASEAN Way' given both representatives' respective roles all the way back to the charter, they were at opposite ends of the spectrum when it came to national positions on human rights. Other representatives such as Indonesia, Malaysia, Singapore, and Thailand were relatively new to formal ASEAN interactions. Vietnam sent lower-level officials as representatives (whom they changed more frequently than the three-year term) so as not to give the AICHR appointment prominence.[29] The trust and familiarity would have to be built up over time, and this hindered the AICHR during its formative stages.[30] Whereas ASEAN is said to work best when it is informal and the atmosphere is collegial,[31] this was not the case in the beginning for the AICHR, with diverse political backgrounds and a lack of familiarity with each other at the outset. (See Table 7.2.)

Thus, the difficulties were not only external. For example, the first AICHR meeting in April 2010 was intended to discuss the 'rules of procedure',[32] and there was an immediate dispute on this matter between Laos and Indonesia.[33] Referring to the procedures as 'rules' was too legalistic for Laos, which asserted that the AICHR could operate without rules of procedure. This deadlock could not be broken during the first meeting, and the failure to publicise the draft was criticised by human rights groups.[34] It was not until the AICHR's fourth meeting in February 2011 that the 'Guidelines on the

---

[29] Interview with ASEAN official, 23 November 2017.
[30] Interview with ASEAN officials, 31 October and 23 November 2017.
[31] Interview with ASEAN official, 5 September 2017.
[32] AICHR, 'Press Statement by the Chair of the ASEAN Intergovernmental Commission on Human Rights on the First Meeting of the ASEAN Intergovernmental Commission on Human Rights' (Jakarta: ASEAN Secretariat, 2010).
[33] Interview with ASEAN official, 31 October 2017.
[34] SAPA TFAHR, *Hiding behind its Limits*, 8–9.

Table 7.2 *Inaugural representatives of the ASEAN Intergovernmental Commission on Human Rights*

Name	Country	Position
Awang Hj. Ahmad bin Hj. Jumat	Brunei	Minister of Culture, Youth and Sports
Om Yentieng	Cambodia	President, Human Rights Committee of Cambodia
Rafendi Djamin	Indonesia	Coordinator, Coalition of Indonesian NGOs for International Human Rights Advocacy
Bounkeut Sangsomak	Laos	Deputy Minister of Foreign Affairs
Muhammad Shafee Abdullah	Malaysia	Director, Asian Finance Bank; member, SUHAKAM (Malaysian human rights commission)
Kyaw Tint Swe	Myanmar	Vice-Chair, Myanmar National Human Rights Commission
Rosario G. Manalo	Philippines	Special Envoy, Department of Foreign Affairs
Richard Magnus	Singapore	Senior District Judge, Singapore Legal Service (retired)
Sriprapha Petcharamesree	Thailand	Director of Human Rights Studies and Social Development, Mahidol University
Nguyen Duy Hung	Vietnam	Director-General, Institute for Foreign Policies and Strategic Studies, Diplomatic Academy of Vietnam

Operations of AICHR' were adopted. The 'Guidelines on the AICHR's Relations with Civil Society Organisations' took even longer to be adopted and were still not ready by the time the AHRD was released in 2012.[35] Nevertheless, work began on the ASEAN Human Rights Declaration.

---

[35] They were eventually adopted on 11 February 2015, more than two years after the AHRD.

The Drafting Group's AHRD Draft

In July 2011, the AICHR established a Drafting Group to prepare the 'basic draft' of the ASEAN Human Rights Declaration, giving them six months to accomplish the task.[36] This group would report to the AICHR, who intended the draft to become the working document for their deliberations. The Drafting Group agreed amongst themselves that they would not share information publicly, and the secrecy with which their ToR and activities were cloaked was criticised by civil society.[37] Most of the representatives were functional mid-level foreign ministry officials without expertise in human rights. (See Table 7.3.) The exceptions were the Thai and Indonesian representatives, although several others had strong legal backgrounds, such as those of the Philippines and Singapore. As ASEAN chair in 2011, Indonesia also chaired the Drafting Group.

The 'zero' draft was started by the ASEAN Secretariat, but this was resisted by the CLMV countries. One ASEAN official characterised the Drafting Group process as 'a repeat of discussions on the ASEAN Charter on the human rights body'.[38] Despite the title of the 'ASEAN Human Rights Declaration' already having been mentioned in the AICHR's terms of reference,[39] the debate was reopened on what to call the declaration, with some insisting that it was a framework for cooperation rather than a declaration of norms and values. Some suggested that these were manoeuvres to slow down the process and prevent it from reaching a conclusion.[40]

As in the AICHR ToR process, the meetings immediately became bogged down in procedural issues. While the Drafting Group had their own ToR, they did not refer to them as they were broad, and, as the chair, Indonesia suggested following the use of international

---

[36] AICHR, 'Press Release of the Sixth Meeting of the ASEAN Intergovernmental Commission on Human Rights (AICHR)' (Vientiane: ASEAN Secretariat, 2011).

[37] SAPA TFAHR, *A Commission Shrouded in Secrecy: a Performance Report on the ASEAN Intergovernmental Commission on Human Rights, 2010–2011* (Bangkok: Forum Asia, 2011).

[38] Interview with ASEAN official, 27 October 2017.

[39] ASEAN, *ASEAN Intergovernmental Commission on Human Rights (Terms of Reference)*, Art. 4.2.

[40] Interview with ASEAN official, 27 October 2017.

Table 7.3 *Representatives of the ASEAN Human Rights Declaration drafting group*

Name	Country	Position
Hjh. Faizah Pangiran Hj. Abdul Rahman	Brunei	Deputy Director, Department of International Organisations, Ministry of Foreign Affairs and Trade
Orn Panhha	Cambodia	Assistant to the Senior Minister, President of the Cambodian Human Rights Committee
Harkristuti Harkrisnowo	Indonesia	Director-General of Human Rights, Ministry of Law and Human Rights
Phongsavanh Sisoulath	Laos	Deputy Director-General, ASEAN Department, Ministry of Foreign Affairs
Nazrin Aznam	Malaysia	Deputy Director-General, ASEAN Political-Security Community, ASEAN–Malaysia National Secretariat
U Nyunt Swe	Myanmar	Deputy Director-General, International Organisations and Economic Department, Ministry of Foreign Affairs (retired)
Irene Susan Natividad	Philippines	Executive Director, Office of Legal Affairs, Department of Foreign Affairs
Loh Tuck Keat	Singapore	Deputy Director-General, Singapore ASEAN National Secretariat
Seree Nonthasoot	Thailand	Legal Counsel, State Enterprise Policy Office, Ministry of Finance
Vu Ho	Vietnam	Deputy Director-General, ASEAN Department, Ministry of Foreign Affairs

conventions to establish the structure of the declaration.[41] However, this was met with resistance by the CLMV countries, which wanted to

---

[41] Interview with ASEAN official, 30 October 2017.

Drafting the ASEAN Human Rights Declaration 207

maintain maximum room for manoeuvre.⁴² As with the charter, however, it was agreed early on that it would not be a declaration that contained reservations, meaning all would have to agree (or at least not object) to every line. One delegate wanted the draft to have novel human rights protections that were not found anywhere else, but the group found it hard to come up with such ideas. Laos submitted two pages of novel rights, but they were deemed impractical, for example a 'right to happiness'.⁴³

Eventually a text was submitted to the AICHR given the deadline, but virtually the entire document was 'bracketed', meaning there were contested lines of text throughout that the Drafting Group had not managed to resolve between the different poles of opinion. It further had an accompanying note to the document, which explained the differences and interpretations of various texts.⁴⁴ It contained both freedoms and fundamental rights and duties and obligations. However, the Drafting Group did at least put the idea of a 'Right to Development'⁴⁵ on the table, and this would eventually make it into the final AHRD as a new right.

The AICHR Draft

At the beginning of 2012, with Cambodia chairing, the AICHR took up the next stage of the negotiating process, meeting nine times through the year before finalising the draft. The Drafting Group's version of the AHRD did not last long with the AICHR. Both the liberal and authoritarian norm circles were unhappy with the large amount of bracketing that would define the fault lines if this document became the working text. Whereas the Drafting Group had conducted its meetings in relative secrecy, the AICHR's hand was forced by an early leak of the Drafting Group's text in January, leading to vociferous public criticism by human rights groups of the alleged positions of various member states. The draft, dated 8 January 2012, marked the text in its raw state, with numerous brackets indicating the proposals

---

[42] Interview with ASEAN official, 27 October 2017.
[43] Interview with ASEAN official, 27 October 2017.
[44] Interview with ASEAN official, 30 October 2017.
[45] Unpublished draft, *Working Draft of the AHRD as of 8 Jan 2012 0400hrs* (Jakarta: ASEAN, 2012), Arts. 71–9. Copy on file with author.

by individual or groups of member states, alternative wordings by those in disagreement, and even attempts at compromise texts.[46]

It was thus agreed to completely restart the process with a brand new draft, dropping the Drafting Group's text entirely.[47] Singapore and Malaysia then led the process in providing a new initial draft of the AHRD.[48] Following the debacle of the leaked draft, brackets and country lines were omitted, and though there were some new arguments, it was agreed that it would be a 'UDHR Plus' document, i.e. not going below the standard of the Universal Declaration of Human Rights, as well as adding at least some novel rights that no other region had yet instituted.

At their second meeting, it was agreed that 'The AHRD is to be a political document that reflects the aspirations and commitments of ASEAN to the promotion and protection of human rights.'[49] The AICHR had been criticised repeatedly by civil society organisations for its lack of transparency.[50] The leaked draft, which displayed the diversity of national positions, heightened fears that the AHRD would significantly dilute human rights standards for the region, and the idea that it was to be a 'political document' raised further fears about what this would mean. On 8 April, concerned human rights NGOs issued a press release calling for the public release of the draft AHRD.[51]

By June, a 'final' draft was released for the seventh AICHR meeting, ahead of a regional consultation that included thirty-six CSOs.[52] While CSOs made numerous recommendations to amend the text to strengthen human rights protections,[53] this draft was basically the

---

[46] Ibid.   [47] Interview with ASEAN official, 30 October 2017.
[48] Ibid. Cf. Magnus, 'ASEAN Intergovernmental Commission on Human Rights: Some Personal Reflections', in *50 Years of ASEAN and Singapore*, ed. Koh, Seah, and Chang (Hackensack: World Scientific, 2017), 376.
[49] AICHR, 'Press Release of the Second Meeting of the ASEAN Intergovernmental Commission on Human Rights on the ASEAN Human Rights Declaration' (Jakarta: ASEAN Secretariat, 2012).
[50] SAPA TFAHR, *Hiding Behind Its Limits*.
[51] Forum Asia, 'Joint Statement on Calling AICHR to Release ASEAN Human Rights Declaration' (Bangkok: Forum Asia, 2012).
[52] ASEAN, 'The Seventh Meeting of the ASEAN Intergovernmental Commission on Human Rights (AICHR) on an ASEAN Human Rights Declaration (AHRD) and the Second Regional Consultation of AICHR on the AHRD' (Kuala Lumpur: ASEAN Secretariat, 2012).
[53] Forum Asia, 'Joint Submission to the ASEAN Intergovernmental Commission on Human Rights on the ASEAN Human Rights Declaration' (Bangkok: Forum Asia, 2012).

version that was adopted, with the notable omission of the words 'and association' from Art. 24 guaranteeing freedom of assembly.[54]

In much the same way that the ToR for the AICHR had to have a political statement appended to explain that the AICHR would not dilute human rights and the terms could be reviewed to strengthen the body in the future, the ASEAN Human Rights Declaration had the Phnom Penh Statement on the Adoption of the AHRD appended. This text reaffirmed ASEAN's commitment to ensure that the implementation of the AHRD be in accordance with the UN Charter, the Vienna Declaration, and other international human rights instruments.[55]

Assessing the Contest

Analysis of the AHRD and the degree to which it upheld or diminished human rights can be found in multiple analyses.[56] It disappointed numerous human rights groups[57] as it represented a qualification of human rights commitments, rather than an aspirational high watermark (which, at least, the charter, for all its ambiguities, did create). Nevertheless, there were some important marks of progress, especially in the context of a region that, until then, had had no regional human rights standards adopted by its members.

In terms of victories for human rights, the Drafting Group text had an entire section on 'Limitation of rights', containing ten variations of wordings on limitations and responsibilities.[58] These would eventually be condensed into Art. 6 of the AHRD (which had been finalised by June[59]), and without the extensive limitations feared by human rights groups, though they did not take up Forum Asia's recommendations to strengthen the article in support of human rights.[60] Regional

[54] ASEAN, *Draft ASEAN Human Rights Declaration as of 23 June, Kuala Lumpur* (Kuala Lumpur: ASEAN, 2012), Art. 24.
[55] ASEAN, 'Phnom Penh Statement on the Adoption of the ASEAN Human Rights Declaration (AHRD)' (Phnom Penh: ASEAN Secretariat, 2012).
[56] For example, Renshaw, 'The ASEAN Human Rights Declaration 2012', *Human Rights Law Review* 13, no. 3 (2013); ABA-ROLI, *The ASEAN Human Rights Declaration: a Legal Analysis* (Washington, DC: American Bar Association, 2014).
[57] Renshaw, 'The ASEAN Human Rights Declaration 2012', 559.
[58] ABA-ROLI, *AHRD: a Legal Analysis*, 15.
[59] ASEAN, *Draft ASEAN Human Rights Declaration as of 23 June, Kuala Lumpur*, Art. 6.
[60] Forum Asia, 'Joint Submission to AICHR on AHRD', 6.

particularities were 'purged',[61] and the Phnom Penh Statement affirmed that any interpretation of human rights would not go below the level of the UDHR and the Vienna Declaration. However, Renshaw argued that Art. 7 was 'a middle path between the Bangkok and Vienna Declarations'.[62]

However, there were several things that did not make it in. Freedom from torture, which had appeared in the controversial January 2012 draft, was left out of the final AHRD.[63] The January draft also included mention of ethnic groups, minority groups, and indigenous populations. All of these were omitted from the final version, although mention is made in Art. 4 of vulnerable and marginalised groups.[64] Forum Asia had recommended mention of 'indigenous peoples, minorities, Lesbian-Gay-Bisexual-Transgender (LGBT) persons, persons deprived of liberty' in the list in Art. 4, but this was declined. Rights related to sexual orientation were deemed too sensitive an issue, especially for an otherwise pro-human rights Malaysia, which also accepted the inclusion of 'public morality' in Art. 8, despite the protests of the other liberal states.

Controlling the Initiative

The process set in motion after the charter meant the timelines were dictated by the ASEAN summits, in which progress had to be submitted at regular intervals. This meant that the HLP, for instance, was required to submit a 'final draft' of the AICHR ToR to the ASEAN Summit by December 2008, while the Drafting Group had to submit its draft to the AICHR by January 2012, and the AICHR needed the final text to be agreed before the Phnom Penh Summit of November 2012. These deadlines were sometimes extended: the ToR was drafted by the December 2008 deadline but spilled into 2009 over remaining issues as Indonesia continued its fight for stronger mechanisms. However, these timelines were also significant as they would determine which chairing country would receive the credit, as seen in the names of the Cha-Am Hua Hin Declaration and Phnom Penh Statement: Thailand's main objective was to deliver the ToR rather than push human

---

[61] Villanueva, 'ASEAN "Magna Carta" Universalizes Human Rights', *Jakarta Post*, 8 January 2013.
[62] Renshaw, 'The ASEAN Human Rights Declaration 2012', 568–9.
[63] ABA-ROLI, *AHRD: a Legal Analysis*, 37.   [64] Ibid., 120.

rights,⁶⁵ and similarly Cambodia wanted to be the country that issued the AHRD.⁶⁶

This also lent itself to some strategies for negotiation. The authoritarian states believed that Indonesia was playing to the domestic audience.⁶⁷ Therefore, one plausible strategy was to stall them until time was running short, after which ASEAN's proclivity to saving face and getting things agreed would take over. The opening salvos in the HLP and Drafting Group discussions over procedural issues can be understood in this light, as progressive members voiced frustration at frequent stalling tactics, over seemingly trivial or already decided issues, such as the naming of the declaration.⁶⁸

One particularly frustrating possibility was to send alternates without a 'full mandate', which meant discussions could not reach consensus as the missing member had not sanctioned a decision. Fortunately, however, this was quickly clarified and only individuals with full mandates were sent. The AICHR, much like the Charter HLTF, also had to invoke a working rule not to reopen any deliberations that had been agreed upon, regardless of any potential new instructions from foreign ministries.⁶⁹

Stalling the process made the relatively tight schedule even tighter, and raised the potential costs of threatened walkouts, with both the Philippines and Indonesia prepared to do so. When the threat of walkout became imminent, 'white knights' were needed to personally persuade the actors to return to the table, with increasing urgency if the time was limited. Thus, a division of goals manifested: the two extreme poles of the furthest norm circles might be overtly concerned with achieving their goals, while those in the middle became overtly concerned with getting them to reach agreement. If ASEAN took a 'lowest common denominator' approach, this gave considerable leverage to the extreme end of a norm circle, as long as they intended to reach eventual agreement.

---

⁶⁵ Muntarbhorn, *Evolving Human Rights Mechanisms in ASEAN*, 126.
⁶⁶ Interview with ASEAN official, 16 October 2017.
⁶⁷ Interview with ASEAN official, 23 November 2017.
⁶⁸ Interview with ASEAN official, 27 October 2017.
⁶⁹ Interview with ASEAN official, 31 October 2017.

Shared Norms

The Vienna Declaration, the Universal Declaration of Human Rights, and the ASEAN Ministerial Meeting's joint communiqué of July 1993 were the guiding texts for the AHRD. The Joint Communiqué was, perhaps surprisingly, the only time ASEAN had explicitly detailed any positions on human rights up to that point.[70] The controversial 1993 Bangkok Declaration, which had established numerous escape clauses from human rights, was disregarded as it was argued that the Vienna Declaration had superseded it and provided the new baseline, given the joint communiqué's commitment to Vienna. This was decisive in removing the controversial escape clause of 'regional particularities'[71] from the AHRD, even as what could arguably have been a shared norm or precedent as such things existed in the Bangkok Declaration, Art. 1.4 of the AICHR ToR, and the Drafting Group's text.[72]

This was moreover a creative use of 'ASEAN minus X' in all but name: the 1993 communiqué affirming the Vienna Declaratiom was issued before any of the CLMV countries joined the grouping, but its existence as a precedent was unassailable. Thus, at the normative level of debating the text, it was difficult for the CLMV countries to argue against the various human rights notions, even when opposed to them ideologically. They thus appealed to past ASEAN decisions to make their arguments. Bounkeut Sangsomak, the Laos delegate who had participated in the HLP and charter processes, was said to continuously frame his arguments as appeals to history. Vietnam also made claims, especially about what ASEAN had purportedly agreed, when arguing against the liberal norm circle. The ASEAN Secretariat officials therefore had to check their accounts to confirm or deny whether these precedents existed.[73]

However, the fundamental basis of all the negotiations was the 'ASEAN Way', including non-interference and ASEAN's corollary,

---

[70] The exhaustive study of ASEAN's early statements related to rights is in Working Group for an ASEAN Human Rights Mechanism, *ASEAN and Human Rights*.

[71] Villanueva, 'ASEAN "Magna Carta" Universalizes Human Rights'.

[72] Unpublished draft, *Working Draft of the AHRD as of 8 Jan 2012 0400hrs*, Preamble, vi.

[73] Interview with ASEAN official, 30 October 2017.

the intergovernmental approach.[74] This precluded supranational structures:[75] the AICHR had no chance of gaining investigative power, and even establishing a communications procedure was deeply controversial. In much the same way that the idea of a regional court suggested by the EPG had been discarded immediately by ASEAN foreign ministers in the charter drafting process, so too had mechanisms to make the AICHR stronger or independent, because it implied supranationality.[76]

It is worth bearing in mind that the EPG had also recommended that the ASEAN Secretariat develop monitoring and investigative functions to enhance compliance to strengthen the Economic Community project, and this too was rejected, even though it was for enhancing arguably the most important community pillar to ASEAN. The defeat of the AICHR's protection powers was not merely because it was a human rights body, but because supranationality anywhere in the RO was not desired.

Metis

The first important difference was that the power of the norm circles varied between different iterations of the various committees. Thailand's HLP representative, while familiar with human rights debates in his role at the UN, was more given to finding consensus and compromise.[77] The Philippines and Indonesia were therefore left to argue these positions.[78] This left the progressive norm circle even weaker than it had been during the charter process. Rachmat Budiman, while quietly uncompromising, was also at a lower rank in the foreign ministry than his respective counterparts, and therefore somewhat isolated amongst the numerous senior officials who knew each other very well through other ASEAN interactions. This weakened his ability to bring other officials to his side.

---

[74] Villanueva, 'ASEAN "Magna Carta" Universalizes Human Rights'.
[75] Ng and Liow, 'The Southeast Asian Dimension: the ASEAN Model of Integration', in *The Regional World Order: Transregionalism, Regional Integration, and Regional Projects across Europe and Asia*, ed. Voskressenski and Koller (Lanham: Lexington Books, 2019), 117–18.
[76] Interview with ASEAN official, 30 August 2017.
[77] Interview with ASEAN official, 23 November 2017.
[78] Muntarbhorn, *Evolving Human Rights Mechanisms in ASEAN*, 125.

Legalistic argumentation was less of an issue at the ToR stage, as the only lawyer present was the Thai representative, an experienced SOM leader who knew ASEAN well. However, the CLMV norm circle believed their countries' legislatures would not accept human rights commitments.[79] Part of the process, according to multiple ASEAN officials, was to offer arguments to use to explain to their own governments.[80] In one instance, the Lao official who had been uncompromising during the charter process was refusing to allow space in the AICHR's ToR for civil society engagement:

> Laos ... were very strict. They were against [including] the civil society role [in the AICHR]. Thailand, Indonesia, and the Philippines were pushing for it. But we told them, 'You don't have a civil society. You can define the "civil society", whether [it is] these Soviet or women's groups. Don't worry so much about the language.' We had to give him some arguments to use with his own government. And he trusted us because we have known each other for thirty years.[81]

His concerns were alleviated when it was argued that there was sufficient ambiguity to define what was implied by 'civil society', which need not necessarily imply human rights groups. With that as an acceptable argument for his home government, he no longer objected to the inclusion of mention of civil society in the ToR. Thus, Art. 4.8 was accepted, which mandates the AICHR to engage with 'civil society organisations and other stakeholders'.[82]

Considering the debate that had gone on within the Drafting Group, and the hundred or so bracketed texts upon which they could not agree, it was perhaps a surprise that the new draft led by Singapore and Malaysia was accepted so much less contentiously. Both states were considered moderates, though Malaysia leaned more progressively on human rights. Richard Magnus, the Singapore representative, was described as 'a walking encyclopaedia',[83] and delivered the logic of the new draft, rationalising its language and why texts were tabled in a specific way. He could often break deadlocks upon his

---

[79] Poole, 'The World is Outraged', 361.
[80] Interviews with ASEAN officials, 5 September, 9 October, and 14 November 2017.
[81] Interview with ASEAN official, 5 September 2017.
[82] Interview with ASEAN official, 5 September 2017.
[83] Interview with ASEAN official, 30 October 2017.

intervention, and belonging to neither the authoritarian nor the liberal circle, he was held to be an objective participant.

The draft AHRD that had been presented (and criticised by civil society groups) took one final twist. Instead of being presented directly to the foreign ministers, it was first reviewed by the Senior Officials Meeting (SOM). Allegedly, Laos (supported by Vietnam) used this opening at the SOM level to make amendments and the progressive circle rushed to ensure there were no changes to the document, or that it would not be the SOM officials adopting it (rather than the foreign ministers or leaders).[84] In comparing the final text with the January leaked draft and the later June Kuala Lumpur draft, it is notable that Art. 24 of the final AHRD[85] drops 'and association' from 'Every person has the right to freedom of peaceful assembly and association,'[86] even though it had not been bracketed as contentious in the controversial January draft.[87]

Civil society participation had a mixed effect. On the one hand, countries that could partner with civil society groups could better brainstorm the positions they would take in the negotiating hall, and Indonesia worked particularly closely with its human rights activists in doing so. On the other hand, ASEAN observers felt that politicisation of the process was bad for the result, as it put the authoritarian circles on the defensive and made themless willing to concede ground.[88] Indonesian Foreign Minister Marty Natalegawa defended the secrecy, arguing that if the text were released, it would harden the positions of certain member states.[89] Manalo (Philippines), who had pushed strongly for a human rights mechanism in the charter and was considered a deeply committed liberal by her ASEAN counterparts, had a complex relationship with civil society groups. She would harangue them on the issues they kept raising, while civil society representatives insisted that this was because the AICHR was not listening.[90] In such public displays, she may have been attempting to build trust to use

---

[84] Interview with ASEAN officials, 30 and 31 October 2017.
[85] ASEAN, 'ASEAN Human Rights Declaration' (Phnom Penh 2012), Art. 24.
[86] *Draft ASEAN Human Rights Declaration as of 23 June, Kuala Lumpur*, Art. 24.
[87] Unpublished draft, *Working Draft of the AHRD as of 8 Jan 2012 0400hrs*, Art. 48.
[88] Interview with ASEAN officials, 23 November 2017.
[89] Ng, 'The ASEAN Human Rights Declaration: Establishing a Common Framework'.
[90] Interview with ASEAN official, 16 October 2017.

internally to persuade the authoritarian norm circle that civil society was not the threat it was suspected to be.

External observers, such as the UN Office of the High Commission for Human Rights, the International Commission of Jurists, the European Union, and the USA, all offered commentary and nudging through the process. The AICHR was invited to the USA and Europe to learn about Western systems of human rights institutions. However, these trips offered lessons that were probably not intended by the hosts.

Richard Magnus (Singapore) recounted the learning of conditionalities in the USA for civil society groups 'not to be concerned with domestic matters' in exchange for federal funding. Similarly, in Europe, other groups received funding that specifically targeted other countries. Meanwhile, he noted the 'inordinate' delays faced by the European Court on Human Rights because of the numerous cases filed by individuals against the member states.[91] The implication in the funding example was that human rights issues could be used as a political instrument, an undesirable outcome for ASEAN member states. The latter case on the court suggested that ASEAN would not have the capacity to deal with human rights cases if it developed a complaints or reporting mechanism.

Conclusion

The creation of an ASEAN human rights body and then a human rights declaration in the space of four years was a remarkable period of transformation for an organisation that had taken ten years to sign its first meeting, and twenty years to establish its Secretariat. Human rights protections were perhaps the strongest test of ASEAN's commitment to sovereignty. As Sriprapha Petchamesree, Thailand's first AICHR representative, writes:

The notion of national sovereignty was pronounced throughout the text in the forms of the reference to national laws, the inclusion of limitation clauses as well as the emphasis on the responsibilities of the individual vis-à-vis

---

[91] Magnus, 'ASEAN Intergovernmental Commission on Human Rights: Some Personal Reflections', 377–8.

society and state and the direct reference and repetition of the principle of non-interference in internal affairs.[92]

Ultimately, the process of norm-setting must be understood not merely as an aversion to human rights, but as an aversion to ceding sovereignty in the RO. While the whole process from the charter to the ASEAN Community 2015 began from the economic domain, with an imperative for creating a more legal, rules-based order to support regional integration, when the respective ideas came into contact with the political and security cultures of the organisation, these legalistic approaches were constantly rebuffed. ASEAN did effect a human rights standard, but one with very ASEAN characteristics, full of compromises and a deep aversion to supranationality. (See Table 7.4.)

The progressive norm circle of Thailand, the Philippines, and Indonesia saw its efforts wax and wane depending on who was sent, so their strategy after conceding ground in the negotiations was to put up a parallel statement as an explanatory note that bound the interpretation of the document to a more progressive reading of the contested areas. Thus, the ToR on the AICHR were coupled with the Cha-Am Hua Hin Declaration on the Intergovernmental Commission on Human Rights, while the AHRD was coupled with the Phnom Penh Statement on the Adoption of the ASEAN Human Rights Declaration. Both statements reiterated that their related document would not go below the level of the human rights norms established in international treaties, and the Cha-Am Hua Hin Declaration provided for review to leave open the possibility for stronger mechanisms to be developed in the future.

It would also be unfair to suggest that ASEAN did not push the envelope with the AICHR and the AHRD. As the previous chapter showed, just seven years earlier, the EPG could not agree on recommending the creation of a human rights body at all, and then the Charter HLTF could not agree even to call the body a 'commission', or agree to any functions that it could undertake aside from the ambiguous 'promotion and protection' line. What ASEAN achieved with the AHRD was unsatisfactory to civil society advocates, who sought improvements on global human rights standards, which were not achieved.

However, ASEAN did socialise its newest members into its particular processes, and by the end of the first tenure, the representatives of

---

[92] Petcharamesree, 'The ASEAN Human Rights Architecture: its Development and Challenges', *Equal Rights Review* 11(2013): 58.

Table 7.4 *Contestation over the ASEAN human rights mechanism*

Factors	Proposing norm circle	Opposing norm circle
Members	Indonesia, Philippines, Thailand, Malaysia	Cambodia, Laos, Myanmar, Vietnam
Control of initiative	• Origins in 1993 communiqué • Scrapping of Drafting Group's draft AHRD (too many reservations) • Tight timeline	• Stalling via procedural disagreements
Norms invoked	• Universal Declaration of Human Rights • Vienna Declaration (non-use of Bangkok Declaration) • Convention on the Rights of the Child (CRC) and Convention on the Elimination of All Forms of Discrimination against Women (CEDAW)	• Non-interference, sovereignty • 'ASEAN Way': Informality, pragmatism, consultation, and consensus • Intergovernmental character of ASEAN • Attempts at framing past decisions in their favour
Metis	• Suggesting arguments for CLMV countries to take home to their respective governments • Walkout threats; enjoinment of ToR/declaration with political statements • Leak of draft document to civil society groups	• Familiarity between ASEAN officials in ToR round • Passing declaration through ASEAN SOM • Clause to review mechanism after five years
Outcome	Intergovernmental body with no protection powers, guided by a political document (qualified)	

the AICHR were said to have increasingly better working relationships with each other.[93] This has further improved with successive commissions as they rotate on three-year terms. Remarkably, the ASEAN

---

[93] Interviews with ASEAN officials, 27, 30, and 31 October 2017. Magnus, 'ASEAN Intergovernmental Commission on Human Rights: Some Personal Reflections', 376.

Declaration on Strengthening Social Protection, a progressive, rights-based approach to the welfare of vulnerable groups, was adopted in 2013. As the shared norms and practices increased and members have become more comfortable with the working styles and national preferences of their counterparts, the newer agreements have become easier to reach. The fear that these instruments might be used to interfere with the domestic politics of certain countries had not come to pass, and resistance was less absolute.

Indonesia, the Philippines, and Thailand were always a minority, and aside from Indonesia, their support for the process waned at times. Depending on the different task forces, they did not always even get support from their fellow member states in the same norm circle to operate as a united group. During the Drafting Group stage, the Philippines representative often sent alternates, which broke the continuity of taking certain positions in various debates. In the HLP on the ToR, the Thai representative was too close to ASEAN norms and the ASEAN Way, and therefore too likely to concede on points the others wanted to push. In the AICHR, the Philippines representative seemed distant and unempathetic towards civil society. Yet despite these occasional breaks in continuity, they managed to push things further than one might have expected given the consensus requirement. However, the strength of the other norm circle was also dependent on their participation. Vietnam and Laos delegates were repeatedly said to be the most vocal participants, while Cambodia was often represented by an alternative, and Myanmar tended not to speak up very much.

While media and civil society groups characterised the AHRD process as a dilution of human rights and condemned its adoption,[94] a deeper undercurrent was resistance to legalism, shared by many members of ASEAN. This is only apparent in tracing how other pre-existing shared norms interacted in the process of contestation, including the contest over the use of economic norms in other parts of the ASEAN Community project. This is the subject of the third ASEAN case study in the next chapter, framed around the debate over the 'ASEAN minus X' principle, and attempts to institute it as a decision-making procedure in ASEAN.

While ambiguities reflected the lack of consensus, it need not only be read as a failure of the regional organisation to institute strongly

[94] Wahyuningrum, *AICHR: Origins, Evolution, and the Way Forward*, 18–19.

enforceable norms. Failure to give a tight and precise mandate meant the AICHR would be a political body with wide interpretative space. Vitit Muntarbhorn, the first Thai AICHR representative, noted that the liberal norm circle understood the AICHR's ToR expansively, 'that what is not prohibited is not forbidden'.[95] Unlike other functional groups in ASEAN, such as the education, finance, or environmental groups, it remained a political grouping with a political mandate. The space for the exercise of metis remains its strongest potentiality.[96]

As many ASEAN observers have noted,[97] standard international relations theories have difficulties explaining ASEAN institutions. Rational choice theory has little to say when the benefits and costs are not quantifiable, but even less so when the regimes created do not create explicit compliance mechanisms. Realist coercion is also difficult to argue, given that, if a state or region were doing so out of obligation, there is no evidence to show a causal pathway between the hegemonic power and coercive force on all ten member states. Moreover, the more relevant hegemon would arguably be China for the authoritarian states, and they would be under little compunction to accede to any such incremental steps.

Meanwhile, an ideational theory that suggests states create the institutions consistent with their values would have difficulty explaining why the CLMV countries, which wield effective vetoes in a consensus-based organisation, did not simply call a halt to the entire process, or indeed how they could be led by a minority norm circle of just three – or sometimes, four – states. Similarly, socialisation theories would have a problem explaining what gains such incremental steps would provide, given that there was so little approval from liberal Western states in whose direction they were moving, or from the influence of a minority of members of the liberal norm circles within the RO with which they were vigorously opposed. The creation of the body for legitimation purposes might be equally hard to sustain, given the fraught nature of relations with civil society groups throughout the process, in which the final text drew sustained condemnation by human rights groups. Its functions and activities since its creation have also not given it such a legitimation role.

---

[95] Muntarbhorn, *Evolving Human Rights Mechanisms in ASEAN*, 130.
[96] Munro, 'The Origins and Regime Design of AICHR', 1194.
[97] Poole, 'The World is Outraged'; Munro, 'The Origins and Regime Design of AICHR'.

Conclusion 221

Instead, what one finds is that there was, first, an aggregate of utilities driving the creation of the human rights body, locked in at various stages through the consensus mechanism. Whether or not diplomats from countries like Indonesia were playing for a domestic audience or personal motivations, they sought strong mechanisms that would reflect what they believed to be a robust human rights institution. The opposite norm circle, led particularly by Laos and Vietnam, maintained that ASEAN was an intergovernmental organisation focused on cooperation in limited areas. If human rights were an area for intergovernmental cooperation, this would be limited to promotional activities. Their main concern was to ensure that the body could not be used to interfere with domestic politics, which was why the debate over civil society participation was so contentious.

Following the decision to create a human rights body in the charter, however, the CLMV states had to work within those constraints. The question was then what it could do, and what norms it would develop. Once this process was in motion, bureaucratic logics and practices took over. Negotiations went as far as the skills of the respective norm circles' negotiators could take their initiatives, mastery of shared norms and practices, and other opportunities for influence. In the control of the initiative, this was largely set by timetables from higher ASEAN levels, and a failure to meet the deadlines was not countenanced. However, that did mean that processes became more urgent and frantic towards the end, requiring more compromises.

The most interesting observation from this episode is the importance that shared norms played in the HLP, Drafting Group, and AICHR processes. Whereas the relative blank slate of the ASEAN Charter had precluded most appeals to anything other than the ambiguous 'ASEAN Way', here the struggle over precedents and decisions was much more decisive in settling arguments. The Vienna Declaration came to be the foundational normative text, bolstered by the 1993 ASEAN foreign ministers' communiqué. The CLMV delegates attempted to argue against it through their characterisations of past ASEAN decisions and processes, aided particularly by the Laotian representative's participation in all the processes since the HLTF on the charter. These had to be fact-checked by Secretariat staff.[98]

---

[98] Interview with ASEAN official, 30 October 2017.

Unlike the more powerful role that the AU Commission (OAU Secretariat) has in Africa, the ASEAN Secretariat is a support service rather than a supranational authority. While it can work on issues, and to some extent can be a custodian of precedents and decisions, it cannot exert an authoritative force in the debate. This was most clearly seen by the rebuff to its 'zero draft' of the AHRD for the Drafting Group.[99] Meanwhile, the diverse political structures of each of the member states made it difficult to argue from common purposes: Brunei did not even have 'citizens', while two of the states were Marxist-Leninist, and two more were authoritarian. These states therefore lacked an understanding of human rights concepts from their particular political discourses, and were suspicious of attempts by the liberal norm circle to persuade them.[100] Therefore, shared norms became the main source of authority within all of the groupings, failing to find a shared logic on which to rest their normative arguments. This then was reflected in the very ASEAN-styled human rights body and declaration that resulted.

Finally, ASEAN's informality provided many opportunities for the exercise of 'metis', and these were carried out by both sides. 'Spa diplomacy', a feature of the ASEAN Charter drafting process, was not absent here.[101] Most notably on the side of the CLMV countries, they intercepted the document during what was supposed to be a formality of submitting it through the SOM level before it reached the foreign ministers, and this led to the omission of the freedom of association. Indonesia and the Philippines, meanwhile, had to introduce the Cha-Am Hua Hin Declaration and Phnom Penh Statement as interpretative texts to the AICHR ToR and AHRD respectively, to ensure that whatever else was conceded in the negotiations, the interpretation of the mandates and texts should not go below accepted human rights standards. Finally, like the charter, the ToR left open the possibility of review to strengthen the AICHR's mandate and functions, a hard-fought point for the Indonesian and Philippine HLP

---

[99] Interview with ASEAN official, 27 October 2017.
[100] Interview with ASEAN official, 31 October 2017.
[101] Villanueva, 'ASEAN "Magna Carta" Universalizes Human Rights'.

Conclusion 223

members. Proposals to open up that review were repeated in 2013, 2014, and 2015.[102] However, despite better working relationships between the latter members of the AICHR, no consensus was reached on reopening it. It seems unlikely that this will happen any time soon, considering the debates about reviewing the ASEAN Charter.

[102] Interview with ASEAN official, 23 November 2017.

8 | Extending the 'ASEAN Minus X' Formula

Consensus should aid, but not impede, ASEAN's cohesion and effectiveness. As the range of activities within ASEAN increases, ASEAN should consider alternative and flexible decision-making mechanisms. In this connection, the EPG recommends: ... The flexible application of 'ASEAN minus X' or '2 plus X' formula may be applied, subject to the discretion of the relevant ASEAN Community Councils.

EPG Report on the ASEAN Charter[1]

Introduction

Human rights are not the only norm capable of limiting sovereignty in a regional organisation. While human rights were the most visibly contested norm in the drafting of the ASEAN Charter, a less visible but potentially more significant debate concerned the decision-making norms of ASEAN. This debate was over a seemingly procedural norm but with far-reaching implications about the nature of ASEAN: the 'ASEAN minus X' formula. ASEAN was built on a foundation of consensus decision-making, and this was designed to restrain transfer of sovereignty to the RO. However, this was not the most effective means of making tough decisions, and there were calls to amend the consensus principle, with the opportunity presenting itself during the process of thinking about an ASEAN Charter. The idea then was that ASEAN, minus 'X' number of countries that were not yet ready to commit to the decision, could still go ahead in specified areas if there were sufficient will to do so. Most commonly, these areas were tariff reduction schedules where the more liberalised or outward-oriented member states would commit to reducing tariffs in certain product categories ahead of the others, even when the others had no specific timeframe for their reduction.

---

[1] ASEAN, *Report of the Eminent Persons Group on the ASEAN Charter*, 6.

Introduction

However, in deciding to move ahead with a 'minus X' decision, this could lead to an expectation that others *must* eventually commit to the same decision, *when*, rather than *if*, they wish to. This form of decision-making thus may lead to a concession of sovereignty, because some national interests could be bypassed under these procedures. For example, if a set of ASEAN members were committed to a strong regional human rights institution, even the 'minus' countries would be forced to accept it once it were established, and this therefore takes the decision about the regional institutional complexion out of their hands once they are marked as a 'minus' country. As Chan asks: 'For the sake of effectiveness of the organisation, would ASEAN governments be ready to relinquish a part of their sovereignty? Would they accept a sacrifice of national interests when overruled by a majority?'[2]

The practice of consensus decision-making had evolved in ASEAN over the years and required all its member states' respective interests to be considered. Yet, as with other things in ASEAN, consensus was not formally institutionalised until the question came up in the process of creating the ASEAN Charter, and a variety of proposals were offered to improve ASEAN's decision-making process.

During the debates on the charter, there was a move to extend the 'ASEAN minus X' formula – wherein ASEAN could make a decision without certain members – beyond its originally limited domain of trade agreements, and formalise it as a decision-making norm of the RO. Ultimately, however, this was rejected and, in formalising the specifics of when it could be used, it ended up with narrower application than it previously had as an informal norm and practice, a rejection of the norm in any political-security or socio-cultural aspect of the ASEAN Community project.

This chapter begins with the background to the debate leading up to the charter, which helps to explain why the 'ASEAN minus X' formula arose amidst ASEAN's informality and consensus-based decision-making preferences from pressures of economic integration and ASEAN expansion. This is then followed by an account of the EPG's recommendations, which favoured stronger decision-making processes. The next phase, however, does not follow with contestation within the Charter HLTF, as the human rights issue did, but rather

---

[2] Chan, 'Decision-Making in the ASEAN Charter Process', in *50 Years of ASEAN and Singapore*, ed. Koh, Seah, and Chang (Hackensack: World Scientific, 2017).

through differences between economic and foreign ministries of certain ASEAN members. Without overdramatising the events that unfolded, however, the ASEAN foreign ministers controlled the process, and attempts to change the decision-making process were rejected, with ASEAN minus X confined to economic matters, a reversal of its previously expanding application.

This case study is perhaps the most unlike the others, in that the norm circles here do not align neatly on national lines, as in the other cases in this book. Instead, the divide is most apparent between functional groupings: the economics ministers and the foreign ministers of their respective states, who differed in their perceptions of the utility of the two norms of decision-making for the region. This case therefore best brings out the importance of utility as an organising principle in the formation of norm circles. The respective utilities are apparent to each circle, and while both acknowledge the other circle's argument, the concession is to create a hierarchy of preferences. In doing so, the status quo was maintained, and the possibility to extend or experiment with other decision-making alternatives was rejected.

Background

ASEAN had started as an informal association, primarily an organised set of meetings, and did not even have a leaders' summit until 1976 in Bali, nine years after its establishment. The upshot of single-party or authoritarian rule in Southeast Asia is that the longstanding leaders of ASEAN's original five members (to which Brunei was added in 1984) grew close and could agree on most decisions between themselves.[3] They also had an understanding to set aside contentious issues if agreement could not be reached. As part of the political project in which ASEAN was created to smooth differences and improve working relationships, this was a suitable norm or *modus vivendi*.

However, two different pressures were exerted on the grouping in the 1990s: first, the drive towards stronger economic integration and, second, the expansion of ASEAN as Vietnam joined in 1995, followed by Myanmar and Laos in 1997, and finally Cambodia in 1999. Both processes led to stronger demand for a more rules-based rather than informal order, and these culminated in the formation of the charter.

---

[3] Acharya, *Constructing a Security Community*, 78.

However, with so much of the 'ASEAN Way' being 'informal', and indeed being seen by its own officials to be highly successful in that regard, formalisation was resisted, even as there were numerous debates as to *what* ought to be formalised if at all. The 'ASEAN minus X' formula came to be one of the central questions, albeit it was resolved not to extend it as a general principle in ASEAN.

Economic Integration

ASEAN's first multilateral experiment with economic integration began with the ASEAN Free Trade Area (AFTA) in 1992. The timing can be understood against the global context: the end of the Cold War, EU negotiations leading up to the signing of the Maastricht Treaty the same year, as well as the negotiations for the North American Free Trade Area (NAFTA) that were well underway by then. Most of ASEAN's trade was with partners outside the region, and the fear was that competition would split the grouping.[4] While there was no ambition to have as formal a grouping as the EU, or as elaborate a trade agreement as NAFTA, the region risked being marginalised by these developments and responded in its own fashion.

Until 1992, ASEAN only had a Preferential Trade Agreement. AFTA involved creating a Common Effective Preferential Tariff (CEPT) for goods of ASEAN origin traded between member countries, with a target tariff of 0–5 per cent.[5] Within the CEPT, there was no expectation of moving at uniform speeds, but that states would initiate their tariff reductions unilaterally or bilaterally, updating the ASEAN Secretariat and meetings accordingly.[6]

Reflecting ASEAN's preference for informality, there were no sanctions or non-compliance mechanisms, and the only institutional provisions were that the monitoring and supervision be performed by the ASEAN Economic Ministers (AEM) meeting, supported by the ASEAN Secretariat and a lower Senior Economic Officials Meeting (SEOM).[7] The Secretariat was therefore strengthened, and the Secretary-General accorded ministerial status, with summits being

---

[4] Ba, *(Re)Negotiating East and Southeast Asia* (Stanford: Stanford University Press, 2009), 152–3.
[5] ASEAN, 'Agreement on the Common Effective Preference Tariff Scheme for the ASEAN Free Trade Area' (Singapore 1992), Art. 4.
[6] Ibid., Arts. 4, 7(2). [7] Ibid., Art. 7.

regularised.[8] Disputes would be handled bilaterally,[9] and emergency brakes were permitted.[10] The resultant norm, while committing all members to full compliance, also allowed that members could move towards compliance at different speeds. Such flexibility, however, meant the rate of tariff reductions was uneven and added little to the existing unilateral measures already undertaken by members.[11] Prior to the ASEAN Charter, just 30 per cent of ASEAN agreements were implemented.[12]

The 1997–8 Asian financial crisis triggered large-scale capital flight from the region. Precipitated by a collapse of property markets and devaluation of the *baht* in Thailand and exacerbated by economic turmoil in South Korea, the entire region was badly hit as investors fled *en masse*, regardless of the differing economic conditions of various East Asian economies. This general reaction by Western investors provided fertile ground for conspiracy theories relating to currency manipulation, including allegations by the Malaysian Prime Minister Mahathir Mohamed. ASEAN members tended to understand the crisis in terms of the differences in power between the West and Southeast Asia.[13] The only readily available solutions came from the International Monetary Fund (IMF), which had a long record of imposing unpopular austerity measures through its structural adjustment programmes in the developing world. Indonesia and Thailand accepted these, while Malaysia opted to reject them. The conclusion again was that Southeast Asia needed strengthening and dovetailed with regional developments elsewhere in the world. As Singapore Prime Minister Goh Chok Tong declared in 1999, 'ASEAN must

---

[8] Ba, *(Re)Negotiating East and Southeast Asia*, 155.
[9] The language of this article, along with many other sections, is lifted from the 1977 Agreement on ASEAN Preferential Trade Arrangements, Art. 14.
'Agreement on the Common Effective Preference Tariff Scheme for the ASEAN Free Trade Area', 1992, Art. 8(2). The key difference is that CEPT was an opt-out scheme requiring justification for exceptions, whereas the ASEAN PTA was a product-by-product scheme, which would take years to implement even with the best intentions.
[10] ASEAN, 'Agreement on the Common Effective Preference Tariff Scheme for the ASEAN Free Trade Area', Art. 6.
[11] Ravenhill, 'Fighting Irrelevance: an Economic Community "with ASEAN Characteristics"', *Pacific Review* 21, no. 4 (2008).
[12] Desker, 'Is the ASEAN Charter Necessary?'
[13] Ba, *(Re)Negotiating East and Southeast Asia*, 202–3.

become more united to stand up to the rise of regionalism in North America, South America and Western Europe.'[14]

ASEAN Expansion

After the Cold War, ASEAN members also began to envisage coalescing the region into a new regional order.[15] There were, of course, underlying interests in the expansion, for example, Indonesia sought the expansion of ASEAN to counter Chinese influence.[16] The new candidate countries also were emerging from socialist systems, and these were opportunities for new markets too. Vietnam had begun market-oriented reforms known as *doi moi* as early as 1986,[17] and its path out of central planning was keenly watched in the region by both the old communist bloc states and the established capitalist economies. However, tensions over its occupation of Cambodia had led to ostracisation by ASEAN, and these were not resolved until 1991 at the Paris Peace Accords, which followed Vietnam's withdrawal from Cambodia. As relations normalised, Vietnam became the first communist state to join the grouping in 1995.

Myanmar and Laos were next to apply to join the grouping, and whereas both were authoritarian states with significant Western concerns relating to human rights, attention was focused on Myanmar. ASEAN members were concerned about whether the EU and USA would suspend cooperation and development assistance to themselves over their acceptance of Myanmar's membership. This led to a serious test of its norms, particularly as to how ASEAN's stance on 'non-interference' could be interpreted and upheld.[18]

The new membership meant that the development gap between states widened in the 1990s. AFTA and CEPT had encountered problems given the varying levels of development of the existing six members, and the challenge to accept the CLMV countries into the

---

[14] Quoted in Goh, 'The ASEAN Community and the Principle of ASEAN Centrality', in *50 Years of ASEAN and Singapore*, ed. Koh, Seah, and Chang, 337.
[15] Acharya, *Constructing a Security Community*, 121.
[16] Ba, *(Re)Negotiating East and Southeast Asia*, 124.
[17] Ng and Giao, 'The Socialist Republic of Viet Nam', in *Rule of Law for Human Rights in the ASEAN Region: a Base-Line Study*, ed. Cohen, Tan, and Mohan (Jakarta: Human Rights Resource Centre, 2011), 285.
[18] See Chapter 7. Acharya, *Constructing a Security Community*, 111–14.

grouping meant that further exceptions were required for the trade tariff reduction schedule. From an economic standpoint, the development gap between the newer and older members necessitated flexibility for the newer members to come to terms with ASEAN agreements, yet, as one diplomat put it, it could not be so flexible that there were no rules at all.[19]

The more globally integrated ASEAN members often had stronger bilateral agreements with external partners than within the grouping, and the ASEAN agreements negotiated thus far were of little use to the private sector.[20] Improving agreements required moving towards a more rules-based organisation and improving the decision-making process, and it seemed then that a move away from consensus and informality needed to occur.

To some extent, questions about ASEAN's identity arose as the communist or left-leaning states joined. The Cold War divide had seen the capitalist economies in ASEAN close ranks, although officially non-aligned.[21] ASEAN's unity had owed a great deal to every member's unequivocal opposition to Vietnam's invasion of Cambodia during the Cold War, and this reasoning no longer existed. It was also apparent in 1995 that consensus would be harder to reach in an expanded grouping.[22] Thus, between the need to break deadlocks and the expansion that made consensus harder to achieve, considerable discussions in the early 2000s revolved around strengthening the decision-making structure.

Alternatives to Consensus and Informality

The expansion of ASEAN heightened the need to allow variable levels of implementation of agreements, but it was not an entirely new debate. Singaporean Prime Minister Lee Kuan Yew first suggested the softening of the consensus-only approach in the 1980s, suggesting (when ASEAN had just five members) that a 'Five minus One' decision,

---

[19] Koh, Manalo, and Woon, *The Making of the ASEAN Charter*, 85.
[20] Ravenhill, 'Fighting Irrelevance'.
[21] During the Cold War, Thailand was the lone formal US ally, while the Philippines had American military bases which were removed in 1991. However, all of the ASEAN countries had closer relations with the West than with the communist bloc.
[22] Acharya, *Constructing a Security Community*, 126.

as long as the one does not object, still constituted a consensus.[23] The corollary to CEPT was the 1992 Framework Agreement on Enhancing ASEAN Economic Cooperation, which provided the framework for creating AFTA. Notably, it also contained notation away from the requirements of consensus, stating:

> All Member States shall participate in intra ASEAN economic arrangements. However, in the implementation of these economic arrangements, two or more Member States may proceed first if other Member States are not ready to implement these arrangements.[24]

This became known as the '2 plus X' formula, permitting individual members to start cooperation in defined areas, without explicitly calling for the permission of other members. Singapore, pushing for stronger economic integration, again argued for more effective ASEAN decision-making in the 1990s to avoid drifting apart.[25] This was an interesting twist because, whereas a 'minus X' argument would, by definition, leave some members behind, the stronger cohesion from economic integration and increasing the overlap of shared interests was argued to increase the benefits and thus the unity of the grouping.

The net result of these pressures was the need for new norms to strengthen economic integration, particularly with new members who were vastly behind in economic development compared with the founding members. Fears that gains made could be lost through non-compliance or non-implementation were exacerbated by China's growing economy, which was taking in most of the new foreign direct investment to the wider region.

The respective utilities of both the 'consensus' and 'minus X' decision-making norms can be described in functionalist terms. Economic integration was intended to boost intra-regional trade and increase overlapping and shared interests. The overarching principle for integration was to extend a clear, rules-based or legal framework to the regulation of economic activities across the region. These should be applied as evenly as possible, but given the various levels of economic development, this could mean some countries could not yet implement

---

[23] Acharya, 'Culture, Security, Multilateralism: the "ASEAN Way" and Regional Order', *Contemporary Security Policy* 19, no. 1 (1998): 63–4.
[24] ASEAN, 'Framework Agreement on Enhancing ASEAN Economic Cooperation' (Singapore: ASEAN Secretariat, 1992), Art. 1(3).
[25] Ba, *(Re)Negotiating East and Southeast Asia*, 138–9.

the rules effectively. Given this predicament, the idea was that some countries that were already ready should be allowed to move first.

Thus, to accelerate the economic community efforts, it might involve leaving some countries out, somewhat contradictorily. Yet, if the purported gains of integration amounted to a public good, then the opposition to allowing for mechanisms that could accelerate integration prevented the attainment of those public goods. Furthermore, this was believed to be necessary for strengthening ASEAN as a grouping against external powers.

Both had competing arguments for their respective utility, and it was not easy to quantify and compare their respective importance. The argument for utility turned on which approach would better promote unity (which all regional actors agreed was a desirable goal), economic integration or political consensus, but this was a value-judgement. ASEAN's consensus-based approach, however, meant every member had a veto,[26] and no member's interests could be ignored. Trying to formally codify this norm, however, was always avoided initially.

Developing the ASEAN Community

At the start of the 2000s, as discussions about the charter gathered pace, the underlying motivation was the need to strengthen economic integration, and a search for the kinds of mechanisms that would permit this without losing sight of the 'ASEAN Way'. It was apparent that ASEAN needed a 'well-developed institutional and legal infrastructure to facilitate greater economic integration',[27] which would require granting the organisation a legal personality.[28] The legal personality, formally, would also provide it with a framework to interact with other entities, such as the EU and USA.

The Hanoi Plan of Action was the first six-year plan established to realise the ASEAN Vision 2020, adopted in 1998 to cover 1999–2004. Largely framed against the backdrop of the East Asian financial crisis, its primary aims were economic recovery and addressing the social impact of the financial crisis.[29] By 2002, the 'agenda towards an

---

[26] Woon, *The ASEAN Charter*, 157.
[27] Hew and Sen, 'Towards an ASEAN Economic Community: Challenges and Prospects', *ISEAS Working Papers, Economics and Finance* (2004): 23.
[28] Acharya, *Constructing a Security Community*, 234.
[29] ASEAN, *Hanoi Plan of Action* (Jakarta: ASEAN Secretariat, 1997).

Developing the ASEAN Community 233

ASEAN Community' was in the works, and the ASEAN Economic Community (AEC) was formally proposed by Singapore at the Phnom Penh Summit.

At the October 2003 ASEAN Summit, the Declaration of ASEAN Concord II (Bali Concord II, an agreement of common ASEAN principles) was adopted, as well as a declaration to form an 'ASEAN Community'. An earlier High Level Task Force (HLTF on Economic Integration, hereafter the Economic HLTF) had been set up and made recommendations on the AEC annexed in the Bali Concord II. The impetus for setting up the AEC was clear, as mentioned in a consultants' report that was among the documents considered for the Vientiane Action Program (VAP)[30]:

> Most importantly, the AEC would therefore build on the AFTA framework using it as a 'building bloc' towards creating a single market and production base. An integrated ASEAN could become an alternative to China as a regional production base for MNCs.[31]

The proposal was about strengthening the ASEAN community to provide a viable alternative to a rapidly rising China, which was swallowing up the bulk of new foreign direct investment to the region. With this as the guiding frame, efficacy in the economic sphere was of utmost urgency.

At that time, the proposed AEC was the centre of discussions, and the political-security and socio-cultural pillars that would form the other two pillars of the ASEAN Community project were still not yet developed. In Bali, the AEC was the only 'community' item on the agenda. However, having raised the AEC at the summit, this, according to sources, brought a fresh suggestion from President Megawati Sukarnoputri of Indonesia – that there should also be a security community alongside the economic one. Philippines then added that the ASEAN Community should also contain a socio-cultural community. Without objecting to the AEC directly, Indonesia and Philippines thus insisted on the other two pillars in order to get on board with the economic pillar.[32] Thus, three community 'pillars' were decided upon, but there were no details on two of

---

[30] 'Vientiane Action Programme' (Jakarta: ASEAN Secretariat, 2004).
[31] Hew and Sen, 'Towards an ASEAN Economic Community: Challenges and Prospects', 3.
[32] Interview with ASEAN official, 9 October 2017.

them; the annex of Bali Concord II only included plans for the AEC, recommended by the Economic HLTF. The Economic HLTF stopped short of explicitly recommending majority voting or the 'ASEAN minus X' formula, stating that the 'Decision-making process by economic bodies [is] to be made by consensus, and where there is no consensus, ASEAN [is] to consider other options with the objective of expediting the decision-making process.'[33] The Bali Concord II also explicitly called for institutions that would increase the rules-based nature of the grouping, meaning sanctions could be imposed for non-compliance, which would operate on a *de facto* 'minus X' formula. These included an ASEAN Compliance Body, enhancing the ASEAN dispute settlement mechanism, and creating a legal unit within the Secretariat to provide advice on trade disputes. It further called for acceleration of liberalisation of various trade and services areas through the ASEAN minus X formula, even those on a 'sensitive list', which would be moved to the temporary exclusion list (wherein their liberalisation was planned for rather than excluded).[34]

The VAP followed Bali Concord II, being the first plan developed around the 'ASEAN Community' idea adopted at the 2003 Bali Summit, with three pillars (economic, political-security, and socio-cultural) for integration. However, even though a year had passed since Bali, a review of the VAP shows how far advanced the plans for the AEC were over those for what became known as the 'ASEAN Political-Security Community' (APSC) and the 'ASEAN Socio-Cultural Community' (ASCC): the plan for the AEC was specific and detailed, and at six pages, twice the length of the other two blueprints.

Crucially, however, the APSC blueprint required the 'shaping and sharing' of norms. This involved embarking on the process of the ASEAN Charter drafting, which would formalise the norms of the RO. Virtually every aspect of ASEAN would be under scrutiny, albeit by distinguished former statesmen of its members, but this would include the oft-criticised decision-making process. The political question initially took a back seat.

---

[33] ASEAN, 'Declaration of ASEAN Concord II' (Bali 2003), Annex, para. 14(iv).
[34] Ibid., Annex, Recommendations.

The Eminent Persons Group

As noted above in Chapter 7 on human rights in the charter, the EPG had been tasked with being 'bold and visionary'.[35] The recommendations they came up with were, in their view, the best options available to the RO,[36] without necessarily considering the implementation of the recommendations. While the EPG considered matters such as human rights too contentious to deal with, they were much bolder on amending the decision-making structures to make ASEAN a more 'rules-based' community.

The overarching recommendation was that the organisation should 'realise an ASEAN Community and ultimately an ASEAN Union'. This involved replacing the Heads of State Summit with a more formal 'ASEAN Council' (although functionally it would be the same group of leaders meeting on a scheduled basis). It identified compliance as the primary barrier to ASEAN achieving its visions. To remedy this, the EPG recommended *inter alia* that:

- Dispute settlement mechanisms (DSM) should be established in all fields of ASEAN cooperation, which should include compliance monitoring, advisory, consultation as well as enforcement mechanisms.
- The ASEAN Secretariat should be entrusted with monitoring compliance with ASEAN agreements and action plans, with the Secretary-General of ASEAN reporting its findings to the ASEAN Council and the Community Councils on a regular basis.
- ASEAN should have the power to take measures to redress cases of serious breaches of ASEAN's objectives, major principles, and commitments to important agreements. Failure to comply with decisions of the dispute settlement mechanisms should be referred to the ASEAN Council. Such measures might include suspension of any of the rights and privileges of membership. Unless otherwise decided by the ASEAN Council in exceptional circumstances, there should be no recourse to expulsion of membership.[37]

---

[35] *Report of the Eminent Persons Group on the ASEAN Charter*, 2.
[36] Interview with ASEAN official, 6 October 2017.
[37] ASEAN, *Report of the Eminent Persons Group on the ASEAN Charter*, 4.

These recommendations, if adopted, would centralise authority within the Secretariat and its institutions, creating a more hierarchical structure. In Chapter V of the EPG's recommendations for inclusion in the charter, it proposed a variety of decision-making procedures. As a rule, consensus and consultation would apply especially on security and foreign policy (it did not preclude exceptions). In other areas, 'if consensus cannot be achieved', it allowed for decisions to be made through voting, whether in simple, two-thirds, or three-quarters majorities. Finally, it provided for the use of the 'ASEAN minus X' and '2 plus X' formulas in cooperation issues or projects, as decided by the community councils (which managed the sectoral arms of the ASEAN Community Project). The EPG argued:

While consensus should always be sought as a first step, it should not be allowed to hold up decisions or create an impasse in ASEAN cooperation. Consensus should aid, but not impede, ASEAN's cohesion and effectiveness. In this regard, economic cooperation is an example of one area where we can adopt a more flexible approach. For instance, the 'ASEAN minus X' or '2 plus X' formula of flexible participation could be used in such situations, subject to the decision of the relevant Community Councils.[38]

This was a fully fledged 'rules-based' community with measures for redress, non-compliance, and streamlined decision-making, controversially built under an umbrella of an 'ASEAN Union'. Dispute settlement mechanisms 'in all fields of cooperation' would mean supranational structures, even if temporary, would need to be created. There would be significant constraints on states and high requirements to uphold their commitments, with possibilities for punishment from non-compliance, even up to expulsion.

Without explicitly stating it, the EPG was suggesting the concession of sovereignty in several areas, to expedite the regional project, particularly economic integration. Nevertheless, the Cebu Summit endorsed the EPG's report, and work now turned to the Charter HLTF to begin the work of formally putting these into action. However, very little of what the EPG recommended that would check member state sovereignty would make its way into the final charter.

---

[38] Ibid., 17.

The Economic and Charter Task Forces

Because each group included representatives from all ten countries, one might ask how they formed norm circles. The answer is that ASEAN's method of reaching consensus at any level of grouping led to the formation of a norm circle. Once any particular ASEAN group made a consensus decision, the grouping spoke with a single voice. Thus, the consensus decision resulted in the creation of the norm circle on the issue area, but this may or may not have been aligned with other groups. Thus, as Chan explains: 'It is important to note that both the EPG and HLTF processes, as well as those of the ASEAN Foreign Ministers and ASEAN Heads of State/Government who mandated, guided, and adopted their outcomes, *were all themselves products of consensus.*'[39] While it would have been possible to try to trace the divisions within each grouping, for the purpose of explaining this contestation over the decision-making mechanism it is not necessary: each group met first, and having reached particular decisions, interacted with the other groups as units (though occasionally some members might be missing), trying to influence or impart instructions as the case may be. Thus, this case study departs from the state-level divisions of other contests examined in the book, into a purely functional contest between economic and foreign ministers.

The norm circle in favour of variable decision-making processes consisted of the EPG, ASEAN economic ministers, and the Economic HLTF. The norm circle favouring consensus and consultation consisted of the ASEAN foreign ministers, to which the Charter HLTF deferred on the matter. One foreign minister explicitly vetoed voting,[40] and this became the consensus of the foreign ministers, who at their second meeting with the foreign ministers instructed the Charter HLTF that 'ASEAN minus X' would be restricted to the economic domain.

The Charter HLTF, therefore, taking instructions from the foreign ministers, were told at their first meeting with them that the term 'ASEAN Union' should be left out and that the basic principle of decision-making was consensus.[41] The Economic HLTF met with the Charter HLTF in April 2007, and asked whether 'the ASEAN minus

---

[39] Chan, 'Decision-Making in the ASEAN Charter Process', 237, emphasis in the original.
[40] Woon, *The ASEAN Charter*, 157.
[41] Koh, Manalo, and Woon, *The Making of the ASEAN Charter*, 54.

X principle could be expanded to become "policy"' and that the Enhanced Dispute Settlement Mechanism should be institutionalised as the mode of dispute settlement in the charter.[42] According to some officials, there was concern that the decisions and processes set in motion after Bali Concord II would be unravelled by the charter if there were a reversion to consensus-only decision-making and informality.[43] However, as Tommy Koh recounts:

> The response of the Charter HLTF was somewhat sceptical. My sense is that there was a certain lack of empathy between some members of the Charter HLTF, all of whom are from their foreign ministries, and our colleagues from the economic track. This could have been due to the fact that in some ASEAN countries, coordination between them is not optimal and there is considerable rivalry between them.[44]

While a 'lack of empathy' may certainly be possible, it does not explain why a division existed in the first place. More simply, the functional reading of the debate was clear: economic integration required a variable-speed approach, and therefore was more amenable to the 'ASEAN minus X' formula compared with the political-security agenda, which saw the formula as only divisive. Thus, in the final charter, the 'ASEAN minus X' principle was included but only as applying to the economic domain, with the caveat that consensus was first required to employ the principle. Meanwhile, stronger powers for the Secretariat, recommended by both the EPG and the economic ministers, were rejected.

The two remaining issues related to non-compliance and the failure to reach consensus. In both cases, it was determined that the ASEAN (heads of state) Summit would decide what to do, though the ASEAN (foreign) Ministers Meeting (AMM) ruled out suspension or expulsion as possible instruments. In the latter case, the argument may be circular,[45] if it is the summit itself that fails to reach consensus (rather than at the sectoral level, where the authority of the summit decides). The experience of the debates in the Charter HLTF itself was an example of this very principle in action, as decisions went higher up the various layers of ASEAN meetings until they could be resolved. However, Charter HLTF questions never needed to be escalated beyond the foreign ministers.

[42] Ibid., 55.   [43] Interview with ASEAN official, 6 October 2017.
[44] Koh, Manalo, and Woon, *The Making of the ASEAN Charter*, 55–6.
[45] Woon, *The ASEAN Charter*, 159.

Table 8.1 *Recommendations on ASEAN decision-making compared with the result*

EPG recommendations	ASEAN Charter
Chapter V: Decision-making process The ASEAN Charter should institute a more effective decision-making process. • The decision-making process in ASEAN shall, as a general rule, be based on consultation and consensus, especially on decisions in more sensitive areas of security and foreign policy. • On other areas, if consensus cannot be achieved, decisions may be taken through voting, either on the basis of a simple majority, or on the basis of a two-thirds or three-quarters majority. • The ASEAN Council [Summit] shall prescribe rules of procedure governing situations when there may be voting by a simple majority, atwo-thirds or three-quarters majority. • On certain ASEAN cooperation issues or projects, the formula for flexible participation of 'ASEAN minus X' or '2 plus X' may be applied, to be decided upon by the relevant Councils of the ASEAN Community. • Decisions on temporary suspension of rights and privileges of membership shall be taken by unanimity, without participation of the Member State or Member States to which the decision shall be applied.	**Art. 20: Consultation and consensus** 1. As a basic principle, decision-making in ASEAN shall be based on consultation and consensus. 2. Where consensus cannot be achieved, the ASEAN Summit may decide how a specific decision can be made. 3. Nothing in paragraph 1 and 2 of this Article shall affect the modes of decision-making as contained in the relevant ASEAN legal instruments. 4. In the case of a serious breach of the Charter or non-compliance, the matter shall be referred to the ASEAN Summit for decision. **Art. 21: Implementation and procedure** 1. Each ASEAN Community Council shall prescribe its own rules of procedure. 2. In the implementation of economic commitments, a formula for flexible participation, including the ASEAN minus X formula, may be applied where there is consensus to do so.

Source: Adapted from Chan, 'Decision-Making in the ASEAN Charter Process', 241.

Controlling the Initiative

The 'ASEAN minus X' formula advanced as long as the frame of the debate related to ASEAN economic integration. From the 2002 Phnom Penh Summit till the 2006 EPG report, it seemed likely that some qualifications to the consensus principle would occur when the charter was drafted. The problems with an informal trade agreement like AFTA were clear: no enforcement mechanisms and variable timetables meant the incentive continued to be that the bulk of trade would occur outside the region with external partners. Stronger agreements could not be created when consensus was necessary, and diplomats and experts at the time were united in believing stronger agreements were the most urgent need for ASEAN.

As the most developed 'pillar', the Economic Community had often offered norms for the rest of the grouping[46] and the push to move it to a rules-based community was perhaps the most ambitious of such attempts. While discussion centred around economic integration and the AEC, the utility of streamlining the decision-making process and avoiding deadlocks was clear. The processes from the VAP to the EPG did not raise substantial objections regarding proposals to change ASEAN's decision-making procedures. Indeed, a plethora of voting rule possibilities was explored by the EPG, and the economic ministers, who had elaborated considerable mechanisms in the Vientiane Action Programme and ASEAN Economic Blueprint, were keen to have these formalised as ASEAN rules of procedure.

However, as the 'ASEAN Community' project grew, and the other two pillars were introduced and elaborated, the political aspects of ASEAN returned to the fray. As the process moved to the Charter HLTF, the influence of economic ministers and the EPG began to wane, as the broader concerns of ASEAN came into view.

Nevertheless, the influence of the EPG started well, as Musa Hitam, chair of the EPG and one of its more progressive members behind many ambitious recommendations such as civil society engagement,[47] addressed them initially at the first HLTF meeting. He briefed them on the areas where the EPG could have gone further, including more elaborate mechanisms such as an ASEAN Parliament, Court of

---

[46] Interview with ASEAN official, 14 November 2017.
[47] Jayakumar, *Be at the Table or Be on the Menu*, 89.

Justice, and of course the human rights commission.[48] However, none of these would eventually make it into the charter, as each was vetoed by the ASEAN foreign ministers, with the exception of the human rights body. These omissions left some EPG members 'disappointed' with the charter.[49]

At the drafting stage, however, foreign ministers had direct authority over the Charter HLTF, and the question of what the HLTF could determine depended on whether there was consensus among the ten HLTF members. If there were no consensus, they would refer the question to the foreign ministers, who were expected to come up with a decision.[50] This in effect meant that the gradual momentum for exceptions to consensus, which had been building under the rubric of ASEAN's informal practices, came to a halt.

Shared Norms

Because ASEAN had adhered to informal processes in the past, the writing of the charter and the dictate to be 'bold and visionary' allowed for substantially wider interpretation of shared norms than normally espoused for the EPG. How much space each EPG member had to recommend novel instruments was left to their own interpretation; Ali Alatas of Indonesia perhaps interpreted it the broadest, and therefore felt the least beholden to existing norms, choosing to draw on organisational forms from other regions such as the EU, AU, and OAS.[51]

The high degree of past informality also meant ASEAN had a lot of formalising to do, with many norms being considered simultaneously in the charter process. ASEAN, with its informal preferences, had already experimented with a variety of alternatives, such as 'ASEAN minus X', '2 plus X', and even questioning what it means to have a consensus – whether it means that everyone agrees about a decision's desirability, or that no one objects strongly enough, for example.

While the consensus was that the EPG report could be drawn on as a shared norm, the HLTF was instructed to follow a set of instructions

---

[48] Woon, *The ASEAN Charter*, 22.
[49] Koh, Manalo, and Woon, *The Making of the ASEAN Charter*, 51.
[50] In theory, if the foreign ministers were deadlocked, they would have referred it to the ASEAN Summit (heads of state level), but no questions went that far.
[51] Chan, 'Decision-Making in the ASEAN Charter Process', 239.

and documents, of which the EPG report was only one. This meant that the HLTF could either selectively pick from the EPG report, rejecting anything contentious, or else defer the question to foreign ministers if necessary. The Cebu Declaration on the Blueprint of the ASEAN Charter, while endorsing the EPG's report, noted that foreign ministers' instructions and 'relevant ASEAN documents' would be part of the norms that the HLTF would consider, alongside the EPG recommendations:

> we endorse the Report of the EPG on the ASEAN Charter and agree that the High Level Task Force should commence the drafting of the ASEAN Charter based on our directions given at the 11th and 12th ASEAN Summits, the relevant ASEAN documents, together with the EPG recommendations ...[52]

The 'endorsement' of the EPG report was thus a relatively weak one. The foreign ministers immediately rejected the notion of an 'ASEAN Union' and reiterated consensus as the basic decision-making process.[53] Moreover, the late addition of the other two pillars – the political-security and socio-cultural communities – meant that these relatively underdeveloped areas received less attention from both the VAP and the EPG. However, they brought back into the picture the fractious origins of ASEAN as an aspirational security community, and the norms required for this to be achieved.

If the primary logic of developing the 'ASEAN Community' was economic integration, then the instruments required for this process would take primacy. This was most apparent to the economic ministers and Economic HLTF, who pushed for the 'ASEAN minus X' formula to become official policy, and the institutionalisation of the ASEAN Enhanced Dispute Settlement Mechanism – both creations necessitated by the needs of the AEC project. Economic goals required streamlining the decision-making norms.

In contrast, the foreign ministers and Charter HLTF had a broader view of ASEAN norms, keenly aware of the need for consensus to drive the ASEAN security community in a way that no national interests could be left out. This meant that the economic-driven norms took a subordinate role to the political norms of consensus, consultation, and sovereignty. The potential for a flexible decision-making

---

[52] ASEAN, 'Cebu Declaration on the Blueprint of the ASEAN Charter'.
[53] Koh, Manalo, and Woon, *The Making of the ASEAN Charter*, 54.

Developing the ASEAN Community 243

formula to override any national interests was considered too risky for the RO.

Politically, ASEAN had informally used the 'minus X' formula with respect to Myanmar in the past. As Singaporean Foreign Minister George Yeo described:

> The fact that we operate on a consensus principle did not prevent us in the past from calling for the release of Aung San Suu Kyi. Members will remember that during the ASEAN Summit in Singapore after the informal dinner hosted by the Prime Minister, nine leaders of ASEAN stood together to issue a statement on Myanmar, following the refusal of Myanmar's Prime Minister to agree to an ASEAN meeting with UN Special Envoy Gambari. So that statement was not a 'consensus statement'. It was a 'minus one' statement and it was a statement about the 'minus one'.[54]

While this was a potential precedent, it was too sensitive to be appealed to as an argument with the Myanmar representative sitting in the room during the charter drafting process. The complication furthermore was that as long as ASEAN retained its informality, such a possibility was not precluded in the future. However, changing the formal principle of decision-making was too contentious,[55] and when the time came for putting down the principle formally in writing, it entrenched the consensus decision-making process to a greater degree than perhaps had existed in reality.

Metis

What of the opportunities to influence the decision-making process? The task had become distant from the imperative of economic integration that had driven the whole process. Attempts were nevertheless made to assert influence from other groups in ASEAN.

Although the first meeting with the ministers stressed the importance of consensus and consultation as the primary decision-making mode of ASEAN, they did not specify further that other alternatives were excluded. The HLTF even considered briefly sub-articles on voting for rules of procedure or how decisions could be made in the absence of members, but could not reach consensus and thus these were omitted from Art. 21 of the ASEAN Charter.[56]

---

[54] Yeo, 'Remarks by Minister for Foreign Affairs George Yeo'.
[55] Interview with ASEAN official, 5 September 2017.
[56] Woon, *The ASEAN Charter*, 160.

The interjections of the Economic HLTF occurred at the fourth Charter HLTF meeting, when they sought clarification about existing economic decision-making processes such as ASEAN minus X and the Enhanced Dispute Settlement Mechanism. The pressure from the economic ministers would continue all the way to the final HLTF meeting in Vientiane. Despite the guarded diplomatic language, Tommy Koh's account is clear that the opportunities to exert influence were not exactly welcome and even divided the Charter HLTF:

> A lot of time was spent on how to respond to the requests of the ASEAN Economic Ministers. They were resisted by several members of the HLTF who, probably for domestic reasons, had no empathy for the AEM. Because of their resistance, compromise language had to be negotiated between those who were supportive and those who were unsympathetic to the requests of the AEM. I would respectfully request our Foreign and Economic Ministers and their respective Senior Officials to meet together and to do so more frequently in order to bridge the gap.[57]

Other ASEAN officials noted that the foreign ministers are not always the most important ministers in their respective countries, and their economic counterparts may outrank them domestically. In some cases, this may have been important within the HLTF, where the final say on the charter would include approval from both the foreign and the economic ministers, a concern noted by Myanmar's Aung Bwa.[58]

Two tangible examples may have framed the debate decisively: the dispute settlement mechanism and the human rights body. On the human rights body, the Philippines had suggested controversially at the eighth HLTF meeting that the ASEAN Human Rights Commission should be established on the 'ASEAN minus X' principle: that the ASEAN member states ready to move forward with a commission could do so, and the others could join when they were ready. This was also supported by Indonesia and Malaysia but rejected by the CLMV countries.[59] Rather than helping establish the desired human rights body, this may have been counter-productive in establishing the decision-making mechanism, as it clarified how the use of the 'minus X' principles in political situations would only heighten controversy.

---

[57] Koh, Manalo, and Woon, *The Making of the ASEAN Charter*, 65-66.
[58] Bwa, 'The Jewel in my Crown', 33–4.
[59] Koh, Manalo, and Woon, *The Making of the ASEAN Charter*, 59.

The dispute settlement mechanism was a core mechanism of the ASEAN Economic Community, established before the charter, and then labelled the 'Enhanced Dispute Settlement Mechanism' (EDSM) in the Vientiane Protocol[60] to distinguish it from the earlier version found in the CEPT AFTA framework. While the EDSM covered economic agreements, other dispute settlement procedures are found in other ASEAN treaties, most notably the High Council provided for by the Treaty of Amity and Cooperation (TAC).

However, in all cases, both parties must first agree to use the mechanism before it will be established. An independent actor such as a disinterested member state or the ASEAN Secretariat cannot invoke it. This mechanism remained unchanged, perhaps to the disappointment of some economic ministers who sought a more robust or apolitical procedure. The difficulty was that such mechanisms would require a more hierarchical and centralised institution, rather than an intergovernmental one, and whenever this question was raised, the intergovernmental form won out.[61] The preference remained for solving disputes through negotiation, mediation, and conciliation.[62] The only hierarchy that was countenanced was the implicit bureaucratic hierarchy of each member state:

> Hierarchy weighed heavily on the HLTF's negotiating process. It seemed difficult to escape the consciousness that the HLTF were drafting provisions that would define the roles of the Ministers and Heads of State/Government. I recall one delegation leader exclaiming, 'Who am I to tell the Leaders what to do?'[63]

A brief attempt within the Charter HLTF was made to define what kinds of areas were 'non-sensitive' to allow more efficient decision-making, but according to Chan, the response was that 'It would be too sensitive to define the sensitive areas.'[64] Thus, in trying to identify the areas for alternatives to consensus, only the pressure from the economic ministers led to formal acceptance of a variable decision-making process in their domain.

---

[60] Woon, 'The ASEAN Charter Dispute Settlement Mechanisms', in *The Making of the ASEAN Charter*, ed. Koh, Manalo, and Woon, 72–3.
[61] Ng and Liow, 'The Southeast Asian Dimension'.
[62] Interview with ASEAN official, 25 September 2017.
[63] Chan, 'Decision-Making in the ASEAN Charter Process', 240.   [64] Ibid., 243.

Yet, as Walter Woon has pointed out, the ASEAN Treaty on Mutual Legal Assistance in Criminal Matters is an example of a non-economic agreement that initially started out on the 'ASEAN minus X' formula: Thailand and Myanmar did not initially join.[65] Similarly, the 1995 Treaty on the Southeast Asia Nuclear-Weapon-Free Zone (Treaty of Bangkok) Article 8(8) allows for two-third majority voting on issues should there be a failure of consensus.[66] Thus, there were non-economic areas that had once been deemed to be *not* too sensitive for the 'minus X' application, but owing either to time constraints or to the nature of how the argument unfolded, the HLTF was not able to create the space for other flexible arrangements to be acknowledged in the charter, potentially a missed opportunity for the HLTF members who were so inclined.

Conclusion

By the time the ASEAN Charter was adopted, ASEAN had showed it would reject any suggestions pointing in the direction of supranationality, even in relatively innocuous name changes, such as the 'ASEAN Council' being rejected in favour of retaining 'ASEAN Summit' for the heads of state meeting. Similarly, any substantial changes to the decision-making procedures, so long criticised for slowing the economic integration process, were rejected if they could potentially override national interests. This pointed to the continued preference that sovereignty would not be conceded if formally suggested, as a matter of principle. Stronger powers for the ASEAN Secretariat, recommended by both the EPG and the economic ministers, were rejected.

Deliberation on decision-making norms was not as contentious as that on human rights, but if the impetus for a charter was accelerating economic integration, there was a very strong argument that a consensus-only approach had to be qualified by more expedient decision-making formulas if it meant ending up with frequent deadlocks. However, it seemed apparent after the EPG process that, despite pressure from the economic quarters, this could end up with a concession of sovereignty. As a senior ASEAN official put it:

[65] Woon, *The ASEAN Charter*, 158–9.
[66] However, a majoritarian vote is unlikely to ever be used, according to some ASEAN officials. Interview with ASEAN official, 23 November 2017.

The political and social community are not so simple, the Charter has mentioned quite clearly. This would give de facto majority decision-making going forward. The 'minus X' [formula] could evolve into a way out, with a *de facto* majority decision-making process. I think some countries understood that this would be the case.[67]

Such a result was perceived to jeopardise the unity of ASEAN, if it permitted the overruling of national interests, even if only on occasion. Political questions, the above official argued, were qualitative, whereas economic ones were quantitative. And in the case of qualitative decisions, there was no adequate formula to justify overriding any national interests. Yet this impasse also meant that ASEAN failed to solve an age-old question. As the former Secretary-General Rodolfo Severino put it: 'ASEAN has fallen short of the ambitions that it has proclaimed for itself, particularly in terms of driving regionalism and regional integration. A major reason for this is the fact that political cohesion and economic integration are pursued independently of each other.'[68]

The economic and political-security spheres tend to operate independently of one another, when they are more interdependent than officials appear to understand. For instance, the potential for strong common economic interests to begin to bring national interests more in line with each other, reducing potential for conflict, is under-recognised. The economic ministers were not trying to undermine unity, but rather forge a different kind of project that they also believed would enhance unity in the long term. However, it was decided that ASEAN had not yet forged enough common cause and good faith, and the risk of a majoritarian decision-making process could unravel the experiment if not handled carefully.

As Ng and Liow argue, ASEAN settled on a 'hierarchy of problems' rather than a 'hierarchy of norms': the cohesion of the political community was more important than economic expediency, and norms that would permit hierarchical structures for more efficient decision-making were therefore relegated or rejected.[69] This applied to both AICHR, which retained its intergovernmental shape determined by political rather than normative decision-making, and the 'ASEAN

---

[67] Interview with ASEAN official, 9 October 2017.
[68] Severino, 'ASEAN beyond Forty: Towards Political and Economic Integration', *Contemporary Southeast Asia* 29, no. 3 (2007): 406.
[69] Ng and Liow, 'The Southeast Asian Dimension', 117.

Council' and ASEAN minus X, which were rejected or confined to a narrow domain.

The push for 'ASEAN minus X' was not a conscious attempt to undermine ASEAN's political norms, only a desire to strengthen the economic decision-making process. However, as the impact of such a change became clear – that there would be an impact on sovereignty, and potentially supranational structures would be required to enforce disputes – ASEAN members turned back from the proposals and retreated from the 'bold and visionary' ideas to the norms that they believed had served them well. If the contest had been, as some hinted, about bureaucratic rivalries between the economic and foreign ministries in certain countries, it could also have precluded room for compromise and resulted in the narrow allowance of 'ASEAN minus X' to only be formalised in the economic community pillar.

Ironically, the creation of the charter and the push for a rules-based community meant formalisation of the decision-making process narrowed the scope of application of certain processes, particularly the 'ASEAN minus X' formula. One ambassador, having urged stronger integration (which the charter had originally been envisaged to enhance), called the charter's commitment to consensus and sidelining of '2 plus X' and 'ASEAN minus X' a 'retrograde step'.[70] Had the minus X application not been politicised, particularly deployed in the human rights commission debate, there may have been more room to apply it in discrete projects. In searching for a general norm or trying to push for its formalisation, however, the decision was that the norm applied very narrowly, and was confined to the economic domain because that was the only sectoral group to push for it. One ASEAN official stated that the mistake was in trying to change the principle: in leaving it informal, the practice would probably have been allowed to drift much further in the direction of minus X rather than strict consensus, but when the principle was challenged, the member states were unwilling to shift it.[71] Notably, '2 plus X' vanished from ASEAN processes, despite it having been a part of ASEAN's 1992 Framework Agreement,[72] after being omitted from mention in the charter, although a more ambiguous 'flexible participation' is included.

[70] Desker, 'Is the ASEAN Charter Necessary?'
[71] Interview with ASEAN official, 5 September 2017.
[72] ASEAN, 'Agreement on the Common Effective Preference Tariff Scheme for the ASEAN Free Trade Area'.

Conclusion 249

ASEAN's lack of a legal culture meant that even as it was making a charter that would create a binding set of rules, some of the codification involved an entrenchment of informality, such as the decision to formally declare negotiation and consensus as the basis of ASEAN decision-making. The more ambitious idea to create a rules-based community, central to the notion of the AEC, was not provided with strong mechanisms to effect it. While every member agreed to 'rule of law' as a value and it appears as both a purpose and a principle in Arts. 1(7) and 2(h) of the ASEAN Charter, the mechanisms for enforcing it do not. To date, attempts to set up a functioning investor–state dispute settlement mechanism across ASEAN have not been possible.

'ASEAN minus X' might have been intended as a means to bridge the gap between member states and bring more of them in line with the needs of an 'economic community', but if certain members were unwilling to countenance the necessary changes to their domestic institutions, then it was not possible to proceed at the multilateral level. While there were clearly different norm circles with different views on the application of the 'ASEAN minus X' or '2 plus X' alternatives to consensus, the utilities split the circles along functional lines, therefore (relatively) neatly lining them up in economic and foreign ministry groups at the ASEAN level. The domain constraints then took over and largely determined the process: with the Charter HLTF taking instructions from their foreign ministers, the avenue for influence from the economic ministers or Economic HLTF was very limited. In the end, the application of 'ASEAN minus X' was granted, but only for the limited domain in economics where it already existed, and it did not mention other alternatives such as '2 plus X'. Table 8.2 shows the factors that affected the contest.

This case study is important because it represents a purely internally driven debate: any external pressure may have been in the form of competitive pressure, but it was not of the sort of direct lobbying or attempts to make ASEAN emulate other institutions. This case also lays bare how overtly functionalist some fault lines can be in an RO, with the divide not falling easily along national lines, but in this case, more apparently along differences between economic and foreign ministries of respective member states.

The three contestation factors – control, shared norms, and metis – played out, albeit in a weaker sense, as the economic groups were not pushing aggressively for an expansive interpretation of a variable

Table 8.2 *Rejection of 'ASEAN minus X' as a procedural norm in ASEAN*

Factors	Proposing norm circle	Opposing norm circle
Members	Economic ministry officials, Economic HLTF, EPG	Foreign ministry officials, Charter HLTF
Control of initiative	• ASEAN economic community needs driving new norms (Vientiane Action Programme) • EPG meetings and recommendations	• Full control during charter drafting process • Centring debate on political-security community considerations
Norms invoked	• Decision-making mechanisms in AEC • EPG report • Minor precedents	• Sovereignty • 'ASEAN Way': informality, pragmatism, consultation, and consensus
Metis	• Attempted meetings with Charter HLTF	• Foreign ministers' decision to exclude most EPG recommendations
Outcome	Option for economic community, if consensus agreed (rejected)	

decision-making process, and the domain constraints that limited their influence with the HLTF were considerable. However, it was clearly observed on a longer arc: while the reference frame was the AEC (as was the case in the VAP and EPG report), the 'ASEAN minus X' principle seemed to be gaining ground for implementation as a decision-making principle. However, by the time of the charter drafting, when the wider regional considerations had to all be considered, it lost its momentum.

Second, shared norms were significant, though a brief argument was attempted to express 'ASEAN minus X' as a shared practice that could be translated into a formal norm of the organisation. However, ultimately, the 'ASEAN Way', comprising informality and intergovernmentalism, held its ground and any innovations in the decision-making process were rejected. The consensus processes in each of the groups – the EPG, the HLTF, and the foreign ministers – were all performed according to the ASEAN practice of consensus and consultation. Even if innovations had been made in the decision-making processes, it is

Conclusion

also possible that these could have been undermined through other means if necessary, such as rules of procedure or controlling the quorum.[73]

Finally, there were few opportunities for external influence, but the interaction by the Economic HLTF may have backfired, in spite of some support for its positions within the Charter HLTF.[74] The debates on use of the formula for the dispute settlement mechanism and the human rights body may have also sealed its fate in being rejected for more extensive application. The net result is that ASEAN continued to make all decisions in a political manner: as Chan says, 'Such a [consensus-based] structure does, however, imply that notwithstanding references to a rule-based organisation, all issues in ASEAN are ultimately decided by a political process.'[75]

Norm circles have proved their strength as a unit of analysis with emergent properties, as norms are decided in smaller groups, aggregating up to larger groups, for the study of the multilayered system of ASEAN and its high-level committees, but not without some caveats. The interaction and outcome recommendations from the EPG to the AMM to the Charter HLTF to the Economic HLTF each differed slightly: their interpretation of the norm and its importance for ASEAN consequently was not completely aligned, certainly not on state lines, and sometimes not entirely on functional lines either. However, where they reached consensus positions, they could form norm circles which then interacted with other potential clusters that were in their own process of forming their own normative conclusions.

Each circle could also either be read as a black box or be studied according to the interaction within it. However, some groups were more accessible than others, and this was the most difficult case for attempting this kind of research, which is contingent on accounts or observations of diplomatic practice in action. While it was known that there was considerable debate at the foreign ministers' level, the nature of this debate was not known, even among members of the HLTF, who only received the consensus decisions of the foreign ministers at the end.

---

[73] Chan, 'Decision-Making in the ASEAN Charter Process', 246.
[74] Bwa, 'The Jewel in my Crown', 33.
[75] Chan, 'Decision-Making in the ASEAN Charter Process', 243.

Yet, in a nod to ASEAN's original informality, some ASEAN initiatives have once again resurfaced, in some cases in a sort of unilateral but multilateral form, where one country proposes, staffs, or funds it, and no one objects. This can be seen of the ASEAN Institute for Peace and Reconciliation in Indonesia or the ASEAN Regional Mine Action Centre in Cambodia, which one ASEAN official sardonically termed a 'One minus Nine' principle;[76] neither of these appears to have any significant support from or obligations for the other nine members. When one considers one original motivation of strengthening ASEAN – to assist in raising support from donors by turning it into a legal entity – these kinds of institutions continue to do just that.

Finally, there is a lesson for international relations theories: the focus on economic reasoning to the exclusion of the political may not always provide the results desired. The quantitative utility gains of the 'minus X' formula, which the economic ministries were largely in agreement on, were rebuffed when it encountered qualitative political considerations. Efficiency considerations could not, it was decided, move faster than the political project, no matter how slow that may be. When economic reasoning is the only logic accepted, decisions may be made that would be unpalatable to other parts of the organisation or their member states. This case study highlighted the importance of studying cases when the economic meets the political, even though because of different methodological approaches, they tend to be kept separate, with nothing to offer the other at worst, or privileging one set of reasoning over the other at best. A good understanding of how competing logics address each other when they clash or seem incommensurable is best achieved through a practice-oriented analysis of contestation.

---

[76] Interview with ASEAN official, 5 September 2017.

PART IV

Comparative Findings

This book set out to investigate the evolution of sovereignty in two regional organisations (ROs) of the Global South, the AU and ASEAN. To differentiate itself from existing theories, the aim was to develop a fully fledged anti-foundationalist account that could incorporate power, explain both stability and change, and resist the privileging of some kinds of norms or norm agents over others. This necessitated a model where a 'functionalist bird's-eye view is combined with the worm's-eye view of actor centered social analysis'.[1] The study thus focused on 'contestation', seeking an understanding of not only significant and successful norms, but also rejected or qualified norms. Having centred the model around actors in a norm circle, it then zoomed in on the practices of those norm circles and how they interacted with their opponents to shape the outcomes.

In specifying the contours of the regional organisation as the domain, the model showed how the rules of the game – i.e. contestation – are significantly constrained by the respective ROs. One could not study the norm absent its proponents and opponents (the norm circles), or the domain's characteristics (such as institutional rules and normative environment). In an RO, the norm(s) rode on a particular text – a proposal – around which the contest unfolded. Some more ambitious proposals contained numerous norms, and were passed wholesale, such as the Conference on Security, Stability, Development, and Cooperation in Africa (at the second attempt). The CSSDCA also showed the importance of the norms beyond its packaging into a proposal. Judged from the label, CSSDCA – the physical conference proper – vanished by 2004, and might be mistaken as a failure. But its impact in the establishment of norms throughout

---

[1] Berger and Offe, 'Functionalism vs. Rational Choice? Some Questions Concerning the Rationality of Choosing One or the Other', *Theory and Society* 11, no. 4 (1982): 523.

the new AU, from the right to intervene, the Peace and Security Council, participatory mechanisms in NEPAD, and even diaspora participation – none of which were present or acceptable in 1991 – showed how influential it was in inserting itself into the everyday structures of the organisation.

Other proposals had much more limited ambitions, such as the mere mention of human rights protection in the ASEAN Charter, which was tightly contested despite omission of tangible institutional mechanisms (which would develop a few years later). The nature of contestation over the presence of norms in a proposal depended on the opposing norm circles' decisions to convert their preferences into overt opposition – turning latent power into influence[2] – and in doing so, creating observable discourses and actions that helped to shed light on the nature of contestation in light of the practices of the respective norm circles. By looking at the nature of sovereignty contests, it showed that given normative diversity, linear models to integration are improbable when political decision-making is paramount and the opposing norm circles are relatively balanced.

In selecting cases of rejected norms, this model illustrated how successful strategies for opposing a norm often went amiss in other theories. In looking at qualified norms, it demonstrated the importance of not privileging the substantive content of a norm in advance, and shed light on neutral actors or brokers who organised compromises between extreme ends of the normative spectrum. The focus in scholarship on successful norms has led to neglect of many characteristics that this book has explored. This section now comparatively assesses the model and how the different cases inform the significance of each variable, before drawing its conclusion.

---

[2] Cox and Jacobson, *The Anatomy of Influence* (New Haven: Yale University Press, 1974), 21–2.

9 | Assessing the Model

The model used the concept of the 'norm circle' not only to act as the causal agents, but also to emphasise the social milieu in which normative agents operated. Individuals or states could play leading roles at times, but they were always operating in a normative environment involving other clusters of norms and norm circles. In the first instance, a proposal that was overwhelmingly useful was unlikely to be contested; a much smaller norm circle would often be unwilling to raise objections, deeming the social costs of objection too high. Significant power inequalities, such as those possessed by a regional hegemon, could also pre-empt contestation, but these circumstances were avoided in the study as it focused on narrower differences and greater contestation. The model did not specify 'utility' to a great degree, partly in recognition of diverse epistemologies and logics of regional actors, but also importantly to conceptually separate it from the contest, preventing the model from privileging one norm over another. If there were significant enough members in a norm circle to oppose the proposal, contestation ensued.

In most of the cases, the relevant norms were explicitly stated in their proposals, but some were more implicit, with the implied utility a matter of perception. This was especially so for the democratic participation entailed by a Pan-African Parliament, and the sovereignty concession involved in allowing for 'ASEAN minus X'. All the norms in their respective proposals would potentially constrain sovereignty in some form, and the proposals entailed substantive changes to the respective organisations. This meant that there was an essential tension in each, as ideational commitment was insufficient to explain support for or opposition to the norm, particularly in the case of the Pan-African Parliament, when democratic states opposed it, and the 'ASEAN minus X' debate, when the division fell along functional ministry lines rather than between member states. Utility, and the concept of 'bracketing' open positions by member states, allowed for observing this phenomenon to map the formation of norm circles as well as changes of alignment or removal of objections (such as Libya on CSSDCA, or Laos on civil society engagement with the AICHR).

Utility and Power

The functional approach – thinking in terms of the implications of norms, even political ones, and their attendant costs – was the best means of understanding the normative contest as 'conflicts of interest over the distribution of those adjustment costs'.[1] The distance that states perceived their own norms or institutions to be from the newly proposed norms gave an indication of the cost their acceptance would entail, though it was possible for them to be persuaded that those costs were not as significant as they seemed.

The model also gave relational power a prominent role in affecting outcomes. Power was observed in two forms. One was the arrangement and size of the norm circles themselves, through a sorting by 'utility', albeit one that was not necessarily quantifiable. The second form played out as relative competencies.

This first form of differential power, manifested by utility, was open-ended, recognising that diverse actors in a domain may deploy different logics (such as logics of consequences, appropriateness, or practice) to choose whether to support or reject a norm. A norm that was particularly useful, however, could amass such a large support from proponents in its norm circle that contestation would be avoided, even in organisations that had institutional rules such as consensus. Utility, however, was not an objective concept owing to the difficulties with quantification. Here, one form of persuasion (or rhetorical action) manifested in convincing non-committal or opposed actors either to join the proposing norm circle – not always through moral or ideational appeals but often on instrumental grounds – or failing that, at least not to coalesce their opposition formally.

Who comprised those norm circles and what power they wielded in the domain was also significant. While Obasanjo and ASEAN's Eminent Persons Group both offered novel solutions to problems in their respective regions, when they were no longer state parties, they had little opportunity to influence the outcome aside from stating their

---

[1] Buthe and Mattli, *The New Global Rulers*, 42.

recommendations. Obasanjo rectified this shortcoming when he returned as head of state, but the EPG never achieved its recommendation to create alternative decision-making norms that could overcome the consensus veto.

The second form of power was observed through diplomatic competencies, specific to the nature of the domains in question, i.e. the respective ROs. These involved the various norm circles' abilities to control the initiative, frame new ideas as extensions or corollaries of other existing shared norms, and metis – 'the agential power to change relations'.[2] This model suggests that a proposal's chance of success was determined first by the formation of norm circles for and against it, followed by a contest between the proposing and opposing norm circles. The likelihood of success was then annotated as:

$$P \text{ (Proposal success)} = P (C_A > C_B) \cdot P (S_A > S_B) \cdot P (M_A > M_B)$$

Where A and B represented the proposing and opposing norm circles respectively, 'C' represented 'Control of the initiative', 'S' their mastery of other 'Shared norms', and 'M' related to their 'Metis' or opportunities to change the relations between norm circles. I now evaluate the respective importance of each of these factors against the overall cases of the book, and try to draw some comparative insights grouped around the respective factors.

Control of the Initiative

Control of the initiative and mastery of a regional organisation's procedures are a core competency for negotiators: the 'first mover' advantage. Understanding the bureaucratic logic of how the organisation works is a necessary condition for success, yet the ability to leverage that control to further an actor's aims may be variable depending on the space each RO allows. 'The ASEAN Way' had become so familiar to ASEAN officials that space to seize the initiative became constrained in the RO. However, in the OAU especially, use of the 'death by committee' method – constant deferrals without overt objection to a proposal – occurred both in deferring Obasanjo's proposal for a CSSDCA in 1991 and in Gaddafi's initiatives relating to the United States of Africa. However, the prevalence of this

[2] Bjola and Kornprobst, *Understanding International Diplomacy*, 126.

particular tactic seems to be organisation-specific, owing to the difficulty in opposing a leader who has committed to throwing all their support behind a particular proposal.[3] Although the same function can be performed by ASEAN, in which referral to the Committee of Permanent Representatives (CPR) or Senior Officials Meetings (SOMs) can cause an item to languish indefinitely out of public view, it is less frequently used, and even more rarely for high-profile proposals.

Both organisations were sensitive to domination, albeit in different ways. Gaddafi's brow-beating style of getting states to align with him worked against him, and even caused his erstwhile ally, Mali's Alpha Konaré, to complain about the attempts at domination and exclusion,[4] and eventually concede one of the federalists' most important goals – the supranational powers of the Pan-African Parliament. In ASEAN, aversion to domination is also mentioned as a key issue.[5] The ability to set the agenda is most apparent when the rotating chair is held by a particular country. Yet in the negotiating process itself, the chair country is expected to play a neutral role and balance the interests of all circles, with a primary national objective being the reaching of an agreement – a very different utility that complicates the pursuit of normative goals. Thailand's representative in the ASEAN human rights body terms of reference (ToR) debate abandoned his advocacy for a robust human rights institution that would be much more actively taken up by his successors as their national positions. The Philippines could not manage both chair and lead human rights advocate roles to its detriment in the ASEAN Charter debate, while Singapore dodged the problem by nominating two representatives, one to perform the chair role and the other to represent the national position, in the High Level Task Force for the charter. Whether this aversion to domination stems from the seriousness with which states treat the putative equality between members, or from their shared history of colonial domination, it suggests that a norm circle can overplay the control of the initiative, hurting its goals.

As a concession to the norm circle that was most unhappy about the outcomes, in both cases the actors of both proposing and opposing

---

[3] Deng and Zartman, *The Kampala Movement*, 125.
[4] Konaré, 'Allocution à Lomé, 2000', 10.
[5] Abdul Razak, 'Facing Unfair Criticisms', 20, 21.

norm circles allowed for the review of their decision or protocols after a stipulated period. This was a key mechanism for overcoming objections and averting any actor from wielding a veto. Yet, given the passage of time, it is interesting that in both organisations, few want to review these debates again: the period of normative openness had passed and it was felt that reopening the debate would have caused conflict again. Furthermore, the ability to wield the consensus-withholding veto against the procedural decision not to re-open the debate is a much simpler and politically-costless act, especially in ASEAN. This suggests that allowing for 'review' might not be as useful a solution to breaking a deadlock as hoped, and some actors may seek to press their cases harder in the future.

One key difference that emerged in the comparison stems from the observation that the officials who understand the procedures of the RO best come from its Secretariat. Because the OAU/AU had a far larger Secretariat, its officials were more influential in brokering compromises, framing the negotiations, and controlling the initiative while appearing to be disinterested actors. Salim Salim's role in quietly introducing norms from the CSSDCA proposal after its rejection in 1991 was a key factor in its later acceptance. In ASEAN, crucial interventions did occur, such as by the Secretary-General in resolving the debate over the ASEAN human rights body at the charter drafting stage by introducing an innocuous phrasing, and by Secretariat officials in fact-checking past decisions. However, these were much fewer in extent and scale than the actions performed by the 'Africrats', per Tieku,[6] whose role in averting deadlocks during the contestation was more significant.

The Mastery of Shared Norms

While 'persuasion' has long been identified as playing a key role in norm change, how or when it works is still not adequately theorised. My model split 'persuasion' as rhetorical action into two forms: first, to try to persuade others about the norm's perceived utility, and second, to centre the new norm around the successful articulation of it as consistent with, or extensions of, other existing norms and practices in the RO. In all the cases, actors were observed appealing to

---

[6] Tieku, *Governing Africa*, 107–20.

other shared norms to make their cases for their new proposals. Furthermore, introducing other norms as an independent variable highlighted the other values and interests of the opposing norm circle, which could be obscured in a one-sided 'norm entrepreneur' model. Moreover, appealing to a norm from outside the domain that was not shared by all members – as Obasanjo did with the Helsinki Process and CSSDCA, and Indonesia attempted by analogising the AICHR to national human rights commissions – could jeopardise the process.

Maverick leaders, seemingly unencumbered by the norms of their international environments, may periodically make radical and potentially revolutionary proposals to transform their institutions. The US of Africa and CSSDCA cases illustrate both unsuccessful and successful attempts respectively, each indelibly linked to the personalities and backgrounds of their respective leading proponents – Muammar Gaddafi and Olusegun Obasanjo. Yet both leaders had to behave in normatively compliant ways to get their points across, and their violations of other agreed practices, procedures, or norms undermined their cases.

A question arises as to why this issue of shared norms is so important. In understanding the logics used by diverse actors, it was clear that there was no single rationale being employed by competing norm circles by which to reach agreement. Instead, some norm circles could be promoting a norm based on rational calculation (such as economic ministers on 'ASEAN minus X'), common identity (Pan-Africanism in the US of Africa), values (human rights in ASEAN regionalism), and so forth. Lacking a common logic for decision-making, the appeal to authority was the only option possible to appeal to all members, and the only such 'authority' available was the shared norms or precedents in the RO.

Finally both organisations have a preference for consensus decision-making, but this may form an effective veto with respect to individual member states in opposition. However, both have similar methods of bypassing this if necessary, which rely on social pressure (though the AU also formally has a majority-voting protocol it can use). For the AU, the desire to support Pan-African solidarity tends to overcome minority positions,[7] while in ASEAN, the appeal to ASEAN unity performs the same function, by which members are frequently urged to unite or face division and weakening in the face of external threats.

---

[7] Ibid., 25.

However, ASEAN rejected a formal workaround, the 'ASEAN minus X' formula, and never came close to discussing a majority-vote process, which might have been much more contentious in such a small RO.

Metis

Understanding the nature of the contest also helped to clarify 'metis' as a concept. Although its initial definition was broad, metis can be specified by understanding the nature of the domain and contest. The model helped to conceptualise contestation around utility for competing norm circles, and once norm circles are introduced, understanding metis as the reconfiguring of the circles became evident: affecting the utility calculus using available, often contingent, means. If the contest involves opposed norm circles formed around different perceived utilities of a norm, then 'metis' involves changing those perceived utilities of the norm for actors, in order to expand support or diminish opposition to the norm.

The 'actor' could be a state, in which case domestic political change may be necessary to change its perceived utility, as was the case of the change of stance of Nigeria on the CSSDCA between 1991 and 1999, or the vigour with which Indonesia, a young democracy, pursued human rights mechanisms regionally. However, the relevant actor could also be a leader or diplomat, in which case personal appeals may be more efficacious (as was the case in persuading Abdoulaye Wade to drop overt support for the US of Africa idea, or in assuring a Lao official to accept civil society engagement for the AICHR on account of the ambiguity permissible in the term 'civil society'). However, not every attempt at personal engagement was successful, such as Muammar Gaddafi's offer to South African Foreign Minister Nkosazana Dlamini-Zuma to be the first Foreign Minister of the United States of Africa.

The larger size of the AU also meant relationships could not be as close as they are in ASEAN. The observed exercises of successful 'metis' tended to be more material in AU, whereas they were more social in ASEAN. For example, NEPAD played an important, material, role in driving a wedge between Gaddafi's federalist norm circle, whom he was also funding in large part. Unable to compete directly with his material support, the promise of long-term solutions to the foreign debt question was a creative way to compete against his influence. In ASEAN, such overt material incentives would likely have been rejected by any of the member states as means of influence. Instead, within the small task forces set up to debate the norms, they used personal relations and persuasive skills to move national positions. However, this was constrained to the degree that such strategies were recognised as ploys or gambits, such as frequent threats to walk out, given a common understanding that all the actors involved had a shared goal of meeting organisational deadlines.

Moving members into one's norm circle or at least averting their opposition can be done either through persuasion – in the sense of arguing for the utility of the norm for the adversary's national interests – or, failing that, by allowing for ambiguity to downplay the prospective costs of acceptance. However, if ambiguity is used to enlarge the norm circle, there are two trade-offs. First, the purported benefits of adherence to the norm would be diluted if enforcement is necessary for its effectiveness. In the case of ASEAN's human rights protection mechanism, the ambiguities permitted resulted in the AICHR only effectively functioning as a promotion vehicle rather than to protect against human rights violations. One could argue that this defeated the purpose and created a 'toothless' mechanism, but it was better than nothing at all, when that would be the price of refusal to compromise. The second trade-off would be that the wide interpretive space permitted by ambiguity would also guarantee a more inconsistent approach to enforcement and implementation. The proponents, rather than achieving a lock-in on commitments, would still have much of their work left in front of them. Arguably, the strategy should shift to deepening human rights values further so that more effective protection mechanisms could be developed later – much in the way the CSSDCA proponents nevertheless promoted the quiet development of collective security norms through other means in the OAU.

Model Inferences versus Empirical Results

In Chapter 2, seven implications were derived directly from the model. One can look back on these inferences considering the empirical cases:

1 *Utility is analytically prior to competence.* It proved to be the case that utilities could most effectively predict the requirement for the

exercise of diplomatic competence in the model. In the second-round debate on the CSSDCA, the lack of opposition was noteworthy, which therefore obviated the need for significant exercise of competencies to push it through. This was because Obasanjo had effectively removed objections from the main opponent, Gaddafi, while Gaddafi required his *quid pro quo* on the 'US of Africa' proposal. Opposition failed to coalesce absent Gaddafi, and it passed without modification.

2 *Outright successes are unlikely under situations of contestation.* This was perhaps best demonstrated in the ASEAN cases because officials were so intimately familiar with ASEAN practices that it was difficult for any member state to wield decisive advantages after the utility arguments had been exhausted. Each of the norm circles tried to push their preferences, but each left dissatisfied with the outcome. The one exception was the control of institutional rules and authority to prevent access to the process, as the Charter HLTF did to its rival Economic HLTF, preventing modifications to the consensus principle.

3 *Veering far from the norm is hard to do.* Despite the ambitions of their initiators, all the normative outcomes ended up as incremental steps, a necessary condition of success. Where the normative gulf was too wide, the proposals were doomed to failure (the CSSDCA in 1991, the US of Africa), and even where precedents could be invoked, the degree to which these could be extended was still limited. While the CSSDCA's impact was arguably the strongest at the second attempt, it took no less than eight years – the longest time period under study in any of the cases – to get OAU norms to shift, largely as a result of the proliferation of civil conflicts on the continent. ASEAN's human rights norms only came in through a slow process over five years, starting with simple wording before institutional structures could be created, and even then far more tepid steps than what the Philippines had been pushing for in 2006.

4 *Strategic ambiguity in the proposal may be used to change the utility perception to prevent opposition from key actors.* The scope for watering down proposals to remove objections depended to some degree on the length of the text. Sometimes a single word could be argued over (e.g. 'human rights *protection*'), while at other times there were such long and extensive arguments for a particular norm (e.g. the Kampala Document) that large swathes of the text could be

altered without necessarily giving up the key norms implied. However, the texts were modified in all cases as a result of the contestation. The most interesting outcome of the contested processes in ASEAN was the use of political declarations alongside the agreed texts of the ASEAN Human Rights Declaration to reiterate that any concessions in the text should not be interpreted as allowing the human rights commitments to go below other international standards, such as the Universal Declaration of Human Rights and other UN conventions.

5 *Not causing the opposing faction to trigger a veto is crucial, and any actor with this capability is especially powerful.* Because of consensus decision-making, virtually every actor had the potential to veto any proposal, and this could be used by both sovereigntists and integrationists. However, there was a clear reticence to exercise this in both regions and associated social costs, even as the threats of such were taken quite seriously. This suggests that the formal structure of decision-making would be subsumed under the social processes unless a state's direct interests were threatened. Because negotiating officials were often not the most senior authorities of their governments, they were also pushed to work towards solutions and secure the achievement of passing out the draft agreements.

6 *The decision not to oppose or convert power into influence guarantees passage of the proposal.* Perhaps this is obvious, but just as Russia and China deferred the use of their vetoes over the Libyan UNSC resolutions, so too did Libya and Sudan over the CSSDCA. The presence of ideological opposition under consensus decision-making did not guarantee failure. Metis here appears to be the only factor capable of influencing such a choice and requires further study.

7 *The domain ensures power is never extremely unequal, and this allows small states to punch 'above' their weight, and potentially block larger states from dictating terms.* The final observation is perhaps hopeful for small states or disheartening for large states. While large states' consent was necessary for all the proposals, the key roles that relatively small states played, whether in the shape of Mali, Senegal, Laos, or Singapore, had significant effects on the outcomes. Investing in diplomatic competency had large payoffs for these states as they manoeuvred around larger states' interests, and in brokering compromises, ensured their own interests were secured in the process.

10 Conclusion

The processes of norm contestation in this book present a picture fundamentally at odds with public or official accounts that usually ascribe such changes in an organisation to a triumph of some moral or ethical principles – and yet these are so rarely the factors involved in any of the cases: they may be part of the proposing norm circle's motivations, but they play virtually no role in determining their success or failure during the process of contestation. Indeed, the more dogmatically held such values are, the more likely they are to fail to be adopted, given the utility function for those who do not yet subscribe to the idea and the domain rules of the organisation. Such official narratives also have the tendency to downplay politics, presenting a victor's narrative that inhibits understanding of the complex processes involved.

This conclusion attempts to draw wider implications from the study and how it relates to international relations debates. First, it draws attention to competing logics, rather than simply contested norms: this pinpoints the problem with the picture presented by linear accounts of change such as institutional mimicry and norm cascades. Such theories require singular logics to apply, yet when norms are contested, they are just the visible manifestation of a clash of logical systems or preference orders. The second broad implication concerns regionalism. Much of regional integration literature derives from economic imperatives, and therefore continuously finds the slow pace of integration in the Global South frustrating. It is also susceptible to a universalising logic problem: for regions that cannot seem to push integration fast enough, this is because ongoing contestation has still not yet resolved the preference order between economic imperatives and other logics. Finally, I discuss the impact that contestation has on institutional legitimacy.

Norms and Logics

Victors' narratives tend to overestimate the value of the norm in the process. However, an anti-foundational account built on utility forces one to think not in terms of the individual norm or its value, but in the logical chains or systems in which the norm resides and plays a fundamental role. In other words, contestation is about looking not merely at the contest as being over acceptance or rejection of a norm, but at the entire process of reconciling a norm with a different logic or casual belief where it did not previously have a significant role. Therefore, normative contestation fundamentally involves a clash of systems, yet the actual debates never extend that deeply into the validity of the respective systems, but focus on individual norms as manifestations of the systems. Presenting the norm as useful to a foreign logic is essential to building the norm circle coalition. Therefore, normative persuasion is usually more successful in embedding the norm in some aspect of the competing belief system or as a means towards a shared goal, rather than overturning the entire belief system in a grand conversion.

This has implications for international relations theories that have correlated with the 'unipolar' moment and presented linear accounts of institutional or normative change such as institutional isomorphism,[1] neo-functionalism,[2] and the norm cascade theory.[3] As DiMaggio and Powell have always stressed, the engine of institutional isomorphism was built on bureaucratic rationalisation: a singular logic that applies across different organisations is required to drive convergence. Such studies are valid where that circumstance applies, as long as that continues to be true: neo-functionalist 'spillover' effects have been attested in the EU, but rarely found elsewhere, and since Brexit, there is now a significant political question about whether some aspects of integration need to be rolled back. In comparative studies finding institutional mimicry (especially in convergence with the EU model) by organisations in the Global South, they have rarely investigated whether the internal logics are similar or different, either assuming

---

[1] DiMaggio and Powell, 'Institutional Isomorphism and Collective Rationality'.
[2] Schmitter, 'Ernst B. Haas and the Legacy of Neofunctionalism', *Journal of European Public Policy* 12, no. 2 (2005).
[3] Risse, Ropp, and Sikkink, *The Power of Human Rights*.

them to be so,[4] or where they are clearly different, claiming the adoption of external norms is done for external legitimation[5] – another singular logic. In actual empirical evidence presented in the cases, where the EU offered guided tours of their institutions to ASEAN representatives, for instance, rather than seek to emulate the EU, they often came to opposite conclusions, because their logic differed from the European one.[6]

Earlier norm theorists' attribution of normative change to an apolitical evaluation borrowed from economics – Pareto optimality – masks the problem and assumes there must be only one version of logical evaluation. Instead, this model used a subjective notion of utility interpreted by the norm agents that allowed for multiple logics and assessments. This model of normative change, unprejudicial to any singular logic, found linearity a very unlikely outcome. The normative diversity of the AU and ASEAN meant that norm circle proponents had to deftly wield domain rules, appeal to shared norms and goals, and find creative ways to get neutrals or opponents on board – using multiple logics and means of persuasion at their disposal. For better or for worse, this left inconsistencies in their institutional landscape, whether in the form of a Pan-African Parliament with no powers or a human rights 'protection' mechanism with no teeth.

Regionalism

This book did not seek to examine every contested norm or regional organisation in the Global South. The research design selected case studies that varied on the normative outcome, to compare the suggested factors in the cases. Each proposal was a single case that did not exhaust the sovereignty debates of their respective ROs, though they were significant ones in a period of normative openness about the entire question of 'regionness'. In focusing on sovereignty norms, it shed light on the continued resilience of sovereignty in regions, given a general expectation that globalisation and growing transnational challenges would increasingly challenge nation-state

---

[4] Navarro, 'The Creation and Transformation of Regional Parliamentary Assemblies'.
[5] Katsumata, 'Mimetic Adoption and Norm Diffusion'.
[6] Magnus, 'ASEAN Intergovernmental Commission on Human Rights: Some Personal Reflections'.

sovereignty. Instead, the outcomes here depended on the splits between contesting norm circles.

The study also showed that the nexus of power relates strongly to the outcomes: while economic imperatives may often be the strongest logic for greater integration, if political power is wielded by decision-makers not convinced by an economic rationale, concessions might not be granted, as the ASEAN minus X case showed. The continued 'failure' of these regions to integrate more quickly (generally in comparison with the EU) suggests that studying the internal layout of power in both the ROs may shed light on broader questions about regionalism. Furthermore, the complex interests within a single member state may emerge even at the regional level if foreign policy is not closely aligned across ministries, but this is still not well understood for its impact on regionalism.

The idea that economic interdependence would lead to increased political integration was questioned here, especially where economic and political units could sometimes be divided and even face bureaucratic rivalries. Comparative regionalism has perhaps advanced furthest using political-economy approaches with broadly comparable economic data, but political-normative questions do not translate well into quantitative metrics, yet remain important. How economic or political logics interact when they are not assumed to be aligned would be an interesting avenue for further study, and is a question raised not only by Brexit from the EU, but in other regions as well. The emergence of distinctive political projects situated in regionalism of the Global South is also understudied in comparative regionalism but, given political diversity, it will surely start from a question about norms.

The domain chosen – the regional organisation or RO – helped to delineate the rules of the game in which contestation unfolded. The model demonstrated the domain constraints that affect norm contestation, particularly through the lens of practices. However, most normative contestation takes place in more unstructured environments, such as through private lobbying, in the media, or via advocacy campaigns. The causal factors relevant to normative contests in other environments would be very different from the ones used here. However, if normative contests are to be studied, then studying norm circles – the nature of their formation, their mobilisation methods, and distinct logics by which they may operate – will continue to be a useful conceptual tool in investigating norm contestation, and therefore normative change, without privileging or underrepresenting any one side unintentionally.

While this study did not manage to capture all parts of the Global South, the question of the inexorability of integration must be studied in the light of potential contestation. Local motivations such as protectionism or populist-nationalist agendas will always be part of the utility function that member states bring to the regional table. A critical step usually occurs when the ROs move from multilateral cooperation to pooling of resources (not yet moving as far as pooling of sovereignty), which leads to a question of responsibility for their management. ASEAN has persisted with an intergovernmental format despite all the associated inefficiencies, and the contests it has experienced have only reinforced this. The AU, much larger in membership, has had little choice but to allow a greater degree of pooling and delegation to its Secretariat. Fundamentally these acts amount to questions about the status of sovereignty itself, though they usually do not come to a head until a critical mass of decisions is reached and stock-taking in the RO occurs. In some cases, formalisation can lead to roll-back of norms that had seemed to have delegated powers or bypassed sovereignty, while in other cases it may finally institute what were already standard norms or practices of the region, and in other cases it may lead to expansion of institutional norms and forms. There is extraordinary potential in attempting to study other regions' normative changes in this way, and those interested as reformists or activists in their region would do well to study contestation for the path dependencies that emerge through contestation to inform their policies or strategies.

One example might suffice. The normative wave of regional human rights commitments during the 2000s extended elsewhere, such as in the Arab Charter on Human Rights (2004) and attempts to form an Arab Peace and Security Council (2006). Much like Pan-Africanism, Pan-Arabism has been a unifying norm in the region, but is potentially at odds with the sovereign political structures in existence. For better or for worse, the Arab human rights charter, condemned by human rights activists as falling below international standards, has failed to attract much interest beyond the region, while the Arab League's weak implementation record has left it as a relatively marginal actor. Yet the dynamics of contestation that allowed a human rights charter to be created at all in 2004 (after a failed attempt in 1994) by a set of monarchies and authoritarian states has important implications for the future of sovereignty and human rights in the Middle East. Standard theories of institutional isomorphism or mimetic adoption for legitimation purposes need to be held up against the lens of direct observation of the contestation process to see if their explanation holds up. If one wants to see whether the charter has potential, the first step should be to study the contestation to determine the strength of the opposing norm circle, the competing logics of justification and utility, and the precedents that were set through organisational decisions.

Legitimacy

Practices were identified as the key domain-specific characteristic affecting contestation outcomes. If practice is such an important factor in the acceptance or rejection of norms, however, this has troubling implications for legitimacy. Legitimacy is often seen as a motivating factor for many actions in international relations. Yet in this study of contestation, the role that moral legitimation plays is limited. It could be a factor in the initial 'utility' calculation of the actors, but it is absent from the contestation process. Legitimation in the sense of fulfilling the organisational mandate and purpose is more significant, but follows a different logic from normative legitimacy. Shared norms at best provide a domain-specific source of legitimation for acceptance by the actors in the decision-making circle, but not the wider legitimacy of the decision. This suggests that there is a tension with respect to the decision to accept, qualify, or reject a norm, and the legitimacy of that decision. Thus, whereas Dietelhoff and Zimmermann are optimistic that justificatory contestation may strengthen the validity of the norm,[7] this study suggests it very much depends on which practices are used to 'win' the contest. Successful use of shared norms, for instance, might strengthen a norm's validity, but successful procedural actions and metis, however, might weaken the validity, being based entirely on contingent non-ideational factors.

The act of contestation, and producing an outcome agreeable to all members, in one sense provides the legitimation for the decision. Yet, as the normative content of the proposal changes as a result of that contestation, it departs from the original motivations of the proposers

---

[7] Dietelhoff and Zimmerman, 'Things We Lost in the Fire', 5.

and potentially loses some of its original legitimacy. The case of the ASEAN human rights mechanism best illustrates this problem, with the Philippines and Indonesia determined to create a mechanism to increase ASEAN's responsiveness to human rights problems in the region and its legitimacy. While ASEAN, in resolving the contest, determined the degree to which it could cooperate on human rights and set new normative standards for itself, both the document and body it produced were widely panned by human rights activists.[8] How we can understand these dual effects for legitimacy is not well understood.

This book began with the observation that regional integration – largely along the lines of the European experience – had once been seen as an inexorable force, until it met the immovable object of populism. While the EU was taking stock of its integration project even as it had to deal with the fallout from Brexit, the AU and ASEAN, once seen as integration stragglers, quietly pushed along with their own experiments and were unafraid to make bold statements such as the signing of the CFTA in Africa and the push for CPTPP and RCEP beyond Southeast Asia. While their domestic politics and the presence of populist leaders are by no means unaffected by the same global trends resisting integration, the AU and ASEAN both continue to push forward with little internal contestation to date.

To explain this final puzzle, I hold up the model of contestation against the more general global governance theory of contestation argued by Michael Zürn. While his factors that set out contestation as endogenous to global governance are different from those of this book (which expects contestation given the presence of political diversity),[9] the process that unfolds from global governance legitimation problems is strikingly similar: Zürn argues that international authorities require legitimation in order to justifiably exercise their authority.[10] As the OAU and pre-charter ASEAN sought to reassert their relevance in a post-Cold War order, they faced legitimation problems while their existing institutional frameworks were insufficient for the

---

[8] Poole, 'The World is Outraged'.
[9] For Zürn, it is the distributional imbalances between decision-making rights and material distribution of power that create tension between member states and international organizations, resulting in contestation. Zürn, *A Theory of Global Governance* (Oxford: Oxford University Press, 2018), 84–5.
[10] Ibid., 11–12.

tasks required by those who sought change. This led to a period of contestation by actors both within and without the ROs.

In this book's case studies, civil society groups such as the Kampala Movement and Southeast Asian human rights activists contested from the outside. The response to that challenge led to internal processes of change, which continued the contestation but with very different kinds of figures – senior government officials – who had different views and logics from the activists on the outside. Nevertheless, Zürn's final point is that response to contestation leads to either a deepening or a decline in the system of governance, depending on the nature of that response. In his model, the development of coalitions to respond to legitimation crises leads to a deepening of global governance as they push through provisions to address the criticisms of the existing structures.[11]

Inasmuch as the contestation processes in the AU and ASEAN elevated debates about sovereignty and regionalism to the fore, their resolution followed Zürn's lines as my model demonstrates: norm circles developed around the perceived utilities of different normative positions, and their contestation outcomes, if the competence model is correct, reflected a certain distribution of power in practice within the ROs. While it could be argued that no one was entirely satisfied with the outcome, the other way of looking at it is that everyone had inserted their interests into the process and it was a fair reflection of an aggregate of values of the member states. The one caveat to Zürn's model is that the manner of 'winning' (i.e. building the winning coalition) may also lead to more or less legitimate institutional outcomes.

Thus, when populist forces began a backlash against globalisation, AU and ASEAN member states could not yet find fault with their regional integration: it had been slow and arduous, but therefore had not exceeded a sufficient number of members' comfort levels and they could indeed continue with integration projects against the global headwinds. In contrast, the bias towards bureaucratic and economic logics that bypassed politics in the EU, i.e. the 'spillover' effect, had pushed integration faster than their publics' acceptable rates of change. It would need a deep and intensely political process to recalibrate to the correct level.

---

[11] Ibid., 196–7.

Policy Implications

Finally, there are several policy implications from this study. The first is that understanding the nature of the contest helps to illuminate the future path of the norm and its corollary mechanisms. Whereas common law practice relies on legal precedents (largely from interpreting a text alone, assuming judicial institutions will implement them uniformly) to understand future implications, international norms are too ambiguous for one to derive consistent interpretations, especially when the institutions for implementation are themselves enmeshed with the norm. Instead, the interpretation of the normative result must take into consideration the historical nature of the contest and the interpretation of the actors who participated in the contest as to the outcome. This is the best way to understand the future trajectory of the institutions that develop. The Pan-African Parliament, read from its legal mandate, would make virtually no sense to an outsider, but represents the compromise between rhetorical entrapment and various interests that did not neatly fall into ideational camps. Evolving it in a legislative direction will require metis that causes actors to reassess its utility as an implementing legislative body, and diminishes the threat of supranationality and federalism that the opposing norm circle understood it to be.

Second, those who are appointed as representatives to participate in these contests plainly matter. This model suggested what kind of core competencies they would need – the independent variables of the model – such as detailed knowledge of the organisational practices and bureaucratic procedures, an understanding and mastery of the other widely shared norms and practices of all the members as well as different logics, and an understanding of the nature of the contest, in order to best identify opportunities to bring uncommitted or opposed actors over to their norm circle. These skills can be learnt, and it should be recognised that actor strategies are not static, and actions such as changing the rules of the domain may be used to create advantages.

Finally, the iterative quality of norms means that a norm must be repeatedly selected to strengthen and embed itself in the domain to be successful. To return to the sporting analogy first raised by Adler-Nissen and Pouliot,[12] winning a game may be satisfying, but winning

---

[12] Adler-Nissen and Pouliot, 'Power in Practice', 6.

the league by winning the most matches over a season should be the overall objective. This model of contestation has only shown how norm circles performed under situations of contestation: each case a singular instance of a win, loss, or draw. One-off victories may not be as useful or significant as they appear, and the long-term goal to increase the chances of repeated selection of the norm must be to keep winning, and that means the greatest payoff will come from improving the norm's utility. This is because utility is what ultimately moves the norm circle configuration decisively and permanently in one's favour. This, the internalisation of the norms by a majority of the members in an RO, remains the most important goal for a norm circle.

Appendix
List of Officials Interviewed

African Union/Organisation of African Unity

Name	Position during study period	Position during interview
Emmanuel Akeh	Foreign Service Officer, Nigeria	Principal Policy Officer, Office of the Chairperson, AUC
Lazarous Kapambwe	Permanent Secretary, Directorate of African/OAU Affairs, Ministry of Foreign Affairs, Zimbabwe	Special Adviser to the Chairperson for Economic Affairs; Director, ECOSOCC, AUC
Kassim Khamis	Consultant, Democratisation and Monitoring, Political Cooperation Division, Political Affairs, OAU	Political Analyst, Strategic Planning Directorate, Office of the Chairperson, AUC
Jean Mfasoni	Head of Political Cooperation, OAU/ Director of Political Affairs, AU	Special Adviser to the Chairperson, formerly Secretary-General, AUC
Dr Musifiky Mwanasali	Field Officer/Conflict Analyst, Conflict Management Centre, OAU	Special Adviser to the Chairperson for Political Affairs, AUC

(*cont.*)

Name	Position during study period	Position during interview
J. Kayode Shinkaiye	Permanent Representative of Nigeria to the OAU/AU	Private consultant; Former Chief of Staff to the Chairperson (2008–12)
Omar A. Touray	Permanent Representative of the Gambia to the OAU/AU	Senior Specialist, Islamic Development Bank

Association of Southeast Asian Nations

Name	Position during study period	Position during interview
Chan Sze-Wei	Assistant Director, Ministry of Foreign Affairs, Singapore; Assistants group for the HLTF on the drafting of the charter	Research associate, Centre for International Law, National University of Singapore
Dr Termsak Chalermpalanupap	Special Assistant to the Secretary-General; Director, Political-Security Affairs, ASEAN Secretariat	Fellow, ISEAS-Yusof Ishak Institute
Rafendi Djamin	Indonesian representative, AICHR	Director, Human Rights Working Group (Indonesia)
Prof. Harikristuti Harkrisnowo	Director-General, Human Rights, Indonesia; Indonesia representative, Drafting Group on the ASEAN Human Rights Declaration	Professor of Law, University of Indonesia

List of Officials Interviewed

(cont.)

Name	Position during study period	Position during interview
Hoang Thi Ha	Political-Security Officer, ASEAN Secretariat	Fellow, ISEAS-Yusof Ishak Institute
Bilahari Kausikan	Second Permanent Secretary, Ministry of Foreign Affairs; Singapore representative to the HLP on the ToR of the AICHR	Ambassador-at-Large, Ministry of Foreign Affairs, Singapore
Prof. Tommy Koh	Chairperson, High Level Task Force on the Drafting of the ASEAN Charter	Ambassador-at-Large, Ministry of Foreign Affairs, Singapore
Ong Keng Yong	Secretary-General, ASEAN (2003–7)	Ambassador-at-Large, Ministry of Foreign Affairs, Singapore
Dr Surin Pitsuwan	Secretary-General, ASEAN (2008-2012)	Chairman, Future Thailand Innovation Institute
Yuyun Wahyuningrum	Senior Adviser on Human Rights and ASEAN, Human Rights Working Group	Senior Adviser on Human Rights and ASEAN, Human Rights Working Group
Kartika Budhi Wijayanti	Technical Officer, Political-Security, ASEAN Secretariat; AICHR support division	Communications Officer, UNESCO
Prof. Walter Woon	Solicitor-General, Singapore; Singapore representative to the HLTF on the Drafting of the ASEAN Charter	Dean, Singapore Institute of Legal Education and Deputy Chairman, Centre for International Law, National University of Singapore

Bibliography

ABA-ROLI. *The ASEAN Human Rights Declaration: a Legal Analysis*. Washington, DC: American Bar Association, 2014.
Abbott, Andrew. 'Linked Ecologies: States and Universities as Environments for Professions'. *Sociological Theory* 23, no. 3 (2005).
Abdul Razak, Ahmad Fuzi. 'Facing Unfair Criticisms'. In *The Making of the ASEAN Charter*, edited by Tommy Koh, Rosario G. Manalo, and Walter Woon. Singapore: World Scientific, 2009.
Acharya, Amitav. *Constructing a Security Community in Southeast Asia: ASEAN and the Problem of Regional Order*. 3rd ed. Abingdon: Routledge, 2014.
    'Culture, Security, Multilateralism: the "ASEAN Way" and Regional Order'. *Contemporary Security Policy* 19, no. 1 (1998): 55–84.
    'Norm Subsidiarity and Regional Orders: Sovereignty, Regionalism, and Rule-Making in the Third World'. *International Studies Quarterly* 55, no. 1 (2011): 95–123.
    'The R2P and Norm Diffusion: Towards a Framework of Norm Circulation'. *Global Responsibility to Protect* 5, no. 4 (2013): 466–79.
    Whose Ideas Matter? Agency and Power in Asian Regionalism. Singapore: Institute of Southeast Asian Studies, 2010.
Acharya, Amitav, and Alastair Iain Johnston, eds. *Crafting Cooperation: Regional International Institutions in Comparative Perspective*. Cambridge: Cambridge University Press, 2007.
Adler, Emanuel, and Vincent Pouliot, eds. *International Practices*. Cambridge: Cambridge University Press, 2011.
Adler-Nissen, R. 'Conclusion: Relationalism or Why Diplomats Find International Relations Theory Strange'. In *Diplomacy and the Making of World Politics*, edited by Ole Jacob Sending, Vincent Pouliot and Iver B. Neumann. Cambridge: Cambridge University Press, 2015.
Adler-Nissen, R., and V. Pouliot. 'Power in Practice: Negotiating the International Intervention in Libya'. *European Journal of International Relations* 20, no. 4 (2014): 889–911.

Bibliography

Africa Confidential. "'My Arabism Tired Me Out'". *Africa Confidential* 39, no. 21 (1998).
⸺ 'Organisation of African Unity: the Last Summit'. *Africa Confidential* 42, no. 14 (2001).
Africa Leadership Forum. *The Kampala Document*. Kampala: Africa Leadership Forum, 1991.
⸺ *Report on a Brainstorming Meeting for a Conference on Security, Stability, Development and Co-operation in Africa*. Addis Ababa: Africa Leadership Forum, 1990.
Africa Research Bulletin. 'Continental Alignments: Conferences: the African Union'. *Africa Research Bulletin* 37, no. 6 (2000).
⸺ 'Gaddafy Seeks United Africa'. *Africa Research Bulletin* 36, no. 9 (1999).
African Union. 'Accra Declaration'. Accra: African Union, 2007.
⸺ 'The Constitutive Act of the African Union'. Lomé 2000.
⸺ 'Decision on the Transformation of the African Union Commission into the African Union Authority' (Assembly/AU/Dec. 454 (XX). Addis Ababa 2013.
⸺ 'List of Countries that Have Signed, Ratified/Acceded to the Protocol to the Constitutive Act of the African Union Relating to the Pan-African Parliament'. African Union Commission, www.au.int/web/en/treaties/protocol-constitutive-act-african-union-relating-pan-african-parliament, 21 December 2017.
⸺ 'Protocol to the Constitutive Act of the African Union Relating to the Pan-African Parliament'. Malabo 2014.
⸺ 'Protocol to the Treaty Establishing the African Economic Community Relating to the Pan-African Parliament'. Sirte 2001.
AICHR. 'Press Release of the Second Meeting of the ASEAN Intergovernmental Commission on Human Rights on the ASEAN Human Rights Declaration'. Jakarta: ASEAN Secretariat, 2012.
⸺ 'Press Release of the Sixth Meeting of the ASEAN Intergovernmental Commission on Human Rights (AICHR)'. Vientiane: ASEAN Secretariat, 2011.
⸺ 'Press Statement by the Chair of the ASEAN Intergovernmental Commission on Human Rights on the First Meeting of the ASEAN Intergovernmental Commission on Human Rights'. Jakarta: ASEAN Secretariat, 2010.
Akinsaya, Olusegun. 'Nigeria at the African Union'. In *Nigeria and the Development of the African Union*, edited by Bola A. Akinterinwa. Ibadan: Vantage, 2005.
Akinterinwa, Bola A., ed. *Nigeria and the Development of the African Union*. Ibadan: Vantage, 2005.

Akokpari, John, Angela Ndinga-Muvumba, and Tim Murithi, eds. *The African Union and its Institutions*. Auckland Park, South Africa: Fanele, 2008.
Alden, Chris. '"A Pariah in our Midst": Regional Organisations and the Problematic of Western-Designated Pariah Regimes – the Cases of SADC/Zimbabwe and ASEAN/Myanmar'. *Crisis States Working Paper Series* 2 (2010).
Alli, W. O. *The Role of Nigeria in Regional Security Policy*. Abuja: Friedrich Ebert Stiftung, 2012.
Amoo, Sam G. 'Frustrations of Regional Peacekeeping: the OAU in Chad, 1977–1982'. *Carter Center Working Paper* 1, no. 1 (1991).
ASEAN. '2005 Kuala Lumpur Declaration on the Establishment of the ASEAN Charter'. Kuala Lumpur: ASEAN, 2005.
  'Agreement on the Common Effective Preference Tariff Scheme for the ASEAN Free Trade Area'. Singapore 1992.
  'ASEAN Human Rights Declaration'. Phnom Penh 2012.
  ASEAN Intergovernmental Commission on Human Rights (Terms of Reference). Jakarta: ASEAN Secretariat, 2009.
  'Cebu Declaration on the Blueprint of the ASEAN Charter'. Cebu, Philippines: ASEAN Secretariat, 2007.
  'Cha-Am Hua Hin Declaration on the Intergovernmental Commission on Human Rights'. Cha-Am Hua Hin, Thailand: ASEAN, 2009.
  'Charter of the Association of Southeast Asian Nations'. Singapore 2007.
  'Declaration of ASEAN Concord II'. Bali 2003.
  Draft ASEAN Human Rights Declaration as of 23 June, Kuala Lumpur. Kuala Lumpur: ASEAN, 2012.
  'Framework Agreement on Enhancing ASEAN Economic Cooperation'. Singapore: ASEAN Secretariat, 1992.
  Hanoi Plan of Action. Jakarta: ASEAN Secretariat, 1997.
  'Joint Communique of the 26th ASEAN Ministerial Meeting, Singapore, 23–24 July 1993'. Singapore: ASEAN Secretariat, 1993.
  'List of Members of the Eminent Persons Group (EPG) on the ASEAN Charter'. ASEAN Secretariat, www.asean.org/storage/images/archive/ACP-EPGMember.pdf, 14 June 2016.
  'List of Members of the High Level Panel on an ASEAN Human Rights Body (HLP)'. ASEAN Intergovernmental Commission on Human Rights, http://aichr.org/about/hpl/.
  'Phnom Penh Statement on the Adoption of the ASEAN Human Rights Declaration (AHRD)'. Phnom Penh: ASEAN Secretariat, 2012.
  Report of the Eminent Persons Group on the ASEAN Charter. Jakarta: ASEAN, 2006.

'The Seventh Meeting of the ASEAN Intergovernmental Commission on Human Rights (AICHR) on an ASEAN Human Rights Declaration (AHRD) and the Second Regional Consultation of AICHR on the AHRD'. Kuala Lumpur: ASEAN Secretariat, 2012.

'Terms of Reference for the High Level Panel on an ASEAN Human Rights Body'. Singapore: ASEAN, 2008.

'Vientiane Action Programme'. Jakarta: ASEAN Secretariat, 2004.

Asplund, André. 'ASEAN Intergovernmental Commission on Human Rights: Civil Society Organizations' Limited Influence on ASEAN'. *Journal of Asian Public Policy* 7, no. 2 (2014): 191–9.

Axelrod, Robert. 'An Evolutionary Approach to Norms'. *American Political Science Review* 80, no. 4 (December 1986): 1095–111.

Ayittey, G. B. N. 'The United States of Africa: a Revisit'. *Annals of the American Academy of Political and Social Science* 632, no. 1 (2010): 86–102.

Azevedo, Mario J. *Roots of Violence: a History of War in Chad*. London: Routledge, 1998; repr., 2004.

Ba, Alice D. *(Re)Negotiating East and Southeast Asia*. Stanford: Stanford University Press, 2009.

Baimu, Evarist, and Kathryn Sturman. 'Amendment to the African Union's Right to Intervene'. *African Security Review* 12, no. 2 (2003): 37–45.

Barnett, Michael, and Raymond Duvall. *Power in Global Governance*. Cambridge: Cambridge University Press, 2005.

Barnett, Michael, and Martha Finnemore. *Rules for the World: International Organizations in Global Politics*. Ithaca: Cornell University Press, 2004.

Berger, Johannes, and Claus Offe. 'Functionalism vs. Rational Choice? Some Questions Concerning the Rationality of Choosing One or the Other'. *Theory and Society* 11, no. 4 (1982).

Bernstein, Steven. 'Ideas, Social Structure and the Compromise of Liberal Environmentalism'. *European Journal of International Relations* 6, no. 4 (2000).

Bjola, Corneliu, and Markus Kornprobst. *Understanding International Diplomacy: Theory, Practice and Ethics*. Abingdon: Routledge, 2013.

Bloomfield, Alan. 'Norm Antipreneurs and Theorising Resistance to Normative Change'. *Review of International Studies* 42, no. 02 (2015): 310–33.

Bob, Clifford. *The Global Right Wing and the Clash of World Politics*. Cambridge: Cambridge University Press, 2012.

Booth Walling, Carrie. *All Necessary Measures: the United Nations and Humanitarian Intervention*. Philadelphia: University of Pennsylvania Press, 2013.

Borzel, Tanja A. 'Comparative Regionalism: European Integration and Beyond'. In *Handbook of International Relations*, edited by Walter Carlsnaes and Beth A. Simmons. London: Sage, 2013.

'Theorizing Regionalism: Cooperation, Integration, and Governance'. In *The Oxford Handbook of Comparative Regionalism*, edited by Tanja A. Borzel and Thomas Risse. Oxford: Oxford University Press, 2016.

Borzel, Tanja A., and Thomas Risse, eds. *The Oxford Handbook of Comparative Regionalism*. Oxford: Oxford University Press, 2016.

Bouteflika, Abdelaziz. 'Discours de son Excellence Abdelaziz Bouteflika, Président de la République Algérienne Démocratique et Populair et Président en Exercice de l'Organisation de l'Unité Africaine à la 36ème Session Ordinaire de la Conférence des Chefs d'Etat et de Gouvernement de l'Organisation de l'Unité Africaine, Lomé 10–12 Juillet 2000'. Lomé, Democratic and Popular Republic of Algeria, 2000.

Bower, Adam. 'Arguing with Law: Strategic Legal Argumentation, US Diplomacy, and Debates over the International Criminal Court'. *Review of International Studies* 41, no. 02 (2014): 337–60.

Brosnan, S. F., and Frans B. M. de Waal. 'Evolution of Responses to (Un) Fairness'. *Science* 346, no. 6207 (2014): 1251776.

Bull, Hedley. *The Anarchical Society: a Study of Order in World Politics*. 2nd ed. London: Macmillan, 1977.

Buthe, Tim, and Walter Mattli. *The New Global Rulers: the Privatization of Regulation in the World Economy*. Princeton: Princeton University Press, 2011.

Bwa, U Aung. 'The Jewel in my Crown'. In *The Making of the ASEAN Charter*, edited by Tommy Koh, Rosario G. Manalo, and Walter Woon. Singapore: World Scientific, 2009.

Caballero-Anthony, Mely. 'The ASEAN Charter: an Opportunity Missed or One that Cannot Be Missed?' *Southeast Asian Affairs* (2008).

Chalermpalanupap, Termsak. 'In Defence of the ASEAN Charter'. In *The Making of the ASEAN Charter*, edited by Tommy Koh, Rosario G. Manalo, and Walter Woon. Singapore: World Scientific, 2009.

'Ten Facts about ASEAN Human Rights Cooperation'. Jakarta: ASEAN, 2009.

Chan, Sze Wei. 'Decision-Making in the ASEAN Charter Process'. In *50 Years of ASEAN and Singapore*, edited by Tommy Koh, Sharon Li-Lian Seah, and Li Lin Chang. Hackensack: World Scientific, 2017.

Checkel, Jeffrey T. 'International Institutions and Socialization in Europe: Introduction and Framework'. *International Organization* 59, no. 4 (2005).

Clark, Ian. *Legitimacy in International Society*. Oxford: Oxford University Press, 2005.

Collins, Alan. 'A People-Oriented ASEAN: a Door Ajar or Closed for Civil Society Organizations?' *Contemporary Southeast Asia* 30, no. 2 (2008).

Cox, Robert W., and Harold K. Jacobson. *The Anatomy of Influence*. New Haven: Yale University Press, 1974.

Dalacoura, Katerina. *Islam, Liberalism and Human Rights*. London: I. B. Tauris, 1998.

Davies, Mathew. 'Explaining the Vientiane Action Programme: ASEAN and the Institutionalisation of Human Rights'. *Pacific Review* 26, no. 4 (2013): 385–406.

de Certeau, Michel. *The Practice of Everyday Life*. Berkeley: University of California Press, 1984.

de Oliveira, Ricardo Soares, and Harry Verhoeven. 'Taming Intervention: Sovereignty, Statehood and Political Order in Africa'. *Survival* 60, no. 2 (2018): 7–32.

De Waal, Frans B. M. 'The Antiquity of Empathy'. *Science* 336, no. 874 (2012).

Deng, Francis, and I. William Zartman. *A Strategic Vision for Africa: the Kampala Movement*. Washington, DC: Brookings Institution Press, 2001.

Desker, Barry. 'Is the ASEAN Charter Necessary?' *RSIS Commentaries* 77 (2008).

Dietelhoff, Nicole, and Lisbeth Zimmerman. 'Things We Lost in the Fire: How Different Types of Contestation Affect the Validity of International Norms'. *Peace Research Institute Frankfurt Working Paper* 18 (2013).

DiMaggio, Paul J., and Walter W. Powell. 'The Iron Cage Revisited: Institutional Isomorphism and Collective Rationality in Organizational Fields'. *American Sociological Review* 48, no. 2 (1983).

Djani, Dian Triansyah. 'A Long Journey'. In *The Making of the ASEAN Charter*, edited by Tommy Koh, Rosario G. Manalo and Walter Woon. Singapore: World Scientific, 2009.

Elder-Vass, Dave. *The Causal Power of Social Structures: Emergence, Structure and Agency*. Cambridge: Cambridge University Press, 2010.

'Developing Social Theory Using Critical Realism'. *Journal of Critical Realism* 14, no. 1 (2015): 80–92.

'Towards a Realist Social Constructionism'. *Sociologia, problemas e práticas* 2012, no. 70 (2012).

Fawcett, Louise. 'Exploring Regional Domains: a Comparative History of Regionalism'. *International Affairs* 80, no. 3 (2004).

Fawcett, Louise, and Helene Gandois. 'Regionalism in Africa and the Middle East: Implications for EU Studies'. *Journal of European Integration* 32, no. 6 (2010): 617–36.

Finnemore, Martha. 'Norms, Culture, and World Politics: Insights from Sociology's Institutionalism'. *International Organization* 50, no. 2 (1996): 325–47.
Finnemore, Martha, and Kathryn Sikkink. 'International Norm Dynamics and Political Change'. *International Organization* 52, no. 4 (1998): 887–917.
Fleming, Neil. 'If an African Cannot Succeed Javier Perez De Cuellar'. *UPI*, 15 September 1991.
Florini, Ann. 'The Evolution of International Norms'. *International Studies Quarterly* 40, no. 3 (1996).
Forum Asia. 'Joint Statement on Calling AICHR to Release ASEAN Human Rights Declaration'. Bangkok: Forum Asia, 2012.
'Joint Submission to the ASEAN Intergovernmental Commission on Human Rights on the ASEAN Human Rights Declaration'. Bangkok: Forum Asia, 2012.
Francis, David J. *Uniting Africa: Building Regional Peace and Security Systems*. Aldershot: Ashgate, 2006.
Gaddafi, Muammar. 'Address of the Leader of the Al-Fatah Revolution, Brother Muammar Gaddafi, at the Opening Ceremony of the OAU Ministerial Meeting on the Establishment of the African Union and the Pan-African Parliament'. Tripoli: Libyan Arab Jamahiriya, 2000.
'Speech by the Leader of the Revolution at the Evening Session of the African Summit (Closed Session) on 10 July 2001'. Lusaka: Libyan Arab Jamahiriya, 2001.
Gathii, James Thuo. *African Regional Trade Agreements as Legal Regimes*. Cambridge: Cambridge University Press, 2011.
Gehlbach, Scott. *Formal Models of Domestic Politics*. Cambridge: Cambridge University Press, 2013.
George, Alexander L., and Andrew Bennett. *Case Studies and Theory Development in the Social Sciences*. Cambridge, MA: MIT Press, 2005.
Goh, Dominic. 'The ASEAN Community and the Principle of ASEAN Centrality'. In *50 Years of ASEAN and Singapore*, edited by Tommy Koh, Sharon Li-Lian Seah, and Li Lin Chang. Hackensack: World Scientific, 2017.
Goldsmith, Jack L., and Eric A. Posner. *The Limits of International Law*. Oxford: Oxford University Press, 2005.
Goldstein, Judith, and Robert O. Keohane, eds. *Ideas and Foreign Policy: Beliefs, Institutions, and Political Change*. Ithaca: Cornell University Press, 1993.
Goodman, Ryan, and Derek Jinks. *Socializing States: Promoting Human Rights through International Law*. Oxford: Oxford University Press, 2013.

Gordon, Neve. 'Human Rights as a Security Threat: Lawfare and the Campaign against Human Rights NGOs'. *Law and Society Review* 48, no. 2 (2014).
Gumede, William Mervin. *Thabo Mbeki and the Battle for the Soul of the ANC*. London: Zed Books, 2007.
Habermas, Jurgen. *Between Facts and Norms*. Translated by William Rehg. Cambridge: Polity Press, 1996.
Hafner-Burton, Emilie M., and James Ron. 'Seeing Double'. *World Politics* 61, no. 2 (2009): 360.
Hettne, Björn, and Fredrik Söderbaum. 'Theorising the Rise of Regionness'. *New Political Economy* 5, no. 3 (2000): 457–72.
Hew, Denis, and Rahul Sen. 'Towards an ASEAN Economic Community: Challenges and Prospects'. *ISEAS Working Papers, Economics and Finance* (2004).
Hindawi, Hussain. 'In the Levant: Libya's Love Affair with Africa'. *UPI*, 28 July 2001.
Hodgson, Geoffrey M. 'What are Institutions?' *Journal of Economic Issues* 40, no. 1 (2006): 1–25.
Huliaras, Asteris. 'Qadhafi's Comeback: Libya and Sub-Saharan Africa in the 1990s'. *African Affairs* 100 (2001): 5–25.
Hurrell, Andrew. *On Global Order: Power, Values and the Constitution of International Society*. Oxford: Oxford University Press, 2007.
  'Norms and Ethics in International Relations'. In *Handbook of International Relations*, edited by Walter Carlsnaes, Thomas Risse, and Beth A. Simmons. London: Sage, 2002.
  'Power, Institutions, and the Production of Inequality'. In *Power in Global Governance*, edited by Michael Barnett and Raymond Duvall. Cambridge: Cambridge University Press, 2005.
Jayakumar, Shunmugum. *Be at the Table or Be on the Menu: a Singapore Memoir*. Singapore: Straits Times Press, 2015.
Jeng, Abou. *Peacebuilding in the African Union*. Cambridge: Cambridge University Press, 2012.
Jetschke, Anja, and Philomena Murray. 'Diffusing Regional Integration: the EU and Southeast Asia'. *West European Politics* 35, no. 1 (2012): 174–91.
Johnston, Alexander. 'Democracy and Human Rights in the Principles and Practice of South African Foreign Policy'. In *South Africa's Foreign Policy: Dilemmas of a New Democracy*, edited by Jim Broderick, Gary Burford, and Gordon Freer. Basingstoke: Palgrave Macmillan, 2001.
Jones, David Martin, and Michael L. R. Smith. 'Making Process, not Progress: ASEAN and the Evolving East Asian Regional Order'. *International Security* 32, no. 1 (2007).

Jones, Lee. 'ASEAN's Unchanged Melody? The Theory and Practice of "Non-Interference" in Southeast Asia'. *Pacific Review* 23, no. 4 (2010): 479–502.

'Democratization and Foreign Policy in Southeast Asia: the Case of the ASEAN Inter-Parliamentary Myanmar Caucus'. *Cambridge Review of International Affairs* 22, no. 3 (2009): 387–406.

Karlsrud, John. *Norm Change in International Relations: Linked Ecologies in UN Peacekeeping Operations*. London: Routledge, 2015.

Katsumata, Hiro. 'Mimetic Adoption and Norm Diffusion: "Western" Security Cooperation in Southeast Asia?' *Review of International Studies* 37, no. 2 (2010): 557–76.

Kausikan, Bilahari. 'Asia's Different Standard'. *Foreign Policy*, no. 92 (Autumn 1993).

Keck, Margaret E., and Kathryn Sikkink, eds. *Activists beyond Borders: Advocacy Networks in International Politics*. Ithaca: Cornell University Press, 1998.

Keohane, Robert O., and Joseph S. Nye. *Power and Interdependence*. 3rd ed. New York: Longman, 2001.

Khamis, Kassim M. *Promoting the African Union*. Washington, DC: Liliane Barber, 2008.

Koh, Tommy. 'The ASEAN Charter at 10: Prospects and Retrospect'. *Myanmar Times*, Yangon, 2017.

Koh, Tommy, Rosario G. Manalo, and Walter Woon. *The Making of the ASEAN Charter*. Singapore: World Scientific, 2009.

Konaré, Alpha Oumar. 'Allocution de son Excellence Monsieur Alpha Oumar Konaré, Président de la République du Mali, Trente-Sixième Session de la Conférence des Chefs d'Etat et de Gouvernement de l'Organisation de l'Unité Africaine (Oua) (Lomé, République Togolaise, 10–12 Juillet 2000)'. Lomé, Republic of Mali, 2000.

Koskenniemi, Martti. 'Human Rights Mainstreaming as a Strategy for Institutional Power'. *Humanity: an International Journal of Human Rights, Humanitarianism, and Development* 1, no. 1 (2010): 47–58.

'International Law and Hegemony: a Reconfiguration'. *Cambridge Review of International Affairs* 17, no. 2 (2004): 197–218.

Krapohl, Sebastian, ed. *Regional Integration in the Global South: External Influence on Economic Cooperation in ASEAN, Mercosur and SADC*. Cham, Switzerland: Palgrave Macmillan, 2017.

Krasner, Stephen D. *Sovereignty: Organized Hypocrisy*. Princeton: Princeton University Press, 1999.

Kratochwil, Friedrich V. *Rules, Norms, and Decisions: On the Conditions of Practical and Legal Reasoning in International Relations and Domestic Affairs*. Cambridge: Cambridge University Press, 1989.

Krehbiel, Keith. *Pivotal Politics: a Theory of US Lawmaking*. Chicago: University of Chicago Press, 1998.

Krook, M. L., and J. True. 'Rethinking the Life Cycles of International Norms: the United Nations and the Global Promotion of Gender Equality'. *European Journal of International Relations* 18, no. 1 (2012): 103–27.

Lenz, Tobias. 'EU Normative Power and Regionalism: Ideational Diffusion and its Limits'. *Cooperation and Conflict* 48, no. 2 (2013): 211–28.

Libyan Arab Jamahiriya. 'Explanatory Notes on the Libyan Proposal for Amendment of the Constitutive Act of the African Union'. Addis Ababa: OAU, 2003.

Magliveras, Konstantinos D., and Asteris Huliaras. 'Understanding Success and Failure in the Quest for Peace: the Pan-African Parliament and the Amani Forum'. *The Hague Journal of Diplomacy* 11 (2016).

Magliveras, Konstantinos D., and Gino J. Naldi. *The African Union (AU)*. Alphen aan den Rijn, Netherlands: Kluwer International Law, 2013.

Magnus, Richard. 'ASEAN Intergovernmental Commission on Human Rights: Some Personal Reflections'. In *50 Years of ASEAN and Singapore*, edited by Tommy Koh, Sharon Li-Lian Seah, and Li Lin Chang. Hackensack: World Scientific, 2017.

Mahoney, James, and Kathleen Thelen, eds. *Explaining Institutional Change: Ambiguity, Agency, and Power*. Cambridge: Cambridge University Press, 2010.

Makinda, Samuel M., and F. Wafula Okumu. *The African Union: Challenges of Globalization, Security, and Governance*. Abingdon: Routledge, 2008.

Manalo, Rosario G. 'Drafting ASEAN's Tomorrow: the EPG and the ASEAN Charter'. In *The Making of the ASEAN Charter*, edited by Tommy Koh, Rosario G. Manalo, and Walter Woon. Singapore: World Scientific, 2009.

Masire, Quett Ketumile Joni, Ahmadou Toumani Touré, Lisbet Palme, Ellen Johnson-Sirleaf, P. N. Baghwati, Hocine Djoudi, and Stephen Lewis. *Rwanda: the Preventable Genocide*. Addis Ababa: OAU, 2000.

Matthews, K. 'The Organization of African Unity'. In *African Regional Organizations*, edited by Domenico Mazzeo. Cambridge: Cambridge University Press, 1984.

Mattli, Walter, and Tim Buthe. 'Setting International Standards: Technological Rationality or Primacy of Power?' *World Politics* 56, no. 1 (2003).

Mays, Terry M. *Africa's First Peacekeeping Operation: the OAU in Chad, 1981–1982*. London: Praeger, 2002.

Mazrui, Ali A. *The African Condition. The Reith Lectures.* London: Heinemann, 1980.
———. 'Soldiers as Traditionalizers: Military Rule and the Re-Africanization of Africa'. *World Politics* 28, no. 2 (1976).
Mbete, Baleka. 'The Pan-African Parliament: Progress and Prospects'. In *The African Union and its Institutions*, edited by John Akokpari, Angela Ndinga-Muvumba, and Tim Murithi. Auckland Park, South Africa: Fanele, 2008.
Mitrany, David. 'The Functional Approach to World Organization'. *International Affairs* 24, no. 3 (1948).
Morris, Justin. 'Libya and Syria: R2P and the Spectre of the Swinging Pendulum'. *International Affairs* 89, no. 5 (2013): 1265–83.
Morse, Julia C., and Robert O. Keohane. 'Contested Multilateralism'. *Review of International Organizations* 9, no. 4 (2014): 385–412.
Moses, Jeremy. *Sovereignty and Responsibility: Power, Norms and Intervention in International Relations.* Basingstoke: Palgrave Macmillan, 2014.
Munro, James. 'The Relationship between the Origins and Regime Design of the ASEAN Intergovernmental Commission on Human Rights (AICHR)'. *International Journal of Human Rights* 15, no. 8 (2011): 1185–214.
Muntarbhorn, Vitit. *Unity in Connectivity? Evolving Human Rights Mechanisms in the ASEAN Region.* Leiden: Brill, 2014.
Museveni, Yoweri K. 'Statement by His Excellency Yoweri Museveni, President of the Republic of Uganda, at the 36th Summit of Heads of State and Government, Lomé, Togo, 10th–12th July, 2000'. Lomé, Togo: Republic of Uganda, 2000.
Myerson, Roger B. 'Justice, Institutions and Multiple Equilibria'. *Chicago Journal of International Law* 5, no. 1 (2004).
Naldi, Gino J. *The Organization of African Unity: an Analysis of its Role.* 2nd ed. New York: Mansell, 1999..
Narine, Shaun. 'Forty Years of ASEAN: a Historical Review'. *Pacific Review* 21, no. 4 (2008): 411–29.
Natalegawa, Marty. *Does ASEAN Matter? A View from Within.* Singapore: ISEAS-Yusof Ishak Institute, 2018.
Nathan, Laurie. 'Towards a Conference on Security, Stability, Development and Co-operation in Africa'. *Africa Insight* 22, no. 3 (1992): 212–17.
Navarro, Julien. 'The Creation and Transformation of Regional Parliamentary Assemblies: Lessons from the Pan-African Parliament'. *Journal of Legislative Studies* 16, no. 2 (2010): 195–214.

Neumann, Iver B. 'Returning Practice to the Linguistic Turn: the Case of Diplomacy'. *Millennium: Journal of International Studies* 31, no. 3 (2002).

Ng, Joel. 'ASEAN Human Rights Declaration: a Pragmatic Compromise'. *RSIS Commentaries* 211 (21 November 2012).

'The ASEAN Human Rights Declaration: Establishing a Common Framework'. *RSIS Commentaries* 114 (3 July 2012).

'The State of Brunei Darussalam'. In *Rule of Law for Human Rights in the ASEAN Region: A Base-Line Study*, edited by David Cohen, Kevin Y. L. Tan, and Mahdev M. Mohan. Jakarta: Human Rights Resource Centre, 2011.

Ng, Joel, and Vu Cong Giao. 'The Socialist Republic of Viet Nam'. In *Rule of Law for Human Rights in the ASEAN Region: a Base-Line Study*, edited by David Cohen, Kevin Y. L. Tan, and Mahdev M. Mohan. Jakarta: Human Rights Resource Centre, 2011.

Ng, Joel, and Joseph Chinyong Liow. 'The Southeast Asian Dimension: the ASEAN Model of Integration'. In *The Regional World Order: Transregionalism, Regional Integration, and Regional Projects across Europe and Asia*, edited by Alexei D. Voskressenski and Boglarka Koller. Lanham: Lexington Books, 2019.

Nguyen, Trung Thanh. 'The Making of the ASEAN Charter in my Fresh Memories'. In *The Making of the ASEAN Charter*, edited by Tommy Koh, Rosario G. Manalo, and Walter Woon. Singapore: World Scientific, 2009.

Nzewi, Ogochukwu. 'Influence and Legitimacy in African Regional Parliamentary Assemblies: the Case of the Pan-African Parliament's Search for Legislative Powers'. *Journal of Asian and African Studies* 49, no. 4 (2014): 488–507.

The Role of the Pan African Parliament in African Regionalism: Institutional Perspectives and Lessons for Africa. Saarbruecken: Verlag Dr Mueller, 2011.

OAU. 'Background Information on the Work of the OAU Charter Review Committee'. Paper presented at the 4th Extraordinary Session of the Assembly of Heads of State and Government, Sirte, 1999.

'CSSDCA Solemn Declaration' (AHG/Decl. 4 (XXXVI)). Lomé 2000.

'Decision on African Economic Community' (AHG/OAU/AEC/Decl. I (II)). Ouagadougou 1998.

'Decision on the Convening of an Extraordinary Session of the OAU Assembly of Heads of State and Government in Accordance with Article 33 (5) of its Rules of Procedure' (AHG/Decl.140 (XXXV)). Algiers 1999.

'Declaration of the Assembly of Heads of State and Government on the Establishment within the OAU of a Mechanism for Conflict Prevention, Management and Resolution' (AHG/Decl.3 (XXIX)). Cairo 1993.

'Declaration on the New Common (Map and Omega)' (AHG/Decl.1 (XXXVII)). Lusaka 2001.

'Declaration of the Year 2000 as the Year of Peace, Security and Solidarity in Africa' (AHG/Decl.2 (XXXV)). Algiers 1999.

'Draft of the Establishment of a State of the United States of Africa'. Sirte, Libya: Organization of African Unity Archives, 1999.

'Draft Sirte Declaration'. Sirte, Libya: OAU Archives, 1999.

'Ouagadougou Declaration' (AHG/Decl. I (XXXIV)). Ouagadougou 1998.

Report of the Secretary General on the Implementation of the Lusaka Summit on the Texts Relating to the Key Organs of the African Union. Addis Ababa: OAU, 2001.

'Sirte Declaration' (EAHG/Decl. (IV) Rev. 1). Sirte 1999.

'Transition of the OAU to the African Union: Institutional Capacity Building Needs and Interim Arrangements: Report of the Consultants, June 14, 2002'. Addis Ababa: OAU Archives, 2002.

'Treaty Establishing the African Economic Community'. Abuja 1991.

Obasanjo, Olusegun. 'Address by His Excellency President Olusegun Obasanjo, on the Occasion of the OAU Ministerial Conference on Conference on Security, Stability, Development and Cooperation in Africa (CSSDCA), Abuja, 8 May 2000'. Abuja: OAU, 2000.

'Collective Security is the Answer'. *Africa Forum* 3, nos. 2–3 (1999).

Oche, Ogaba. 'Nigeria, the AU, and the Challenge of Regional Integration'. In *Nigeria and the Development of the African Union*, edited by Bola A. Akinterinwa. Ibadan: Vantage, 2005.

Omorogbe, Eki Yemisi. 'The African Union, Responsibility to Protect and the Libyan Crisis'. *Netherlands International Law Review* 59, no. 2 (2012): 141–63.

Ong, Keng Yong. 'ASEAN: Managing Egos and National Interests'. In *50 Years of ASEAN and Singapore*, edited by Tommy Koh, Sharon Li-Lian Seah, and Li Lin Chang. Hackensack: World Scientific, 2017.

'At Close Quarters with the Drafting of the ASEAN Charter'. In *The Making of the ASEAN Charter*, edited by Tommy Koh, Rosario G. Manalo, and Walter Woon. Singapore: World Scientific, 2009.

Pan African Parliament. 'Pan-African Parliament Hansard Report, Second Session – Third Parliament'. Midrand, South Africa: African Union, 2013.

'Strategic Plan 2006–2010: "One Africa, One Voice"'. Midrand, South Africa: African Union, 2005.

Panke, D., and U. Petersohn. 'Why International Norms Disappear Sometimes'. *European Journal of International Relations* 18, no. 4 (2011): 719–42.
Patrick, Stewart. 'The Evolution of International Norms: Choice, Learning, Power, and Identity'. In *Evolutionary Intepretations of World Politics*, edited by William R. Thompson. New York: Routledge, 2001.
Petcharamesree, Sriprapha. 'The ASEAN Human Rights Architecture: Its Development and Challenges'. *Equal Rights Review* 11 (2013).
Pibulsonggram, Pradap. 'The Thai Perspective'. In *The Making of the ASEAN Charter*, edited by Tommy Koh, Rosario G. Manalo, and Walter Woon. Singapore: World Scientific, 2009.
Poole, Avery. '"The World is Outraged": Legitimacy in the Making of the ASEAN Human Rights Body'. *Contemporary Southeast Asia* 37, no. 3 (2015).
Ramos, Jennifer M. *Changing Norms through Actions: the Evolution of Sovereignty*. Oxford: Oxford University Press, 2013.
Ravenhill, John. 'Fighting Irrelevance: an Economic Community "with ASEAN Characteristics"'. *Pacific Review* 21, no. 4 (2008): 469–88.
Reno, William. *Warlord Politics and African States*. Boulder: Lynne Rienner, 1999.
Renshaw, C. S. 'The ASEAN Human Rights Declaration 2012'. *Human Rights Law Review* 13, no. 3 (2013): 557–79.
Risse, Thomas, Stephen C. Ropp, and Kathryn Sikkink, eds. *The Persistent Power of Human Rights: From Commitment to Compliance*, Cambridge Studies in International Relations. Cambridge: Cambridge University Press, 2013.
———, eds. *The Power of Human Rights: International Norms and Domestic Change*. Cambridge: Cambridge University Press, 1999.
Roberts, George. 'The Uganda–Tanzania War, the Fall of Idi Amin, and the Failure of African Diplomacy, 1978–1979'. *Journal of Eastern African Studies* 8, no. 4 (2014): 692–709.
Romer, Thomas, and Howard Rosenthal. 'Political Resource Allocation, Controlled Agendas, and the Status Quo'. *Public Choice* 33, no. 4 (1978).
Ryu, Yongwook, and Maria Ortuoste. 'Democratization, Regional Integration, and Human Rights: the Case of the ASEAN Intergovernmental Commission on Human Rights'. *Pacific Review* 27, no. 3 (2014): 357–82.
Salim, Salim A. 'Statement by Dr Salim Ahmed Salim, Secretary General of the OAU at the Experts Meeting on the Establishment of the African Union and the Pan-African Parliament'. Addis Ababa: OAU, 2000.

'Statement by Dr Salim Ahmed Salim, Secretary General of the OAU to the Ministerial Conference on Security, Stability, Development and Co-operation in Africa (CSSDCA), Abuja, Nigeria, 8th May 2000'. Abuja: OAU, 2000.

Sandholtz, Wayne. 'Dynamics of International Norm Change'. *European Journal of International Relations* 14, no. 1 (2008).

SAPA TFAHR. *A Commission Shrouded in Secrecy: a Performance Report on the ASEAN Intergovernmental Commission on Human Rights 2010–2011*. Bangkok: Forum Asia, 2011.

Hiding behind its Limits: a Performance Report on the First Year of the ASEAN Intergovernmental Commission on Human Rights (AICHR) 2009–2010. Bangkok: Forum Asia, 2010.

Scanlon, Thomas M. *What We Owe to Each Other*. Cambridge, MA: Harvard University Press, 1998.

Schimmelfennig, Frank. 'The Community Trap: Liberal Norms, Rhetorical Action, and the Eastern Enlargement of the European Union'. *International Organization* 55, no. 1 (2001): 47–80.

Schmitter, Philippe C. 'Ernst B. Haas and the Legacy of Neofunctionalism'. *Journal of European Public Policy* 12, no. 2 (2005): 255–72.

Seabrooke, L. 'Epistemic Arbitrage: Transnational Professional Knowledge in Action'. *Journal of Professions and Organization* 1, no. 1 (2014): 49–64.

Searle, John R. *The Social Construction of Reality*. London: Allen Lane, 1995.

Sending, Ole Jacob, Vincent Pouliot, and Iver B. Neumann. *Diplomacy and the Making of World Politics*. Cambridge: Cambridge University Press, 2015.

Severino, Rodolfo C. 'ASEAN beyond Forty: Towards Political and Economic Integration'. *Contemporary Southeast Asia* 29, no. 3 (2007).

Sikkink, Kathryn. 'Transnational Politics, International Relations Theory, and Human Rights'. *PS: Political Science and Politics* 31, no. 3 (1998).

'The United States and Torture: Does the Spiral Model Work?' In *The Persistent Power of Human Rights: From Commitment to Compliance*, edited by Thomas Risse, Stephen C. Ropp, and Kathryn Sikkink. Cambridge: Cambridge University Press, 2013.

Söderbaum, Fredrik. 'Old, New, and Comparative Regionalism: the History and Scholarly Development of the Field'. In *The Oxford Handbook of Comparative Regionalism*, edited by Tanja A. Borzel and Thomas Risse. Oxford: Oxford University Press, 2016.

Söderbaum, Fredrik, and Björn Hettne. 'Regional Security in a Global Perspective'. In *Africa's New Peace and Security Architecture*, edited by Ulf Engel and Joao Gomes Porto. Farnham: Ashgate, 2010.

Solomon, Hussein, and Gerrie Swart. 'Libya's Foreign Policy in Flux'. *African Affairs* 104, no. 416 (2005).

Stensland, Andreas, Walter Lotze, and Joel Ng. *Regional Security and Human Rights Interventions: a Global Governance Perspective on the AU and ASEAN*. Nupi Security in Practice. 8. Oslo: Norwegian Institute of International Affairs, 2012.

Stimmer, Anette, and Lea Wisken. 'The Dynamics of Dissent: When Actions are Louder than Words'. *International Affairs* 95, no. 3 (2019): 515–33.

Stinchcombe, Arthur L. *Contructing Social Theories*. Chicago: Chicago University Press, 1987.

Strange, Susan. *The Retreat of the State: the Diffusion of Power in the World Economy*. Cambridge: Cambridge University Press, 1996.

Strom, Kaare W., and Benjamin Nyblade. 'Coalition Theory and Government Formation'. In *The Oxford Handbook of Comparative Politics*, edited by Carles Boix and Susan C. Stokes. Oxford: Oxford University Press, 2009.

Sturman, Kathryn, and Aissatou Hayatou. 'The Peace and Security Council of the African Union: From Design to Reality'. In *Africa's New Peace and Security Architecture*, edited by Ulf Engel and Joao Gomes Porto. Farnham: Ashgate, 2010.

Tan, Hsien-Li. *The ASEAN Intergovernmental Commission on Human Rights*. Cambridge: Cambridge University Press, 2011.

Tan, See Seng. 'Whither Sovereignty in Southeast Asia Today?' In *Re-Envisioning Sovereignty: the End of Westphalia?*, edited by Trudy Jacobsen, Charles Sampford, and Ramesh Thakur. Aldershot: Ashgate, 2008.

Tieku, Thomas K. 'Explaining the Clash and Accommodation of Interests of Major Actors in the Creation of the African Union'. *African Affairs* 103, no. 411 (2004): 249–67.

Governing Africa: 3D Analysis of the African Union's Performance. London: Rowman and Littlefield, 2016.

'Theoretical Approaches to Africa's International Relations'. In *Handbook of Africa's International Relations*, edited by Tim Murithi. Abingdon: Routledge, 2014.

Touray, Omar A. *The African Union: the First Ten Years*. London: Rowman and Littlefield, 2016.

Towns, Ann E. 'Norms and Social Hierarchies: Understanding International Policy Diffusion "from Below"'. *International Organization* 66, no. 2 (2012): 179–209.

UN. 'Report of the Regional Meeting for Asia of the World Conference on Human Rights' (A/Conf.157/ASRM/8). Bangkok 1993.

UNECA. *Report on Status of Regional Integration in Africa: Progress, Problems and Perspective*. Addis Ababa: UNECA, 2003.

Unpublished draft. *Working Draft of the AHRD as of 8 Jan 2012 0400hrs*. Jakarta: ASEAN, 2012.

van Kersbergen, Kees, and Bertjan Verbeek. 'The Politics of International Norms: Subsidiarity and the Imperfect Competence Regime of the European Union'. *European Journal of International Relations* 13, no. 2 (2007).

van Walraven, Klaas. 'Heritage and Transformation: From the Organization of African Unity to the African Union'. In *Africa's New Peace and Security Architecture*, edited by Ulf Engel and Joao Gomes Porto. Farnham: Ashgate, 2010.

Villanueva, Kevin H. R. 'ASEAN "Magna Carta" Universalizes Human Rights'. *Jakarta Post*, 8 January 2013.

Wade, Abdoulaye. 'Contribution de Sénégal à l'Union Africaine, Sommet de Lomé du 10 au 12 Juillet 2000'. Lomé: Republic of Senegal, 2000.

Wahyuningrum, Yuyun. *The ASEAN Intergovernmental Commission on Human Rights: Origins, Evolution and the Way Forward*. Stockholm: International IDEA, 2014.

Wawro, Gregory J., and Eric Schickler. 'Where's the Pivot? Obstruction and Lawmaking in the Pre-Cloture Senate'. *American Journal of Political Science* 48, no. 4 (2004).

Weingast, Barry R. 'A Rational Choice Perspective on Congressional Norms'. *American Journal of Political Science* 23, no. 2 (1979).

Wiener, Antje. 'Contested Meanings of Norms: a Research Framework'. *Comparative European Politics* 5, no. 1 (2007): 1–17.

The Invisible Constitution of Politics: Contested Norms and International Encounters. Cambridge: Cambridge University Press, 2008.

A Theory of Contestation. Heidelberg: Springer, 2014.

Wigstrom, Christian W. *'Beyond Theatre Regionalism: When Does Formal Economic Integration Work in Africa?'* PhD dissertation, University of Oxford, 2013.

Williams, Paul D. 'From Non-Intervention to Non-Indifference: the Origins and Development of the African Union's Security Culture'. *African Affairs* 106, no. 423 (2006): 253–79.

Wolff, Jonas, and Lisbeth Zimmermann. 'Between Banyans and Battle Scenes: Liberal Norms, Contestation, and the Limits of Critique'. *Review of International Studies* 42, no. 3 (2015): 513–34.

Woods, Ngaire. 'Good Governance in International Organizations'. *Global Governance* 5, no. 1 (1999).

Woods, Ngaire, and Walter Mattli, eds. *The Politics of Global Regulation*. Princeton: Princeton University Press, 2009.

Woon, Walter. *The ASEAN Charter: a Commentary*. Singapore: NUS Press, 2016.
'The ASEAN Charter Dispute Settlement Mechanisms'. In *The Making of the ASEAN Charter*, edited by Tommy Koh, Rosario G. Manalo, and Walter Woon. Singapore: World Scientific, 2009.
Working Group for an ASEAN Human Rights Mechanism. *ASEAN and Human Rights: a Compilation of ASEAN Statements on Human Rights*. Makati City, Philippines: Working Group for an ASEAN Human Rights Mechanism, 2003.
Yeo, George. 'Remarks by Minister for Foreign Affairs George Yeo and his Reply to Supplementary Questions in Parliament during Cos Debate (MFA) on 28 February 2008'. Singapore: Ministry of Foreign Affairs, 2008.
Zartman, I. William, and Jeffrey Z. Rubin, eds. *Power and Negotiation*. Ann Arbor: University of Michigan Press, 2000.
Zürn, Michael. *A Theory of Global Governance*. Oxford: Oxford University Press, 2018.

Index

Abuja Treaty, 71, 75, 80–1, 83, 87, 89–90, 98, 101, 140–1, 146–7
AEC. *See* African Economic Community (Chapters 3–5)
ASEAN Economic Community (Chapters 6–8)
Africa Leadership Forum, 109–18, 122, 124, 130
African Charter on Human and Peoples' Rights, 57, 149
African Economic Community, 37, 80, 87–94, 135–52, 157–60
African Union. *See* AU
Africrats, 150–1, 259
AICHR. *See* ASEAN Intergovernmental Commission on Human Rights
ALF. *See* Africa Leadership Forum
ASEAN, 2–4, 11, 15–17, 37, 40–1, 44–5, 51, 163–8, 253–4, 256–64, 266–9, 271–2
   ASEAN Way, 163, 170, 182–4, 191–2, 199–200, 203, 212, 218–19, 221, 232, 250, 257
   Economic Community, 67, 166, 232–4, 242, 245, 249–50
   Eminent Persons Group, 64, 165, 170–7, 184–5, 187, 189–92, 196, 213, 217, 224–5, 235–42, 246, 250–1, 257
   Free Trade Area, 227, 229–31, 233, 240, 245
   High Level Panel, 167, 187, 198–203, 210–13, 219, 221–2
   High Level Task Force (Charter), 165, 167, 170–3, 176–92, 196–7, 199, 202, 211, 217, 221, 225, 236, 240–6, 249–51, 263
   High Level Task Force (Economic Integration), 166, 233–4, 236–9, 249–51, 263

   Human Rights Declaration, 63–4, 66, 165–8, 173, 194–6, 202–12, 216–19, 222
   Intergovernmental Commission on Human Rights, 62–4, 67, 165–8, 187, 195–222, 247, 256, 260–2
   Secretariat, 164, 175, 181, 205, 212, 216, 222, 227, 234–5, 238, 245–6, 259
Association of Southeast Asian Nations. *See* ASEAN
AU, 3–4, 9–11, 17, 40–1, 44–5, 56–61, 65–8, 71–7, 241, 259–60, 271–2
   Commission, 73, 77, 94, 140, 150, 152–5, 222
   Peace and Security Council, 59, 103, 128–9, 254

Bali Concord, 61, 169, 188, 233–4, 238
Bangkok Declaration, 62, 166, 197, 212, 218
Banjul Charter. *See* African Charter on Human and Peoples' Rights
Bouteflika, Abdelaziz, 95–6, 142

Cambodia, Laos, Myanmar, Vietnam. *See* CLMV
Chadian Civil War, 81–2, 104–10, 114, 118, 120
CLMV, 164, 171, 173, 179–81, 184, 187, 198, 212, 214, 218, 220–2, 229, 244
coalitions, 7, 23, 32–3, 44, 53–4, 68, 123, 129, 266, 272
cognitive prior, 48, 170, 184
competence, 3, 7, 15–16, 40, 46–53, 95, 98, 102, 132, 134, 262, 272
Conference on Security and Cooperation in Europe, 110, 113

Index 297

Conference on Security, Stability, Development, and Cooperation in Africa. *See* CSSDCA
Constitutive Act of the AU, 9–10, 58–9, 65, 71–7, 84, 88, 93–4, 98, 101–2, 128, 132, 140, 144–50, 152, 156–8
control of the initiative, 3, 7, 15–16, 47–8, 50–1, 257–9
  cases of, 83, 86–9, 97–9, 104, 113, 115–16, 123, 130–2, 143–5, 158, 160, 182–3, 189–92, 210–11, 218, 221, 239–41, 250
CSSDCA, 60, 67, 75, 96, 99, 103–32, 138, 150–1, 159, 253, 256–7, 259–64

Declaration of ASEAN Concord. *See* Bali Concord

East African Community, 80, 136
Economic Community of West African States. *See* ECOWAS
ECOWAS, 10, 40, 59, 80, 92, 120, 136–7, 155
  Monitoring Group (ECOMOG), 120
EPG. *See* ASEAN Eminent Persons Group
Essy, Amara, 72, 76
European Union, 1–3, 37, 39, 87, 90, 163, 169–71, 173–4, 227, 229, 232, 241, 265–8, 271–2

functionalism, 4, 6, 231, 249, 253, 266

Gaddafi, Muammar, 10, 58–61, 67, 71–4, 79–102, 106–8, 121–2, 127, 131, 133–4, 138–52, 156–61, 257–8, 260–3

HLP. *See* ASEAN High Level Panel
HLTF. *See* ASEAN High Level Task Force

International Criminal Court, 35, 39, 49

Kampala Movement, 60, 75, 103, 111–17, 120–31, 138, 263, 272

Koh, Tommy, 178, 180–1, 183, 185–7, 189, 238, 244
Konaré, Alpha Oumar, 73–4, 92–4, 99, 145, 157, 258

legitimacy, 3–4, 12–16, 18, 25, 48–50, 55, 79, 97, 106, 117, 131, 136, 139, 151, 157, 159, 177, 192, 220, 267, 270–2

Manalo, Rosario G., 178, 181–2, 192, 199–200, 204, 215
Mbeki, Thabo, 58, 84, 87–9, 94–6, 111, 122, 127, 131, 159
metis, 3, 7, 15, 49–54, 257, 261–2
  cases of, 88, 95–8, 101, 123–4, 127, 130, 150–2, 158, 185–7, 191, 213–16, 218, 222, 243–6, 250
Millennium Africa Recovery Plan, 95–9
Museveni, Yoweri, 18, 91, 114–15, 117, 122, 124

NEPAD, 76, 95–9, 104, 121, 127–9, 254, 261
New African Initiative, 76, 95–6
New Partnership for African Development. *See* NEPAD
Nkrumah, Kwame, 56, 58, 60, 72, 84, 98–9, 119
norm
  cascade/spiral, 11, 18–20, 23, 30, 35, 60, 63, 129, 169, 193, 265–6
  contestation theories, 3, 6–7, 11–16, 19–20, 38–51, 253–4
  foundational/anti-foundational approaches, 23–9, 253
  functions, 23–7, 30–1, 34–6
  localization, 12, 48, 52, 111, 170
  'norm circle' model, 3, 6–7, 14–16, 31–5, 42–4, 51–5, 255–62
  utility, 13, 15, 24, 27–9, 34–8, 42–4, 51–3, 55, 69, 255–6, 258–64
Nyerere, Julius, 56, 111, 118–19, 122–3

OAU, 1, 9–10, 37, 40, 56–60, 66, 68, 71–7, 91–102, 134–9, 142–54, 158, 160, 190, 221, 257, 259, 262–3, 271

OAU (cont.)
  Mechanism on Conflict
    Management, Prevention, and
    Resolution, 58, 128, 149
  Secretariat, 68, 72, 81, 111, 113–14,
    121, 125, 130, 132, 143, 146,
    149–50, 154, 157, 160, *see also*
    African Union Commission
Obasanjo, Olusegun, 60, 76, 87–90,
  95–6, 103–5, 109–27, 130–2,
  137–40, 150, 152, 159, 256–7,
  260
Omega Plan for Africa, 95, 98–9
Ong Keng Yong, 164, 179–80, 185–6,
  188, 190, 198
Organization for Security and
  Cooperation in Europe. *See*
  Conference on Security and
  Cooperation in Europe
Organization of African Unity.
  See OAU

Pan-African Parliament, 4, 61, 66, 72,
  77, 87, 93, 99–100, 133–61
power, 7, 13–17, 20–8, 30–8, 41–54,
  80, 97, 132, 151, 160, 170, 180,
  184, 186, 192, 213, 220, 228,
  253–4, 264, 268
  in practice, 7, 20, 46–50, 272

regional integration, 1, 6, 38–42, 86,
  90, 103, 135, 159–60, 217, 247,
  265, 271–2
regionalism, 3, 5, 7, 15–17, 36–41, 71,
  91, 103, 229, 247, 265,
  267–70
responsibility to protect, 9–10, 35

SADC, 40, 80, 136, 155
Salim, Salim Ahmed, 58–9, 72, 110,
  114, 122, 124–6, 130–2, 142–4,
  147–52, 259
shared norms, 3, 7, 15–16, 39, 41, 48,
  50–2, 257, 259–61, 267, 270, 273
  uses of, 83, 89–94, 97–100, 104,
  116–20, 123–7, 132, 146–50,
  154–5, 160, 183–5, 192, 200,
  212–13, 219–22, 241–3, 249
Sirte Declaration, 72, 76, 83–4, 90,
  100, 121, 141–2, 145–8, 158
Southern African Development
  Community. *See* SADC

Treaty Establishing the African
  Economic Community. *See* Abuja
  Treaty
Treaty of Amity and Cooperation, 61,
  188, 245

United Nations, 9–10, 40, 60–1, 124,
  209, 213, 216, 243, 264
  Economic Commission for Africa,
    110–11, 113, 122, 131, 135–6,
    140, 158
  Security Council, 47–9, 59, 264
United States of Africa, 4, 56, 58, 60,
  67, 72–6, 79–103, 122, 130, 133,
  138–9, 144, 148, 157–8, 160, 257,
  260–1
Universal Declaration of Human
  Rights, 191, 208, 210, 212, 218,
  264

Wade, Abdoulaye, 74, 84, 91, 94–5, 98,
  145, 261

Printed in the United States
by Baker & Taylor Publisher Services